RESTful Rails Development

Building Open Applications and Services

Silvia Puglisi

Beijing · Boston · Farnham · Sebastopol · Tokyo

RESTful Rails Development

by Silvia Puglisi

Printed in the United States of America.

Published by O'Reilly Media, Inc., 1005 Gravenstein Highway North, Sebastopol, CA 95472.

O'Reilly books may be purchased for educational, business, or sales promotional use. Online editions are also available for most titles (*http://safaribooksonline.com*). For more information, contact our corporate/ institutional sales department: 800-998-9938 or *corporate@oreilly.com*.

Editors: Simon St. Laurent and Allyson MacDonald
Production Editors: Colleen Lobner and
Kristen Brown
Copyeditor: Rachel Head
Proofreader: Charles Roumeliotis

Indexer: Ellen Troutman-Zaig
Interior Designer: David Futato
Cover Designer: Ellie Volckhausen
Illustrator: Rebecca Demarest

October 2015: First Edition

Revision History for the First Edition
2015-10-06:   First Release

See *http://oreilly.com/catalog/errata.csp?isbn=9781491910856* for release details.

978-1-491-91085-6

[LSI]

To Aaron. For being an inspiration.

To Sara. My friend and partner in life and mischief. For always being there.

To my family for being so supportive no matter what.

To everybody else. Friends above all. For sticking around.

Table of Contents

*"We can only see a short distance ahead,
but we can see plenty there that needs to be done."*
—Alan Turing

*"Be curious. Read widely. Try new things. What
people call intelligence just boils down to curiosity."*
—Aaron Swartz

*"The Semantic Web is not a separate Web but an extension of the
current one, in which information is given well-defined meaning,
better enabling computers and people to work in cooperation."*
—Tim Berners-Lee

*"What sets this framework apart from all of the others
is the preference for convention over configuration
making applications easier to develop and understand."*
—Sam Ruby, ASF board of directors

"Rails is the killer app for Ruby."
—Yukihiro Matsumoto, creator of Ruby

*"Life is a distributed object system. However, communication among
humans is a distributed hypermedia system, where the mind's intellect,
voice+gestures, eyes+ears, and imagination are all components."*
—Roy T. Fielding

Preface

This book is focused on designing and developing Representational State Transfer (REST) platforms in Rails. REST is the architectural style of the Web, consisting of a set of constraints that, applied to components, connectors, and data elements, constitute the wider distributed hypermedia system that we know today: the World Wide Web.

There are a few good reasons why it makes more sense to build platforms instead of just products or applications. Platforms are like ecosystems interconnecting different applications, services, users, developers, and partners. Platforms foster innovation through the inputs of their direct collaborators. By providing application programming interfaces (APIs) and software development kits (SDKs), platforms are more customer driven. Another reason for building platforms instead of just applications is that the Web is slowly but surely changing from a model in which a human reader would browse some content on web pages, to a model in which services and clients (not necessarily humans) exchange information. This was certainly, although only partially, what Tim Berners Lee envisioned in 2001 in his famous *Scientific American* article, "The Semantic Web." The Web is becoming more semantic. In the past, a software agent would not have been able to "understand" an HTML document. It could parse some parts of it, but it would not process whether that document was referring to a blog post or something else, like the London bus schedule.

We used to think of the Web as hypertext documents linked to one another; nowadays web documents are instead becoming more like data objects linked to other objects, or *hyperdata*. Applications can either display hyperdata in a human-readable form or parse it so that other services or applications can consume that information. The Semantic Web can be easily explained by considering it as a normal evolution of hypertext. When hyperdata objects are explored through an API, different communication protocols are implemented to allow several technologies to access them independently. To enable this exchange of information among heterogeneous systems, the API implements a language-neutral message format to communicate. This might be XML or JSON, used as a container for the exchanged messages. If we think about it, a "hypermedia API" is one that is designed to be accessed and explored by any device or application. Its architecture is hence similar to the architecture of the Web and we apply the same reasoning when serving and consuming the API as when surfing a web page.

There are also reasons for choosing Rails over other web development frameworks. The first of them is having to develop in Ruby rather than another language. Ruby is easy to use, especially from a web developer's perspective. It is totally object oriented and open source and has a vibrant community working on a variety of diverse and interesting projects and language libraries, making development easier. Ruby on Rails is a pragmatic framework, cleanly and perfectly implementing Model-View-Controller (MVC) patterns, which makes it easy to model real-world scenarios. Rails makes it easier to bootstrap an application, avoiding repetitive coding and speeding up feature development. Rails also follows agile methodology, promoting flexibility, evolutionary development, and iterative delivery.

This book wants to encourage developers to organically design platforms instead of products and to develop them quickly, in the hope that the new services added to the Web of tomorrow will be more easily discovered and eventually integrated, fostering open information exchange and stimulating partnerships between organizations. At the end of every chapter, the reader will have learned something new regarding how to build and organically extend a multiservice platform spanning different devices. Hopefully, at the end of this book you will have a better idea of how to build an architecture composed of different services accessing shared resources through a set of collaborating APIs and applications.

Why Rails and Not Node.js

Many articles have been written about Rails versus Node.js in the last few years. Although both can be used to build web applications, there are some fundamental differences between Node.js and Rails.

First of all, Rails is a complete and highly opinionated web framework, while Node.js is a (nonopinionated) framework based on Chrome's JavaScript runtime for building network applications. In short, Node.js is a server-side JavaScript implementation.

Interaction within the MVC architecture in Rails is clean, concise, and efficient. In Node.js you will need to work with plug-ins and helpers to achieve the same level of integration that in Rails you get *out of the box*. Also, programming both the backend and frontend in JavaScript doesn't necessarily mean you will be able to develop your product faster. While this is probably true for fast prototyping, you should really consider whether Node.js is a technology that will allow you to scale your product down the line. Keep in mind that developing a full application in Rails is as fast as, if not faster than, developing the same app with Node.js. We will see how quickly and easily you can build a REST API in Rails.

The Rails community is quite mature at this point, while still being fresh. There are still a lot of new things happening in the Rails world, both in terms of exciting projects being created and modules being written. If you start programming in Rails, you will also learn Ruby. The Ruby developer community is vibrant, and a good number of new products are written in Ruby. These include technologies like Logstash (*https://www.elastic.co/products/logstash*), Chef (*https://www.chef.io/chef/*), Puppet (*https://puppetlabs.com/*), Homebrew (*http://brew.sh/*), and many others. Also, Ruby programmers are still experiencing a growth in demand. In conclusion, while Node.js is an interesting technology to use and to play and prototype with, Rails is both more mature and more suitable for long-term stable projects.

Why (I Think) You Should Read This Book

There are certainly many reasons to read a particular book, and many more to write one. When I started writing *RESTful Rails Development*, I imagined a world of micro-communicating applications, feeding and sourcing from the so-called Web of Data.

I thought of RESTful principles, and I imagined device-independent services that would just consume, process, and create streams of data. Before writing this book, I had several discussions with friends and colleagues about the future of the Internet and how hypermedia could be considered the true Semantic Web. The same discussions can be found online in blog posts, forums, and social-network threads. Programmers, architects, marketers, and normal people seem to have a spectrum of diverging and colliding opinions on the matter. Some people complain about possible business adoption, others about poor design and lazy development practices. Some others are thoroughly excited about unleashing the full potential of RESTful services.

This book is about:

- How to *develop* RESTful applications
- How to *design* RESTful architectures
- How to *deploy* RESTful services

Therefore, you should read this book if:

- You want to dive into RESTful development.
- You want to learn about how to design a small application ecosystem.
- You just want to design an API to connect to some external services.

You could be a developer with some years of experience, or you could be a student eager to get started with an exciting new project. You could be an engineer exploring different possibilities to create ambitious applications or wanting to convince your manager of the possibilities of RESTful services and hypermedia. You could be a project manager with some technical background looking to understand the logic behind RESTful services, or you could work in marketing but be willing to learn how to open up your platform to services on the World Wide Web.

You should read this book if you are passionate about the future of the Web, if you feel strongly about keeping it open, if you envision the Semantic Web as a mesh of communicating services, or if you want to start writing software that just implements these paradigms. If you have read about API design and hypermedia paradigms, if you are just enthusiastic about the Web of Data, or if you have wondered how you could quickly prototype a new service or apply hypermedia models to a commercial project, then this book is also for you. I hope this book will help you in your present and future projects; I also hope it will be your guide to building amazingly disruptive applications, creating services that will make the Web more open and accessible to a wide range of devices, and providing beautifully designed hypermedia APIs that will make data easier to explore and process. This book is for you—and I hope you thoroughly enjoy it.

What You Will Find in This Book

This is not a book that you have to read from beginning to end, although you certainly can if you want. Every chapter can be considered a standalone unit that will present an aspect of RESTful architecture and Rails development:

Chapter 1, From Hypertext to Hyperdata
    This chapter introduces the shift that has been occurring in the way the Web is accessed and consumed, from hypertext documents that were intended to be human readable, to web applications that can either display information for their human users or provide endpoints for software agents that are designed to consume data.

Chapter 2, Getting Started with Ruby on Rails
    This chapter introduces Ruby on Rails. It guides you through setting up your development environment, and then introduces some RVM and rbenv basics and outlines some simple concepts in Rails application architecture. We will then set up our first application. This will be a "Hello Rails" app with a twist, since it will not strictly be an app but an API instead.

Chapter 3, First Adventures in API Design
    This chapter leads you through some API design considerations by creating a simple API using a Wikipedia categories and category links database dump. The result will be an API with two endpoints. Given a keyword, the API will return the category information or the category graph from Wikipedia in JSON.

Chapter 4, The REST of the World

This chapter covers the basics of REST versus CRUD (Create, Read, Update, Delete) design, introducing architectural constraints, resource and representation concepts, and HTTP protocol semantics. Our categories API will be extended and used to illustrate the concepts.

This chapter also covers how Rails plays with REST logic, since it was designed with CRUD in mind.

Chapter 5, Designing APIs in RoR

This chapter extends what has been introduced thus far regarding REST architectures with hypermedia paradigms.

Practical examples will be implemented over our categories API model. The API introduced in Chapter 3 and extended in Chapter 4 will be further developed to illustrate API architecture and design concepts in Rails. Category links will be used to extend the API in order to make it explorable.

Chapter 6, Asynchronous REST

This chapter explores aspects of REST architecture that concern asynchronous operations. Asynchronous operations on resources are usually applied when your app has to perform some actions that need some time to complete. We will see what the best practices are in these cases.

Chapter 7, Testing RESTful Services

This chapter is about testing, and specifically testing RESTful services in Rails. What are doubles? What are stubs, and what are mocks? These are the questions that will be answered in this chapter. You will also learn about integration testing and best practices in testing.

Chapter 8, Microservices and Microapplications

This chapter is focused on the basics of service-oriented architecture (SOA) and distributed systems design. It takes the approach of envisioning fine-grained collaborating microservices, or better microapplications. A set of applications and APIs accessing shared resources will be used as an example.

In our example, an API will return geographical points of interest within cities. These will be mapped to categories of preference returned from our first API, then data will be correlated to obtain possible thematic city walks.

Chapter 9, Mapping Data Streams onto an Application UI

In this chapter, we consume the APIs built in the previous installments through an application built in RoR plus Ember.js. The chapter is particularly focused on mapping different resources onto an application UI. Our Walks application resources will be mapped to a user interface.

Chapter 10, Deploying an API

This chapter is centered on deploying and building middleware for external customers to connect to the APIs. It will answer questions like "How is an API deployed?" and introduce concepts like the reverse proxy. It will configure a reverse proxy on Heroku and use it to connect the APIs built in Chapter 5 with the applications consuming them.

Chapter 11, Managing an App Ecosystem

This chapter introduces API management solutions. It will help you to make the choice between developing in house or relying on external services. It will also introduce concepts like key provisioning and role management, traffic monitoring, and the API and application lifecycle.

Chapter 12, Consuming Data Streams: Integrating External APIs in Your Application

This chapter explains how to integrate external services and APIs and display them in your application, by using open data or simply importing the Wikipedia, YouTube, or Twitter APIs, thus making the imported resources available to a distributed platform without having to repeatedly call them.

Chapter 13, Device-Independent Development

This chapter expands our case study to different devices: mobile platforms and the Internet of Things. How can we include devices like mobile phones, Arduinos, or Raspberry Pi's in our web apps and organically integrate the generated data? We will build a simple weather app to access, consume, and generate data.

Chapter 14, Data Analytics

This chapter focuses on maintaining control over data flows and analytics. What tools can we develop or integrate to keep control over our platform's data flows?

Chapter 15, Scaling Gracefully

This chapter is about scaling gracefully. It focuses on scaling by design. This chapter is of particular interest with regard to Rails development, because scalability in Rails is a big issue.

Chapter 16, Privacy and Security

This chapter is particularly concerned with security and privacy. How do we secure our platforms, and how do we make sure user data is safe?

What You Will Not Find in This Book (And Where You Can Go for Answers)

This is neither a Ruby nor a Rails book, specifically. This book is about Rails development, but if you want to learn core concepts of the Ruby programming language or the Rails platform, you should also read a book focused on Ruby on Rails or Ruby.

This is not a book about JavaScript or Ember.js, or any other framework, although we will use some JavaScript and we will set up an Ember environment.

This is not specifically a book about Nginx, or Redis or Lua, although we might use or mention some of these technologies when going through API management, scaling, and analytics-related issues.

This book isn't about privacy or security either, though an entire chapter is focused on these topics (and it is important to keep in mind that "with big data comes big responsibilities"). I will redirect you to more authoritative resources in the last chapter, should you want to start learning about these topics.

 Additional resources where you can find information regarding topics that are outside the scope of this book will be provided in notes like this one.

Resources

All code used in this book will be made available on GitHub and released under the GPLv3 license. I will also redirect to authoritative resources on specific topics throughout the book: at the end of each chapter you will find some links that you can follow to start diving into specific sets of technologies relevant to that chapter.

Coding Style

There aren't many coding style guides for Ruby or Ruby on Rails, like you could probably find for other languages—or maybe there are too many, meaning everyone follows their own.

Throughout this book I will use some simple conventions that I hope will make the code more readable and self-explanatory.

These are:

- UTF-8 as the source file encoding.
- Two spaces per indentation level (aka soft tabs); no hard tabs.
- Unix-style line endings.
- One expression per line.
- Single-line format for class definitions with no body.
- Avoid single-line methods.
- Use spaces around operators; after commas, colons, and semicolons, around { and before }.
- Never use *unless* with *else*.

- Keep the controllers skinny.
- Logic resides in the models.

I would also like to underline the simple concept that this won't be a book merely about coding. While it is certainly a book centered on development, coding should also be seen as the medium to explain concepts and design choices. I am also sure most of the readers will be able to find better ways to rewrite the code examples presented. Therefore, I completely encourage you to fork the repositories and get creative creating new apps and products.

RuboCop

RuboCop is a Ruby static code analyzer that enforces many of the guidelines outlined in the community Ruby Style Guide (*http:// bit.ly/ruby-styleguide*) out of the box.

You can find out more about RuboCop at its GitHub repository (*http://bit.ly/rubocop-repo*).

Conventions Used in This Book

The following typographical conventions are used in this book:

Italic
: Indicates new terms, URLs, email addresses, filenames, file extensions, keywords, and variable names.

`Constant width`
: Used for code examples, programming snippets, and function statements.

`<italic>`
: Shows text that should be replaced with user-supplied values or by values determined by context.

Bold
: Shows commands or other text that should be typed literally by the user.

This element signifies a tip or suggestion.

This element signifies a general note.

This element indicates a warning or caution.

Using Code Examples

Supplemental material (code examples, exercises, etc.) is available for download at *http://hiromipaw.github.io/RESTful-Rails-Development/*.

This book is here to help you get your job done. In general, if example code is offered with this book, you may use it in your programs and documentation. You do not need to contact us for permission unless you're reproducing a significant portion of the code. For example, writing a program that uses several chunks of code from this book does not require permission. Selling or distributing a CD-ROM of examples from O'Reilly books does require permission. Answering a question by citing this book and quoting example code does not require permission. Incorporating a significant amount of example code from this book into your product's documentation does require permission.

We appreciate, but do not require, attribution. An attribution usually includes the title, author, publisher, and ISBN. For example: "*RESTful Rails Development* by Silvia Puglisi (O'Reilly). Copyright 2016 Silvia Puglisi, 978-1-491-91085-6."

If you feel your use of code examples falls outside fair use or the permission given above, feel free to contact us at *permissions@oreilly.com*.

All the code and simple apps provided with this book are released under the GNU General Public License version 3. GPLv3 is a free, copyleft license for software and other kinds of works. The GPLv3 license is intended to guarantee your freedom to share and change all versions of a program to make sure it remains free software for all its users.

I encourage you to visit the license document at *http://www.gnu.org/copyleft/gpl.html*.

I also encourage every reader of this book to fork, rewrite, and use the code examples provided to create new and amazing projects.

Rails is released under the MIT license (*http://opensource.org/licenses/mit-license.php*) and Ruby under the Ruby license (*https://www.ruby-lang.org/en/about/license.txt*).

How to Contact Us

Please address comments and questions concerning this book to the publisher:

O'Reilly Media, Inc.
1005 Gravenstein Highway North
Sebastopol, CA 95472
800-998-9938 (in the United States or Canada)
707-829-0515 (international or local)
707-829-0104 (fax)

To comment or ask technical questions about this book, send email to *bookques-tions@oreilly.com*.

For more information about our books, courses, conferences, and news, see our website at *http://www.oreilly.com*.

Find us on Facebook: *http://facebook.com/oreilly*

Follow us on Twitter: *http://twitter.com/oreillymedia*

Watch us on YouTube: *http://www.youtube.com/oreillymedia*

We have a web page where we list errata and corrections; you can access this page at: *http://bit.ly/RESTful_rails_development*.

We also have a GitHub page where all the coding examples and applications used in this book can be accessed: *http://hiromipaw.github.io/RESTful-Rails-Development/*.

Acknowledgments

Thanks to everyone who has made this book possible.

Thanks to the editors that have guided me through this, I'd say, adventure. To all the reviewers who took the time to send me feedback. To all my friends that supported me. To my family and partner, who bore with me while I was *always* writing and rewriting.

I hope it will be a guide to many who are starting their adventures in the REST and Rails worlds.

## CHAPTER 1

From Hypertext to Hyperdata

In this chapter, we will start exploring the basics of REST and HTTP, beginning with some concepts of REST architectures and the role of hypermedia.

This will be an introductory chapter on the architectural foundation blocks of REST and how these map to the HTTP protocol.

REST and HTTP

The Hypertext Transfer Protocol (HTTP) protocol has a predominant role on the Web. It represents the only protocol designed specifically to transfer resource representations, to abstract over lower-layered transport protocols such as TCP or UDP, and to act as the primary application-level protocol for web components.

Everything Started with Hypertext

In the Appendix of this book you can find an introductory section on the HTTP protocol and hypertext. Although web programmers tend to be very familiar with the protocol, recalling some deep concepts can be useful when reasoning about RESTful programming.

Representational State Transfer (REST) architectures are a generalization of the WWW architecture based on the HTTP protocol, where the World Wide Web represents an Internet-scale implementation of RESTful architectural style. In RESTful architectures agents implement uniform interface semantics, instead of application-specific components, implementations, and protocol syntax.

REST therefore represents an abstraction of the actual architecture of the Web, in a similar way to how the Web itself represents an abstraction of HTTP. REST is mostly a model of how the Web should work, a framework to make sure that any development to the protocols or more generally any components that make the Web possible respect the core constraints that make the Web as a whole a successful application.

Architectural Abstractions

Abstraction is an important concept in software architectures, and more generally in programming paradigms. A software system is designed to solve a problem by abstracting the problem scenario, reducing the problem into smaller subproblems, and computing accurate results.

The process of abstracting over a problem scenario is actually extremely common in engineering.

My university professor for a course in complex system analysis used to tell his class that every model is just an approximation of reality, able to produce an outcome (i.e., a solution to a problem) that can be considered somewhat satisfactory.

A software architecture contains different level of abstractions, and each level probably contains its own architectures with its own levels of abstractions. Think of the ISO/OSI model or the TCP/IP stack protocols. These are actual conceptual models that try to standardize a problem—the internal functions of a communications system—by dividing it into abstraction layers. Each layer contains its own specifications, protocols, and interfaces to exchange information with the other layers.

Each system will also have many different phases of operations that will define its behavior in any possible situation presented by the problem scenario.

Architectures define how the various modular *components* are linked through *connectors*, how data is exchanged between these components using a set of defined *interfaces*, and how these are configured within a system.

There are also different possible configurations of components and connectors; these are called *architectural styles*.

Architectural styles can be viewed like design patterns, or in other words as general and reusable approaches to solving recurring problems in a certain context.

It is also possible to break down a system architecture from different *viewpoints*. The idea of an architectural viewpoint is to represent a system from a certain perspective, to permit its comprehension.

The Web is a particularly interesting example of a complex distributed system whose architecture needs to be analyzed via different viewpoints, or by considering its different layers and components, from the actual physical connections that make each communication possible to the various protocols involved in every HTTP message sent or received by every server, computer, and device connected to the Internet.

In 2003, the W3C defined the "Architecture of the World Wide Web," (*http://bit.ly/w3c-architecture*) describing the properties of the Web and the design choices that had been made to apply those properties to protocols, standards, and interfaces developed up to that moment.

Introducing REST

The RESTful architectural style (or just REST) was used by the W3C to design both the HTTPv1.1 protocol and the so-called modern web architecture constraints.

The W3C Technical Architecture Group identifies three architectural foundations of the Web. These are:

- The identification mechanism, where each resource is identified by a uniform resource identifier (URI)
- The actual communication process between agents, where representations about resources are exchanged
- The representations of data being exchanged, and how these are built from a pre-determined set of data formats

These are also the three bases of REST architectures (Figure 1-1).

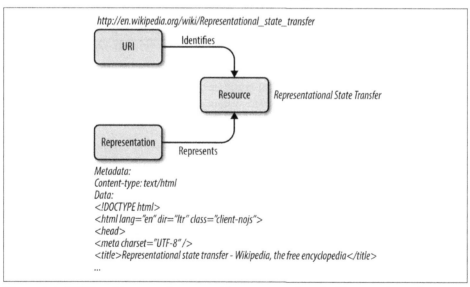

Figure 1-1. REST architectures interact with resources identified by URIs by exchanging data representations (HTML, XML, JSON, etc.)

An important aspect of the Web's architecture is that identification, representation, and format are independent concepts. A URI can identify a resource without knowing what formats the resource uses to exchange representations. Likewise, the proto‐cols and representations used by the resource to communicate can be modified independent of the URI identifying the resource.

This property of orthogonality within the Web's architectural foundations makes sys‐tems easy to modify, extend, and scale. Communication interfaces can be defined only in terms of the communication protocols used, the specified syntax and seman‐tics, and the sequences of interchanged messages.

The principles and architectural details of REST are discussed in practical terms in Chapter 3, but in this chapter we will introduce some theoretical concepts regarding the architecture of the Web and RESTful programming in general. Also note that some more detailed aspects of the HTTP protocol are covered in the Appendix.

RESTful Programming and Hypermedia

The W3C defines the World Wide Web as a *network-spanning information space of resources interconnected by links*. Within this information space, shared by several information systems around the world, other systems and agents create, retrieve, interpret, parse, and reason about resources.

The architecture of the Web is therefore that of a networked, distributed hypermedia information system, where clients access resources by "calling" them through their URIs. Resource states are communicated through some representation of the resource itself via some widely understood data format (HTML, XML, CSS, PNG, scripts).

Distributed systems is a vibrant field of study in computer science. In fact, everything hip and new seems to involve distributed systems, from the proliferation of web apps, to the newest mobile computing trends, to the Internet of Things (IoT).

A distributed system can be roughly defined as a *collection of independent computers that appears to its users as a single coherent system*.

 This definition is from Andrew S. Tanenbaum and Maarten Van Steen's *Distributed Systems: Principles and Paradigms*, 2nd ed. (*http://bit.ly/distributed-systems*) (Upper Saddle River, NJ: Prentice-Hall, 2006). Their book is a milestone in the literature of dis‐tributed systems, enabling readers to understand past, present and future development.

A very important aspect of distributed systems is that differences between the indi‐vidual components and the ways in which they communicate are almost completely transparent to the final user. The same principle applies for the internal organization of each component, as long as the external communication protocols and interfaces are implemented per specifications.

Single components are hence able to operate autonomously and cooperate with one another by exchanging information, so that a hypothetical user can interact with the system in a consistent and uniform way, regardless of where and when the interactions take place.

This aspect makes distributed systems easy to scale, in principle.

Design Concepts

REST is an architectural style crafted for and upon a particular distributed system, the Web. The primary goal of any distributed system is to facilitate access to remote resources.

REST was therefore designed with low entry barriers and with simplicity in mind, to enable quick user adoption and speed up development.

All protocols designed for the Web were conceived as text protocols. Communications between web components could be tested using existing network tools and underlying protocols.

REST was also designed to be easily extended if needed. The Web was built as an Internet-scale application. This means that no central control was considered in the initial design. Anarchic scalability and independent development were (and still represent) two core elements of the Web's architecture.

REST carries the basis for hypermedia applications. Application control information is embedded within representations, or one level above.

RESTful Architectures

RESTful architectures carry some architectural constraints that were inherited from various networked distributed architectural styles.

Client and server in RESTful architectures are orthogonal, meaning there is a clear separation of concerns and functions between them. User logic is moved completely to the client side and server components are kept simple to improve scalability.

This separation also allows the two components to be developed and evolve independently, so long as they respect the communication protocols and defined interfaces.

In a RESTful architecture, each request is treated independently. This means the architecture of the server is stateless and requests cannot take advantage of any stored context and must carry all the necessary information to be understood and processed.

Each response also needs to be labeled as cacheable or noncacheable. If a response is cacheable, the client can store and reuse the data for network efficiency (i.e., cache the data to reduce round-trips).

REST is built on the idea of uniform interfaces between components. This way, the architecture and design choices are simplified in favor of simple interactions. The internal implementations of the components are separated from the services provided, which also encourages independent evolution and development.

REST architectures are layered. This idea of hierarchical systems is deeply rooted in networked architectures and software development in general.

There are a few advantages to developing a hierarchical architecture. The primary benefit is that it keeps the overall system design simple, since each component "sees" and operates only with the layer with which it is immediately interacting.

A last constraint introduced by REST is that of code on demand. Clients in a RESTful architecture can download and execute code in the form of *scripts*. This allows for system extendibility and simplification of the client architecture by reducing the number of features that must be preimplemented and allowing features to be added later, when needed.

Central elements of REST architectures are data, components, and connectors.

The *data* elements described in the definition of REST are the actual *resources* and the exchanged *representations*. With components instead we identify the *clients*, *origin servers*, and any *intermediate parties*. *Components* can communicate and exchange messages through connectors. *Connectors* are specifically used to communicate between RESTful interfaces and any other type of interface. For example, a RESTful service can communicate with a database that doesn't possess a REST interface through a REST connector.

Each of these elements can be used to define an architectural *view*, an abstraction that will help us understand how REST components interact and communicate.

A view describes a layer within an architecture. The need to define layers or views comes from the old controversy around the concepts of client and server. In the HTTP protocol, a component acting as server for a specific call can act as client for another call (for further details on this, see the Appendix). Describing architectures in terms of clients and servers is therefore not always ideal.

Sometimes, to describe architectural views, it is considered that the ultimate goal of an application or client software is accessing some data in a database. In this case, three main levels are considered:

- The interface level
- The process level

- The data level

While these levels can certainly also be identified in REST architectures, it is more convenient to use REST core elements to describe REST architectural views.

Process view

The process view of a REST architecture describes the data flow between client and server for a certain communication. The user agent makes a request to the server, and the message travels through the network and is processed by a series of intermediaries. Intermediary blocks are used for different reasons, from latency reduction to encapsulation of legacy services and from security enforcement to traffic balancing. Intermediaries in REST architectures can be added at any point in the communication without having to modify any interfaces between components.

Recall that the REST architectural style advocates for independent deployment, scalability of components and interactions, and generality of interfaces. The message flow between client and server is also completely dynamic. This has two major implications. The first, and most obvious, is that the path followed by the request message can be different from the path followed by the response message (Figure 1-2). The second implication is that it is not necessary for each component to be aware of the whole network topology to route messages.

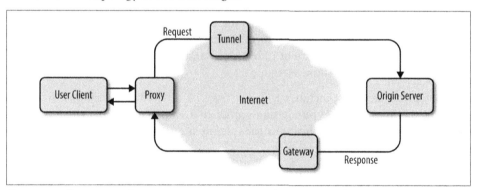

Figure 1-2. Request and response messages can go through an arbitrary number of intermediary blocks

Connector view

The connector view of a REST architecture is somewhat equivalent to the interface level, describing the actual communications between components.

Because REST represents an abstraction of the Web's architecture, communication is not restricted to a particular protocol. REST instead specifies the scope of interaction and implementation assumptions that need to be made between components.

For example, although the Web uses HTTP as its transfer protocol, its architecture can also include services using other protocols, like FTP. REST delegates interaction with those services to a REST connector. The REST connector is responsible for invoking connections to other (non-REST) architectures in parallel.

This aspect of REST preserves its principle of generality of interfaces, allowing for heterogeneous components to communicate seamlessly (Figure 1-3).

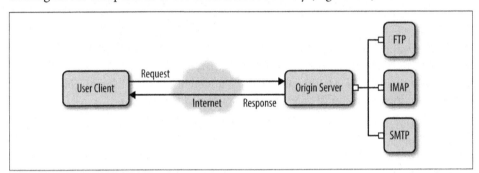

Figure 1-3. A REST connector is able to interface with non-REST services, allowing for different components to easily communicate.

Data view

The data view of an architecture concerns the application state. REST is an architectural style designed for distributed information systems, so a RESTful application can be loosely defined as a structure of information and control alternatives performing some specific tasks under some user input.

This definition certainly includes a wide range of different applications, from an online dictionary to a ticket purchasing service to a social networking site to a video streaming service. These applications each define a set of goals to be performed by the underlying systems.

Components within applications interact to accomplish such goals. Interaction happens by exchanging messages used for control semantics, or exchanging complete resource representations. Messages are dynamically sized.

A frequent form of interaction between components is a request for retrieving a representation of a resource—i.e., the GET method in HTTP (Figure 1-4). The representation received in response contains all the control state of the RESTful resource.

One of the goals of REST is to eliminate the need for the server to maintain any awareness of the client state beyond the current request. This improves server scalability, but also makes every request independent from the previous or the next one.

The application state will therefore be defined by its pending requests, the topology of any connected components, the active requests on any connectors, and finally the data flow of resource representations in response to all its requests.

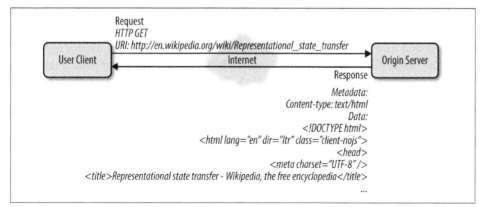

Figure 1-4. The client makes an HTTP GET request and receives an HTML document in response from the server

Part of the application state is also any possible processing of the resource representations as these are received by the user agent.

When an application has no outstanding requests, it is said that the application is in the *steady state*. It is also said that the user-perceived performance is a measure of the latency between consecutive steady states of the application.

Because the control state of an application resides in the requested resource representation, obtaining the first representation is a priority. Once the first representation is obtained the user will be able to jump to another resource representation via a link and manipulate the state directly.

RESTful Interfaces: Hypermedia and Action Controls

The concept of uniformity of interfaces is central to REST architectures. As long as each component implements this simple general principle, each module within the architecture can be developed and deployed independently; the overall architectural complexity is reduced, while server technology can be more easily scaled. Simple interfaces also allow for an arbitrary number of intermediary blocks to be placed between server and client within a communication.

RESTful interfaces

The uniformity of REST interfaces is built upon four guiding principles. These are:

- The identification of resources through the URI mechanism

- The manipulation of resources through their representations
- The use of self-descriptive messages
- Implementing Hypermedia as Engine of Application State (HATEOAS)

The use of the URI mechanism to identify resources is particularly central to the Web, and more generally to REST architectures. When the Web was being designed, it was proposed that each document would be identified by a *Universal Document Identifier* (UDI), to stress the importance that, although the UDI could eventually change, it should nevertheless be considered the unique identifier for that particular document.

The acronym UDI was later replaced by the more general URL (*Uniform Resource Locator*) and then URI (*Uniform Resource Identifier*). The URI still provides a means of identifying a resource that is simple, defined, and extensible.

The uniformity principle assures that different types of identifiers can be used in the same context, allowing a uniform semantic interpretation, even though the actual mechanisms used to access those resources may be different. At the same time, it permits us to introduce new types of resource identifiers without having to modify the way existing identifiers are used, while also permitting reuse of identifiers in different contexts.

It is important to note that not all URIs are URLs. The terms URI and URL actually refer to two different things, although they are often used interchangeably. Strictly speaking, a URI is just an identifier of a resource; it can be a locator or a name (URN, or Uniform Resource Name), or both. A URL therefore refers to a URI that, in addition to identifying a resource, also provides its network location—i.e., a means of locating the resource by providing its access mechanism.

URNs are location-independent resource identifiers that are intended to be persistent. The term URN has now been included in the URI definition: "URI" is used to refer to URIs as intended by the URN scheme and any other URI with the properties of a resource name.

We have introduced the term *scheme*, referring to the URN scheme. A scheme can introduce a protocol or data format that makes use of a specific URI syntax and semantics. The URI specifications provide a definition of the range of syntax permitted for all possible URIs, including schemes that haven't been defined yet. The scheme makes the URI syntax easily extensible, since each scheme can modify and restrict syntax and semantics accordingly to its particular set of rules.

Each URI starts with the scheme name. The scheme name refers to a specification for assigning identifiers within the same scheme. Some scheme examples are:

- *http*
- *ftp*
- *mailto*

- *telnet*
- *news*
- *urn*

Once again, the principle of uniformity allows for independent evolution and development of protocols and data formats from identification schemes and the implementations that make use of the URIs.

The URI parsing mechanism is scheme independent. This means that the URI is first parsed according to the general syntax and semantic specification, while scheme-dependent handling of the URI is postponed until the scheme-dependent semantics are actually needed.

Although URIs are used to identify resources, it is not guaranteed that the URI itself provides a means to access the resource. This is in fact a common misunderstanding of URIs. URIs provide identification. Any other operation associated with a URI reference is associated with the protocol definition or data format that makes use of the URI.

The resource identified by the URI is a general object that is not necessarily accessible either. A resource can be either an electronic document or a service, an abstract concept or a relationship.

A resource is modified by manipulating its representation. The representation in REST contains the actual resource state, and this is what is exchanged between client and server. This means that users interact with a particular resource through representations of its state.

A RESTful application may support more than one representation of the same resource at a certain URI, allowing clients to indicate the preferred representation type.

Resource representations are requested through messages between client and server. Messages in REST architectures are said to be self-descriptive. This means that all the information needed to complete the task is actually contained in the message.

How to include control

Hypermedia as the Engine of Application State (HATEOAS) is a distinguishing element of REST architecture, describing how hypermedia controls can be used to interact with an application to modify its state.

Literally, it means that hyperlinks included within resource representations can be used to control how the user interacts with an application, in a similar way to how a user surfs through the content of a website.

This concept of designing the way a user explores resource states as we would a web page can be compared to the task of designing an application flow or a user interface.

A designer would implement a certain number of tasks that can be completed by the user and would present them in a certain way. The designer's goal, in this case, would be to make the use of the application as intuitive as possible for the end user.

In a similar way, HATEOAS provides the possibility to create semantically rich interfaces for machines and humans alike.

Links are flow control

When designing a simple application, the developer (or architect, if it is particularly complex) will make a number of choices to define the different tasks that a user can accomplish by using the application. Let us think for example about a web email client. The user of our client needs to be able to receive messages, read messages, write messages, and send messages. These are four simple actions that an email client needs to accomplish.

Because our email client application is web-based, the user will probably access it through a certain URL. The user will be presented with a login window to authenticate herself. After the user has authenticated, she will be presented with her list of unread messages. Each message can be opened through a link requesting the full text of the email.

Sound familiar? Each link in the application defines a task that the user can accomplish. Now let us think of the same application as an API.

An API of our web email client will contain all the actions of our application. The API itself will only respond to certain actions—for example, a given call will return the list of unread messages and a different call will return the latest unread message.

We can make this clearer with a few concrete examples. An HTTP GET request to *api.ouremailclient.com/v1/client/list/unread* returns a list of unread messages:

```
"inbox":
{
  "message":
  {
    "id": "Dfvsafaf1479",
    "title":"example message",
    "sender":"john@rubyonrails.org",
    "received_on":"2014-08-19 03:14:07"
  }
  "message":
  {
    "id":"8gryyfav13gT",
    "title":"hello from kathy",
    "sender":"kathy@wikipedia.org",
    "received_on":"2014-08-19 04:23:31"
  }
  "message":
```

```
    {
      "id":"FrT3gqewQ2Ry",
      "title":"let's go surfing",
      "sender":"info@surfingvacation.net",
      "received_on":"2014-08-19 08:45:13"
    }
  }
```

An HTTP GET request to *api.ouremailclient.com/v1/client/messages/Dfvsafaf1479*
returns the full text of a certain message identified with its ID:

```
"message":{
  "id": "Dfvsafaf1479",
  "title":"example message",
  "sender":"john@rubyonrails.org",
  "received_on":"2014-08-19 03:14:07"
  "text":"Hello, this is a sample message to test your new email.
  We hope it works!"
}
```

Although the API itself performs the actions, we would also need to include more
logic in some other software component. The result would allow us to perform all the
functionality of a web application through a set of API calls.

What if a link to the next message was included in the resource representation? Following a simple *next* field would lead the user to the next unread message without
having to go back to the list.

Actions, or operation control

Now imagine that you would like to reply to a single message. You will have to send
another request to another endpoint, specifying at least sender and title.

Although the action seems quite intuitive, especially if you are thinking about it from
a programmer's perspective, having to code the logic to create and send the message
means that if something in the API changes, you will have to update your code so that
your application can continue to function.

This is certainly not ideal. In a perfect world, you would have to send a request specifying only the text you would like to include in your reply message.

To accomplish this simple task, we could create a different endpoint called *reply* that
takes the message ID and the text that the user would like to include and just sends
the email. In this case the user, or the application using our API, would need to know
the right endpoint in order to use it. However, this again means that if something
changes in the endpoint, all the clients using it will need to be rewritten, even if only
partially, in order for them to continue to work.

Another possibility is to include a link to the *reply* action in the message representation. This way a client would only need to send the text in the call to the reply end-

point. The client would not have to include any logic that specifies the endpoint for the reply call; it would just find it in the resource representation and call it as it calls any other resource in the API.

Beyond HTTP

The goal of REST architecture, and hypermedia, is to go beyond the limitations of the Web as we have known it. When the Web was being developed, HTTP and web pages were said to bring semantics to a world of standalone documents. The experience of a user surfing the Web was described as that of our brain seeing an image and *linking* that image to something else we have known or done in the past, like a sound or a smell or a specific place on Earth.

Hypermedia builds on the definition of hypertext as interlinked information and on the HTTP protocol as the primary transport protocol for the Web.

A RESTful application, or a REST API, should in fact be protocol independent. Instead, the API's descriptive efforts should be invested in the definition of the media types used to represent resources.

Hypermedia applications do not simply link objects and make HTTP calls, but also allow clients to interact with those objects through actions.

Ideally, a user would access a hypermedia API only through its main URL. It would then be the role of the server to present the user with the accessible resources and their possible operations.

Information is simultaneously presented with controls, allowing the user to act on it, by selecting actions. Links, therefore, are only a tiny aspect of HATEOAS and REST.

Wrapping Up

This chapter explored the HTTP protocol, the architecture of the Web as a distributed hypermedia system, and the bases of RESTful architectures and hypermedia interfaces. In the next chapter, we will start building a Rails application. This will be an API with actual data with some hypermedia flow control.

## CHAPTER 2

Getting Started with Ruby on Rails

This is a "getting started with Ruby on Rails" chapter—although it will not entirely be a "how to get Rails working" chapter. Our starting point will be exploring Rails by setting up the environment; I will then introduce the Rails application architecture, and finally we will create our first "Hello Rails" API.

Getting to Know Ruby on Rails

Ruby on Rails is a Model-View-Controller (MVC) framework. MVC is a software architectural pattern that divides a given application into three interconnected logic blocks. In the three blocks, the internal representation of some information or object (the model) is separated from the way the user interacts with this information (the controller) and the way this information is presented to the user (the view).

This means that in Rails there is a place where each line of code belongs: all the different models and controllers in your application interact in a standard way. Rails is also designed with the philosophy of favoring convention over configuration. Generally speaking, the developer doesn't need to write any external metadata; everything just works.

Rails is also agile by design, and it handles changes very well. As a framework Rails was built around individuals and interactions rather than processes and tools; it favors working code over extensive documentation, transparency over complex configurations, customer collaboration over elaborate processes. Rails is built around the idea that a group of developers and their favorite editors can just start coding, and this is immediately reflected in what the users see. Rails has been lowering the barriers of prototyping and deploying for programmers and startups, and we are going to see how it can do the same for the next generation of RESTful web APIs.

Setting Up Ruby and Rails

Setting up your Rails environment is probably the hardest part of getting started with Rails. If you are familiar with Rails or with programming in general, you probably know the joy and frustration of setting up a working coding environment on a new computer. That's exactly what we are going to do now.

The version of Ruby recommended for the current version of Rails (4.2 at the time of writing) on *rubyonrails.org* is 2.2. If you have an older working version of Ruby and you do not feel like updating it right now, just bear in mind that some things might be slightly different. You should also consider that Ruby 1.8.x has not been supported since Rails 3.2, while Ruby 1.9.3+ will be supported until Rails 5.

The procedure to install Ruby will vary depending on the system you are using. Generally speaking, there are three possibilities:

Install from source
    You can download Ruby and compile it yourself.

Use an installer
    Windows users can use RubyInstaller (*http://rubyinstaller.org/*). For Mac OS X users, Ruby is included with the developer tools.

Use a version manager
    Like rbenv or RVM.

rubyonrails.org recommends managing your Ruby installation through rbenv, although there is some controversy on the matter. Both rbenv and RVM are extremely easy to use: rbenv is lighter and has fewer features; RVM is more complete and mature.

In reality, rbenv "only" manages Ruby environments, allowing you to switch quickly between them, either locally or as a system-wide default. RVM manages not only the Ruby environment but also Ruby gems. Some say this is too much work for RVM, especially when Rails provides another tool to manage gems, Bundler (*http://bundler.io/*).

If you are interested in the differences between RVM and rbenv, I recommend you start reading some of the endless discussions in the community. It is always interesting to get to know different points of view. We will follow *rubyonrails.org*'s suggestion and consider rbenv our standard Ruby environment manager; nevertheless, we will go through RVM installation as well, in case you prefer that option.

RVM

RVM (*https://rvm.io/*) is a command-line tool that allows you to easily install, manage, and work with multiple Ruby environments from interpreters to sets of gems.

The website provides a quick guided install option as well as detailed documentation explaining the different ways in which users can install RVM on their machines.

There are three installation modes for RVM:

Single user
RVM is installed within a particular user's *$HOME*.

Multiuser
RVM is usable by every user on the system. This is usually needed by server administrators.

Mixed mode
RVM is usable by all users on the system, but it will also provide isolated rubies/gemsets within a user's *$HOME*.

We are going to assume you will be installing the latest release version in single-user mode. If this is the case, you just have to execute a simple command to install *rvm* with *ruby* and *rails*:

```
$ \curl -sSL https://get.rvm.io | bash -s stable --ruby --rails
```

 If you wish to find out more, or you need other installation options, the RVM website (*https://rvm.io/rvm/install*) will guide you through the installation procedures.

RVM is a powerful tool that does much more than just managing Ruby versions. In fact, it has been developed as a collection of tools to solve problems that Ruby developers often face. I recommend you read the documentation and project FAQ before making any decision regarding which is your perfect environment manager tool (if you haven't got one already).

The important thing to note is that RVM is a complete package manager. This means it will manage both your Ruby and your Rails versions, unlike rbenv, which is mainly a Ruby manager.

rbenv

rbenv manages your Ruby installation. For Rails and gemset management, you should rely on Bundler. Bundler is an environment manager for Ruby projects that allows you to track and install the exact needed gems and versions. We will talk about Bundler when configuring our "Hello Rails" app in a few pages.

Unfortunately, you cannot use both rbenv and RVM; you need to pick one of the two. So, if you already have RVM installed and you would like to try rbenv, please make sure to fully uninstall RVM and remove any references to it from your shell initialization files before proceeding.

rbenv works by intercepting Ruby commands using shim executables injected into your *PATH*. It will then determine which Ruby version has been set for a particular application, and will pass your commands to the specified Ruby installation.

A *shim* in computer programming is a small library that intercepts API calls, changes the arguments passed, and handles or redirects the operations transparently.

rbenv inserts a directory of shims at the beginning of your *PATH*:

```
~/.rbenv/shims:/usr/local/bin:/usr/bin:/bin
```

rbenv then matches every Ruby command across every installed version of *irb*, *gem* (the Interactive Ruby Shell), *rake*, *ruby*, and so on.

Shims are used to pass the command along, so that if you run:

```
$ rake
```

with rbenv installed the following will happen:

1. The operating system will search your *PATH* for an executable file named *rake*.
2. It will find the rbenv shim named *rake* at the beginning of your *PATH*, because this is where all the rbenv shims are located.
3. It will run the shim named *rake*, which will pass the command along to rbenv, which in turn will forward it to the correct Ruby version.

To install rbenv you need some basic Git knowledge, or if you are on OS X you can use Homebrew. Homebrew is a package manager for OS X, a little bit like *apt-get* if you are familiar with the Debian system. You can download Homebrew from *http://brew.sh*.

Assuming that you are using Git, the first step will be to check out rbenv into a folder you have created beforehand by using the command:

```
$ mkdir ~/.rbenv
```

Note that this is a *dot folder*. A dot folder is a hidden directory that is not displayed by default. Hidden folders (or files) are usually used for user preferences or to store some utility state.

Now, execute the `git` command to clone the rbenv remote repository:

```
$ git clone https://github.com/sstephenson/rbenv.git ~/.rbenv
```

Then add *~/.rbenv/bin* to your *PATH* for access to the rbenv command-line utility:

```
$ echo 'export PATH="$HOME/.rbenv/bin:$PATH"' >> ~/.bash_profile
```

If you are using Ubuntu Desktop you'll need to modify your *~/.bashrc* instead of *~/.bash_profile*. If you are using Zsh, you should modify your *~/.zshrc* file instead of *~/.bash_profile*.

The next step is adding *rbenv init* to your shell to enable shims and autocompletion:

```
$ echo 'eval "$(rbenv init -)"' >> ~/.bash_profile
```

As pointed out in the previous step, you should use *~/.bashrc* on Ubuntu, or *~/.zshrc* for Zsh.

Finally, you can restart your shell to apply the *PATH* changes. Opening a new tab or window usually will do.

To check if rbenv has been set up successfully, run:

```
$ type rbenv #=> "rbenv is a function"
```

As an optional step you can also install *ruby-build*, an rbenv plug-in that provides the `rbenv install` command, which simplifies the process of installing new Ruby versions. I recommend installing *ruby-build*.

To do this, run:

```
$ git clone https://github.com/sstephenson/ruby-build.git
~/.rbenv/plugins/ruby-build
```

After *ruby-build* is installed, you can run `rbenv install -l` to check the list of available Ruby versions.

To install the latest Ruby version, simply run:

```
$ rbenv install 2.2.2
```

Now that you have a fresh version of Ruby installed, you might want to set it. To set a local application-specific Ruby version, simply run the command:

```
$ rbenv local 2.2.2
```

To unset the local Ruby version, run this instead:

```
$ rbenv local --unset
```

You can also decide to set a global default Ruby version. This is easily accomplished with the commands:

```
$ rbenv global 2.2.2
$ rbenv rehash
```

The `rbenv rehash` command is used to make sure that the shims in the *rbenv* directory match the correct Ruby commands across every installed version of Ruby.

Finally, do a system-wide gem update to make sure that all your gems are at the latest version:

```
$ gem update --system
```

 Please refer to the rbenv (*https://github.com/sstephenson/rbenv*) repository for specific rbenv documentation.

Using an Installer

Using an installer can be the quickest way to set up your Ruby on Rails environment. All you have to do is download a package, and wait for the installer to do the hard work while you are pouring yourself some tea.

RailsInstaller (*http://railsinstaller.org/en*) can do this for you.

The Architecture of a Rails App

Rails is an open source web application framework built in Ruby. It is a full stack framework created by David Heinemeier Hansson in 2004–2005.

Rails is designed as a Model-View-Controller framework (Figure 2-1). MVC can be considered an architectural abstraction of object-oriented programming. The idea behind MVC is that it is possible to create a direct connection between what the user sees and what the programmer actually writes. The user-facing interface of the MVC framework—i.e., what the users see—is the view part. The model is the actual application logic: models describe the objects within an application. The controller defines the actions happening between views and models. In other words, controllers define how models are accessed from the views.

Model-View-Controller

MVC is a pattern for graphic user interface (GUI) software design, formulated by Trygve Reenskaug in 1979 while he was visiting the Xerox Palo Alto Research Center (PARC).

MVC was conceived as a solution to the problem of a user having to deal with large and complex data sets, creating the illusion for the user of seeing and manipulating the domain information directly. We can see how the MVC approach seems natural for RESTful applications and Rails.

In an MVC architecture, the model is where the state of the application resides. This state can either be transient or permanent. When the state is permanent it can be stored outside of the application—for example, in a database.

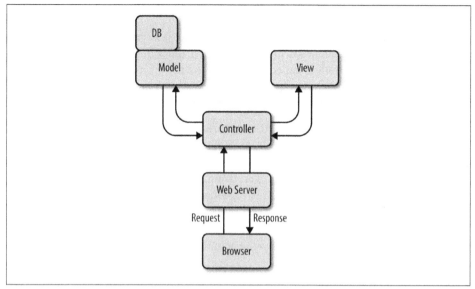

Figure 2-1. The MVC abstraction

The model is more than just the data it describes, though. You can think of the model as both the data object and the constraints associated with it.

The view, simply put, is the user interface. This is based on the data contained in the model and the actions passed by the controller.

The view itself never modifies the data; it just displays it. Many views could access the same model, and one view could ideally access more models.

The view creates all or some parts of a page that is displayed by the browser. Simply put, the most basic view is just some HTML code that displays some text.

Dynamic content in Rails is handled through templates. At the time of writing there are many (maybe countless) templating schemes available, the most common of which are *Erb*, *slim*, and *haml*. We will cover templating schemes in more detail in Chapter 9, when we map data streams into the application UI.

The controller is the logical center of a Rails application. It receives and handles events from the outside world, interacts with the model, and displays data back to the user through the appropriate view.

Most of the interaction between the user (view), controller, and data (model) is handled by Rails transparently. As a developer you can comfortably concentrate on application functionality. This aspect particularly makes Rails applications easy to develop and maintain.

The controller is also responsible for managing caching, helper modules, and user sessions.

In Rails applications, the web server will send requests to a *router*, which will forward the requests and parse them accordingly. The router identifies a particular method in the controller, which in Rails is called an *action*. The action might retrieve or interact with some data in the model, invoke other actions, and so on. The final result is sent to the view to be rendered for the user.

The MVC architecture provides a clear structure for programming and designing an application. Ruby on Rails is no different. Rails provides and enforces a structure; models, views, and controllers are developed separately with different functionality. The icing on the cake of Rails is that everything is put together as the program executes by using intelligent defaults already provided in the framework. This means the developer can concentrate on creating the application logic and forget about the rest. We will better understand how models, views, and controllers work in the next chapter, when we get our hands dirty with some actual development.

Object-Relational Mapping

Object-oriented programming (OOP) has always found it difficult to translate the object model into entity–relationship tables like those used in database management systems such as *MySQL*.

Object-relational mapping (ORM) is the process of converting data models built following OOP paradigms into entity–relationship database records. Using ORM, the properties and relationships of an object can be easily written to the database without having to translate programming logic into SQL statements, which means less database access code is required.

In Rails this is accomplished by *Active Record*, an implementation of the Active Record pattern introduced by Martin Fowler for objects carrying both persistent data and behavioral logic that operates on the data.

Active Record is responsible for handling all the operations that Rails uses to persistently store data. It provides several mechanisms related to the creation and use of model objects. For example, it allows us to:

- Represent models and their data.
- Represent associations between models.
- Represent inheritance hierarchies through related models.
- Validate models before they get persisted to the database.
- Perform database operations in an object-oriented fashion.

The last point is particularly important for Rails developers. Although you should always have a clear picture of the database supporting your application and how your code uses it, with Rails you can design your app by only thinking in terms of programming objects, without having to create an entity–relationship diagram.

Rails achieves this by providing some standard conventions that, if followed, do not require the programmer to write much configuration—and in some cases, no configuration at all—when creating Active Record models.

The idea is that explicit configuration should be needed only when you cannot follow the standard conventions. It is assumed that most web applications will use the default configuration.

ORM assumes you are using a relational database. There are also object-oriented databases available, and if you plan to use one of these you won't be using Active Record; instead, you'll use a different gem with a similar API to Active Record that provides object document mapper (ODM) functionalities for NoSQL database systems.

Bundler

Bundler (*http://bundler.io/*) is the default gem manager for Rails. Its stated mission is to "[manage] an application's dependencies through its entire life, across many machines systematically and repeatably."

Getting Bundler set up on your system is quite easy. Open a terminal window and run:

```
$ gem install bundler
```

With Bundler, dependencies are declared in a file at the application root. This file is called the *Gemfile*.

A *Gemfile* requires at least one gem source, a URL for a RubyGems server. If you run:

```
$ bundle init
```

a *Gemfile* with the default *rubygems.org* source will be generated:

```
# A sample Gemfile
source "https://rubygems.org"
# gem "rails"
```

If possible, use *https* so your connection to the *rubygems.org* server will be verified with SSL. When you generate a new Rails application, this is done for you by Rails.

You can declare with Bundler the gems that you need, including version numbers:

```
source 'https://rubygems.org'
gem 'rails', '4.1.0.rc2'
```

```
gem 'rack-cache'
gem 'nokogiri', '~> 1.6.1'
```

Most of the version specifiers are self-explanatory, but others have a special meaning.

For example, >= is self-explanatory, whereas ~> 2.0.3 is identical to >= 2.0.3, and < 2.1. ~> 2.1 is identical to >= 2.1 and < 3.0. ~> 2.2.beta will match prerelease versions like 2.2.beta.12.

Choosing an Editor

Ruby on Rails doesn't have a so-called standard IDE that the majority of programmers use. Rails programmers tend to use all kinds of editors to write their code; we all have our particular tastes and preferences.

A noncomprehensive list of editors used, in no particular order, includes:

- Vim
- Emacs
- RubyMine (the closest thing to an IDE, probably)
- Aptana RadRails
- TextMate
- NetBeans
- Sublime Text 2
- RDT (Ruby Development Tools plug-in for Eclipse)

Choosing your perfect editor is really a matter of personal taste, though developers often get into editor wars.

If you don't believe me, check out *https://xkcd.com/378/*.

Hello Rails

To make sure that everything was installed correctly and to familiarize ourselves a bit with Rails, we are going to generate a simple "Hello Rails" API. This is like the standard "Hello Rails" app, except at this point we are not creating a view but an API returning a JSON representation of the "Hello Rails" string.

Start by verifying that Ruby was installed correctly:

```
$ ruby -v
ruby 2.1.2p95 (2014-05-08 revision 45877) [x86_64-darwin13.0]
```

Also, make sure that SQL is installed on your system. Most *nix systems will already have SQLite installed; if you are using Windows, you can check the SQLite website (*http://www.sqlite.org/*) for installation instructions. This command:

```
$ sqlite3 --version
```

should return the version of SQLite that is installed.

If you have set up your environment with RVM, chances are you already have Rails installed. If not, you can install it by using the gem install command provided by RubyGems:

```
$ gem install rails
```

To verify that everything has been installed correctly, run the following:

```
$ rails --version
```

Rails comes with a set of scripts, called *generators*, designed to make developement easier and faster. The new application generator creates everything that is necessary to start working on a new app. To use the generator, navigate to your workspace directory in a terminal window and type:

```
$ rails new hello_rails
```

Rails will create a skeleton app for you and run bundle install at the end with a default *Gemfile*. You will see a list of create actions, and then Bundle fetching gems and resolving any dependencies:

```
create
create README.rdoc
create Rakefile
create config.ru
create .gitignore
create Gemfile
create app
...
run bundle install
Fetching gem metadata from https://rubygems.org/..........
Fetching additional metadata from https://rubygems.org/..
Resolving dependencies...
Using rake (10.3.2)
...
Your bundle is complete!
Use `bundle show [gemname]` to see where a bundled gem is installed.
```

The list of autogenerated files and folders constitutes the Rails app structure:

app/
> This folder contains the controllers, models, views, helpers, mailers, and assets for your application.

bin/

This folder contains startup scripts and other scripts used for deploying or running your app.

config/

Files in this folder are used to configure aspects like routes and databases. We will incrementally discover files in this folder as we start developing different aspects of our applications.

config.ru

This file contains the Rack configuration for Rack-based servers used to start the application.

db/

This folder is where the current database schema is stored, as well as all database migrations.

Gemfile

This file specifies the gem dependencies needed for your Rails application.

Gemfile.lock

This is where Bundler records the exact versions of all the gems that were installed. When the same library/project is loaded on another machine, running `bundle install` will look at *Gemfile.lock* and install the exact same versions, rather than just using the *Gemfile* and installing the most recent versions.

lib/

This folder contains extended libraries.

log/

This folder contains the application logs.

public/

This folder contains static files and compiled assets.

Rakefile

This file locates and loads tasks that can be run from the command line. Rather than changing the *Rakefile*, you should add your own tasks by adding files to the *lib/tasks* directory of your application.

README.rdoc

This is a brief instruction manual for your application. You should edit this file to tell others what your application does, how to set it up, and so on.

test/

This folder contains unit tests, fixtures, and other test apparatus. These are covered in "Testing RESTful Services" on page 96.

tmp/

This folder holds temporary files (such as cache, PID, and session files).

vendor/

Third-party code goes in this folder. In a typical Rails application, this includes vendored gems.

Now we want to check if the newly generated app works. To do this, we will just start the Rails server:

```
$ rails server
=> Booting WEBrick
=> Rails 4.0.4 application starting in development on
   http://0.0.0.0:3000
=> Run `rails server -h` for more startup options
=> Ctrl-C to shutdown server
[2014-07-21 13:29:27] INFO WEBrick 1.3.1
[2014-07-21 13:29:27] INFO ruby 1.9.3 (2013-11-22)
[x86_64-darwin13.0.2]
[2014-07-21 13:29:27] INFO WEBrick::HTTPServer#start:
pid=25171 port=3000
```

WEBrick is a web server distributed with Ruby by default. To see your application in action, open a browser window and navigate to *http://localhost:3000*. You should see the page in Figure 2-2.

Figure 2-2. The default index screen of a Rails app

It's now time for Rails to say hello in JSON format. The idea is to write an extremely simple API with a single endpoint. When this is called it will just say *"hello."*

The first step is to write a simple model. It doesn't need to be stored in the database; it just needs to produce a JSON "hello" string. Create a file called *hello.rb* in *app/ models/*.

We are going to define a `Hello` class with a simple `to_json` method. The method will simply return a JSON-formatted string, `"{"hello": "<text>!"}"`:

```ruby
require 'json'
class Hello
  def to_json(text)
    return JSON.parse("{\"hello\": \"#{text}!\"}")
  end
end
```

We are also going to generate a controller for our app. In a terminal window, type:

```
$ rails generate controller say hello
```

This will generate a controller called *say* with an action *hello*:

```
create app/controllers/say_controller.rb
route get "say/hello"
invoke erb
create app/views/say
create app/views/say/hello.html.erb
invoke test_unit
create test/controllers/say_controller_test.rb
invoke helper
create app/helpers/say_helper.rb
invoke test_unit
create test/helpers/say_helper_test.rb
invoke assets
invoke coffee
create app/assets/javascripts/say.js.coffee
invoke scss
create app/assets/stylesheets/say.css.scss
```

Note that not only the controller file was generated—Rails also took care of generating possible HTML, test, helper, JavaScript, and CSS files, to make sure your app skeleton is kept consistent with a standard configuration.

Of course, you can always delete the files you do not need and will not use. Or, if you don't want Rails to generate the controller and the associated files, you can create a new *say_controller.rb* file in *app/controllers/* and take it from there.

In your favorite editor, navigate to *app/controllers/say_controller.rb*, and modify it like this:

```ruby
class SayController < ApplicationController
  def hello
    @hello = Hello.new
    if params[:user]
      render :json => @hello.to_json(params[:user])
```

```
      else
        render :json => @hello.to_json("Rails")
      end
    end
  end
```

This will produce a controller answering only to JSON format with a hello message. If you add a *user* param to the URL, it will say *"Hello <user>."*

To try it out, with the Rails server running, visit *http://localhost:3000/say/hello.json?user=John* in your browser.

Test-Driven Development

Test-driven development (TDD) is an approach to software development suggesting that you should first write the tests for some code, and then go ahead and write the actual code that would make those tests pass.

TDD has been embraced by many companies and developers for a while, especially in the Rails world. With time, though, some people have realized that TDD can best be applied to static testing done via *unit testing*. Unit testing is a testing procedure that takes individual units of a software application, such as one or more modules or procedures, and applies a set of tests to check if these are correct.

While unit testing verifies that individual modules are correct in isolation, facilitates incremental development and refactoring, and allows for bugs to be discovered early, many applications are data driven, and issues are often found at the intersections of particular data circumstances, configurations, and actual code. In this case, although models can still be unit tested efficiently, functional testing of the app as a whole, with actual data, is needed to consider the code sufficiently tested.

Testing was embraced by the Rails framework from the early days. In a way, we could say TDD is part of the DNA of Rails. Because every application interacts with a database, Rails relies on a test database populated with sample data for efficient testing. Functional testing is also possible to simulate browser requests, so you do not have to click through your application several times in your browser to make sure it works.

Rails creates a test folder called *test/* every time a new Rails project is created using the command `rails new` *application_name*. The *test* folder is already structured so that the *models* directory contains tests for the models, the *controllers* directory contains tests for the controllers, and the *integration* directory contains tests involving a number of controllers interacting.

There is also another folder nested under *test*. This is the *fixtures* folder, and it will contain test data. The *test_helper.rb* file in *test* contains the default test configuration for the Rails application.

When our controller was generated, a test class was also created in *test/controllers/ say_controller_test.rb*. By default the file contains a simple test asserting that calling the defined method succeeded:

```
require 'test_helper'
class SayControllerTest < ActionController::TestCase
  test "should get hello" do
    get :hello
    assert_response :success
  end
end
```

To run all of the tests for the application (in our case, just this single one), run `rake test` in a terminal window:

```
$ rake test
# Running:

.

Finished in 0.045843s, 21.8136 runs/s, 21.8136 assertions/s.
1 runs, 1 assertions, 0 failures, 0 errors, 0 skips
```

The test is running and succeeding. How exciting. Let's write some more!

The first test we are going to write is going to assert that if no parameters are passed to the `hello` method, the response will be `"{"hello":"Rails!"}"`:

```
require 'test_helper'
class SayControllerTest < ActionController::TestCase
  test "should get hello" do
    get :hello
    assert_response :success
  end
  test "should say hello rails in json" do
    get :hello
    assert_equal "{\"hello\":\"Rails!\"}", @response.body
  end
end
```

Let's run it again:

```
$ rake test
# Running:

.

Finished in 0.011128s, 179.7268 runs/s, 179.7268 assertions/s.
2 runs, 2 assertions, 0 failures, 0 errors, 0 skip
```

Now we want to make sure that if we pass a `user` parameter, the response is going to be `"{"hello":"<user!>"}"`:

```
require 'test_helper'
class SayControllerTest < ActionController::TestCase
  test "should get hello" do
    get :hello
    assert_response :success
```

```
      end
      test "should say hello rails in json" do
        get :hello
        assert_equal "{\"hello\":\"Rails!\"}", @response.body
      end
      test "should say hello john in json" do
        get(:hello, {'user' => "John"})
        assert_equal "{\"hello\":\"John!\"}", @response.body
      end
    end
```

Let's run it one last time:

```
$ rake test
# Running:

.
Finished in 0.015381s, 195.0458 runs/s, 195.0458 assertions/s.
3 runs, 3 assertions, 0 failures, 0 errors, 0 skips
```

Our tests are running, and we have verified that our code behaves the way we intended! I personally believe in TDD, although there is a bit of controversy around the issue and some developers have started to write blog posts claiming that TDD is dead. We are going to keep writing simple tests for our code to keep up the habit, but if you think the exercise is tedious, you can just skip the testing part.

Wrapping Up

In this chapter, we started to experiment with Rails development. I hope you had some instant gratification and you are now ready to roll up your sleeves and start creating and designing amazing RESTful services.

## CHAPTER 3

First Adventures in API Design

RESTful architectures follow a set of principles defining how agents can communicate by exchanging resource representations.

This set of general rules has created tremendous possibilities for applications to exchange streams of data and contribute to building a Web that is more open and accessible.

In the Dark Ages of the Web it was common to meet websites that would declare their preferred, or best supported, browsers. "This website is best viewed with <browser_name_and_version>" was a popular tagline to insert in your page.

It wasn't only a matter of preferences. Every browser would parse and display HTML code differently, and some features wouldn't work as expected. Although we have left the Middle Ages of the Internet (mostly), web developers continue to struggle to create web applications that behave consistently across a wide range of devices.

It is important to note that the Web was invented to make computers able to communicate with each other easily, so that humans and software agents alike could act on the information shared across the system. The Web, and subsequently REST, was therefore designed with the core principles of simplicity and uniformity repeated and implemented at different layers of its architecture.

Application Programming Interfaces

An API is an *interface* specifying how some software components should interact with each other. A RESTful API is therefore just a REST interface exposing some internal functionality of a software system to developers and external applications. These can now consume and interact with specific resources through the API itself.

APIs are not exactly a novelty, or something that has been developed only in the web world. In fact, an API simply specifies a set of functions that can be used to interact with some components. These actions and components can be a database system that needs to be accessed by a web server, or a video card exposing some of its functionality through a software library. In REST architectures, APIs define actions that access or modify resources through the exchanged representations (Figure 3-1).

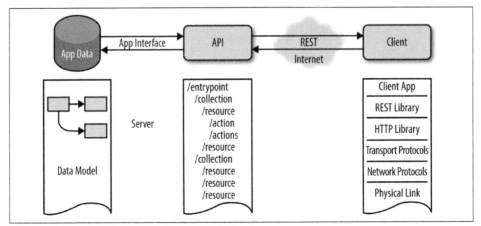

Figure 3-1. An API exposing some application data to a client through a RESTful interface

The API design process therefore starts with some application data that needs to be accessed by one or a collection of clients or services that need to act on the data.

APIs have become a fundamental aspect of software development. Exposing some functionality through an API hides internal system complexity from the user and enforces separation of concerns.

APIs are starting to be fundamental to product development and business execution, so much so that the concept of API-first development is rapidly being adopted.

Developing the product API before anything else actually means defining how users are going to interact with our platform. The API is the skeleton of an application, and in the case of distributed applications, the API defines the way the app interacts with the outside world.

Designing the API before anything else will enable you to start customer discussions and create user stories early on, and use the API to quickly create your app interface mockups.

API-first development can be summarized as the idea that a service should be exposed as a RESTful API to the outside world before anything else. An API-first strategy encourages the use and adoption of your platform amongst developers, while also making access and integration easier for potential customers and partners.

Rather than having to import a specific library or plug-in in their code bases, developers can interface through the API to consume all the required functionality. The API is an application interface that enables developers and services to use your product, consume your data, and easily integrate your service.

One of the easier examples of API-first development is the separation of the backend of an application from its frontend. An API could be built to expose the application data and the actions to act on the app modules, hence operating at the backend level, while the application frontend could just consume the API and present the data to the final user.

There are many more possible examples. For instance, microservices architectures expose different components of their systems through APIs that are implemented and consumed not only by external applications, but also by other components.

In this chapter we are going to start designing an API. Although we are not going to implement hypermedia controls just yet, we will start building our API as a RESTful service, implementing all the principles and architectural constraints of the REST architectural style.

Our service will be developed organically and incrementally. We will start mapping our application data to resources and actions, proceeding with modularity and possible encapsulation of different modules in mind to easily enable resource exploration.

Although there are different opinions and lively discussions on what the best practices are for designing and developing an API, our objective is to adopt a pragmatic approach and cover the topics that will lead to informative decisions through the process of creating and deploying a simple application and its programming interface.

Throughout this chapter and the next ones, we will take the point of view of building microapplications while adopting many microservices paradigms and borrowing some service-oriented architecture (SOA) patterns. We will see how these microapps can cooperate in more complex systems and integrated together with external APIs.

That said, let's start designing and developing our first API.

Dos of API Development

There are many dos (and don'ts) of API development, but some essential requirements revolve around just a few points that can be considered the "good coding standards" of API development. These are the basics that every programmer should take into consideration.

Do KISS and DRY

For every complex problem there is an answer that is clear, simple, and wrong.
—Henry Louis Mencken,
American journalist

KISS is an acronym that stands for "Keep It Stupid Simple" or "Keep It Simple, Stupid," or even the more polite "Keep It Simple and Straightforward." KISS describes a design principle according to which simplicity should be a key goal, and unnecessary complexity should be avoided. KISS is a mantra that is sometimes repeated over and over and can be easily abused.

Although keeping any design neat, clean, and uncomplicated is usually a good thing, you will sooner or later face a case in which a software project or IT system carries an inherent complexity that cannot be eliminated and inevitably will be carried over from the initial requirements to the final result.

Also, any API grows in size and complexity as the number of use cases grows, and maintaining a clear interface that users can feel comfortable with over time is certainly a challenge. However, this does not mean that size and complexity are fundamentally related and it will not be possible to scale the methods and actions of a large or complex API.

Therefore, the KISS concept could be described as stating that a good API is easy to read, to use, and to extend, and is complete and consistent.

Another acronym often encountered in software development is "Don't Repeat Yourself" (DRY). The DRY principle was formulated by Andy Hunt and Dave Thomas in their book *The Pragmatic Programmer*, and states that "Every piece of knowledge must have a single, unambiguous, authoritative representation within a system."

Rails provides a set of tools to "DRY up your code" and avoid duplication, including partials and filters. Partials are used in views and filters in controllers.

From a REST architectural point of view, KISS and DRY translate at the API level to the constraints of uniformity, modularity, and extendability. Both can be summarized into two fundamental principles of API design in particular and system development in general:

- Do simple syntax.
- Do simple semantics.

Do simple syntax

Adopting a simple syntax means making any user's life easier. Start from a base URL that is simple and intuitive. A straightforward base URL will encourage early adopters to just try simple operations with your API (without needing to dive into tedious documentation), thus creating a sense of instant gratification. The rule of thumb in this case is: if you cannot call your API from cURL with a neat and quick line of shell, then maybe your API isn't ready yet and you should rethink one or two of your design choices.

Another aspect to consider is that different people will find different syntax more or less natural to use and remember. A number of syntax choices might just be subjective, so you should always be consistent, and once you choose a convention, stick with it. Don't use mixed upper- and lowercase characters to name a resource; be consistent by using lowercase only. Don't confuse your users with the use of dashes and underscores; keep your resource names short and concise. Another good habit is to use concrete plural nouns when defining resources, avoiding, for example, verbs. If you try to describe method calls to address possible actions regarding a certain resource, you will end up with a long list of URLs and no consistency.

Resource URLs need to be focused on two main things:

- Accessing a collection of elements
- Accessing a specific element

Do simple semantics

Create a small number of powerful commands. Your API methods should be self-documenting, and hence easy to understand. Your users should not need to read several pages of documentation to start using your service, and you should not have exposed your internal models and methods. Use HTTP verbs to operate on collections and elements, and avoid putting verbs in your base URLs.

Do URI Design

URI design is a problem of syntax and semantics. URIs define a hierarchical and logical structure for accessing resources in your API and acting on them through actions.

The very first step in URI design is deciding on your API endpoint and versioning method (i.e., subdomain or directory):

- *api.example.com/*
- *dev.example.com/api*

With subdomain consolidation you can easily run your API completely decoupled from everything else and concentrate all API requests under one API subdomain. Generally speaking, subdomain consolidation makes things cleaner, easier, and more intuitive, while also providing an API gateway for developers wishing to explore the documentation and start using your service.

Another option is to serve all your API documentation with your *dev* subdomain and use the *api/* directory as your endpoint. This is also a common approach.

Versioning is usually indicated right after the endpoint through directory structures. This way, if you were going to build a different version of your API, the API version, like *v1/* or *v2/*, would be the root of your URI tree.

Versioning deals with the problem of keeping your API both forward and backward compatible, at least for a certain amount of time. This is particularly important so that you can make the changes you need to your service, without telling your developers they will lose access or their applications will be unusable if they do not update within a certain time of the release date of your upgraded product. API versioning opens up some issues regarding API compatibility and the future of the service you are designing and planning to develop. You are in fact trying to plan for and foresee an unknown future that will inherently bring unknown changes to the service you are designing at present. Generally speaking, you can adopt two opposite strategies: not doing any versioning and actually doing versioning. Of course, you are free to decide not to do any versioning, but in case you will want to provide different versions of your API, here is what you should consider.

First of all, you should decide where you want to version your API. Some APIs are versioned directly in the endpoint, but versioning with a directory makes it easier to change and evolve your URI structure. There are several possibilities here. You can version in the URL:

- Through the hostname: *v1.api.example.com*
- With a path prefix: *api.example.com/v1/*
- With a path suffix: *api.example.com/products/21345/v1/*
- With a query parameter: *api.example.com/products/21345?version=v1*

Or you can version in the HTTP request:

- With the content negotiation
- With a custom header

HTTP content negotiation is a mechanism defined by the HTTP protocol specification that allows a web server to return a different version of a document (or, more generally, a different resource representation) through the same URI. It was designed such that a user agent, like an application or a web browser, can specify which version of the same resource best fits its capabilities. This is defined in the Accept header of the HTTP request.

An interesting read about content negotiation is provided by the Mozilla Developer Network (*http://bit.ly/mdn-content-negotiation*).

You can also version through the content of your response, like with XML namespaces or HTML doctype declarations. This can be done through server-side or transparent content negotiation techniques.

Another aspect you should consider is what you want to version. For example:

- You can version through the release date: 2013-04-12
- You can version through the version number: v1, v1.1, v1.1.2

Usually a single version digit is used, although the common software practice of decimal notation sometimes extends into API versioning and most of the time there are minor changes for minor versions.

Always, always, always version your API. Versioning is one of the most important (yet sometimes overlooked) aspects of designing an API. Versioning appropriately makes iterating faster, preventing invalid requests from hitting outdated endpoints.

It also helps in providing a smoother service through any API version transition, since you can continue offering the old version for a given period of time, while your users update their applications.

Following the API version, the URI structure starts identifying resources. It is often said that concrete names to identify resources are better than abstract ones, although API architects are sometimes obsessed with abstraction. In general, taking a pragmatic approach can help in situations like this. If you think about your users, they would probably prefer to see self-documenting URIs like *api.example.com/v1/products* or *api.example.com/stores* instead of something more abstract like *api.example.com/v1/objects* or *api.example.com/v1/items*, even if by going through your documentation they will eventually understand that every item or object in your application is either a product or a store.

Abstraction is hence not always useful to developers, and could actually lead to confusing URI structures. The level of abstraction that you might want to achieve will vary based on your application or service architecture.

A pragmatic API architect should consider a balance between concrete names and abstraction, keeping the number of resources in the namespace from growing beyond a healthy limit of maybe 20 or 30 different resources in most cases. A good approach in this case is considering that users will have to remember what URIs they should use to consume a specific resource (or at least, that they will probably try to do so). Limit your URI space as much as possible for the sake of simplicity and usability.

During the API design process, and specifically while you are deciding on your URI structure, you should concentrate on the resources you want developers to access, and how this should be accomplished, always remembering that good URI design improves usability and therefore community adoption. Let's look at a few examples. This will list all products:

```
$ curl api.example.com/v1/products
```

This will show product 21345:

```
$ curl api.example.com/v1/products/21345
```

And this will list all sneaker products for brand "sneak":

```
$ curl api.example.com/v1/products?type=sneakers&amp;brand=sneak
```

This last example illustrates the use of a search query to list all products of a certain type and manufacturer. That is, we used attribute parameters to search through and filter our products resource. One might thus think that query parameters can also be used to alter the state of a resource. You must not do this! You must instead use HTTP verbs to alter state. Remember that anyone can call a URI through a browser (or a crawler), so you do not want to use GET requests to delete or modify resources. Otherwise, even a simple crawler, or the Google bot, could end up compromising your service and deleting resources from your database simply by visiting a URI.

Why You Should Use Rails to Build APIs

The API created in the previous chapter was a simple "Hello Rails" application with a small twist. If a parameter user is passed to the URL, the API will say "Hello <user>" instead. In this chapter we are going to design a more complex API, starting from some application data.

You may have been asking yourself if using Rails just to generate some JSON isn't maybe overkill. Why not use something more lightweight like Sinatra instead?

While this may be true, especially for very simple APIs, there are two aspects of developing a RESTful API to take into consideration:

- Designing a RESTful API presumes more code logic than any application just replying to HTTP requests in JSON format.
- Rails provides a set of defaults that speed up prototyping and development and allow the programmer to concentrate on the application logic, hence avoiding many trivialities.

Rail's *default middleware layer* handles many aspects of an application's lifecycle. It includes the following features:

- It supports transparent reloading.
- Smart defaults are available in development mode.
- Test-driven development is provided out of the box.
- Logging verbosity is always appropriate for the current mode: development/test/ production.
- You have the freedom to decide if you want to specify parameters as JSON, or as a URL-encoded string. Also, if you prefer to use nested URL-encoded parameters, Rails handles this for you.
- Rails handles all the HTTP protocol details to make conditional GET requests; it processes request headers by returning the correct response header and status quote.
- It provides automatic response caching. The cache store can be easily configured in Rails.
- HEAD requests are transparently converted to GETs.

While these features can certainly be built in Rack middleware, the default Rails middleware stack already provides them out of the box. Therefore, even if your application is "just generating JSON," Rails delivers value from the moment you run `rails new <myapp>`.

 Rack provides a minimal interface between web servers supporting Ruby and Ruby frameworks. Rack wraps HTTP requests and responses in the simplest way possible; it unifies and distills the API for web servers, web frameworks, and software in between (the so-called middleware) into a single method call.

More information on Rack can be found at *https://github.com/rack/ rack*.

Rails also provides a framework for handling and responding to web requests: Action Pack (*http://bit.ly/rails-actionpack*). In the MVC paradigm, Action Pack represents the VC part. Therefore, some aspects handled at the Action Pack layer are:

Routing and URLs
This means you will not have to spend time thinking about how to design your API in terms of HTTP requests. You will not have to think about URL generation either. Everything will be cleanly and conventionally mapped from HTTP to controllers by the Rails router.

Headers and redirection responses
You do not have to manually add response headers.

HTTP authentication
> Rails supports three types of authentication out of the box: basic, digest, and token.

Active Support instrumentation
> Active Support provides an instrumentation API allowing developers to provide hooks that other developers may subscribe to.
>
> Also, ActiveSupport provides generators to quickly create models, controllers, routes, and test stubs, and supports plug-ins and third-party libraries that reduce the cost of setting up an application or prototyping a new feature.

In short, Rails has a lot to offer even if we strip out the view layer.

The WikiCat API

The application we are going to design uses the Wikipedia category system to produce the category tree of a given keyword. The Wikipedia category system is a taxonomy, or classification of concepts (in this case, the Wikipedia articles).

The Wikipedia category system is the result of the activity of all users editing and classifying Wikipedia entries. The result is a graph of categories that isn't strictly a tree or a hierarchy, but allows multiple classifications of topics simultaneously, meaning some categories might have more than one supercategory.

The Wikipedia category system can be considered as a thesaurus that is collaboratively developed and used by crowds for indexing Wikipedia articles.

We are not going to use Wikipedia's entire database for our API; we are just going to pretend we have some prepopulated data with category extracts and links between categories.

Given this data, we are going to import it in our app, and subsequently we are going to create the models and controller to access and act on it.

With our API, we will aim to find all subcategories of a given category that is passed as a parameter in the URL. In the next few chapters we will continue extending our API and develop it incrementally as a RESTful interface for the Wikipedia category system.

Preparing the Database

Free copies of all available content on Wikipedia are available for users and multi-licensed under the Creative Commons Attribution-ShareAlike 3.0 License (CC-BY-SA) and the GNU Free Documentation License (GFDL).

Snapshots of Wikipedia categories and Wikipedia category links pre-prepared to be imported into this application can be found at the WikiCat GitHub repository (*http://bit.ly/wikicat-github*).

Because the English category links table contains a large number of records, an extract of the whole dump has also been prepared for testing purposes, so that you do not have to wait several hours for the dump to be imported into your development database.

Wikipedia uses MySQL for its database, so although the dumps can be translated to another SQL dialect or NoSQL language, we are going to use MySQL for the WikiCat API.

The first step is making sure that MySQL is installed on your system. Run:

```
$ mysql --version
mysql Ver 14.14 Distrib 5.6.20, for osx10.9 (x86_64) using
EditLine wrapper
```

It may be the case that MySQL is not installed on your system. In this case, you will have to install it.

Mac OS X users can use *brew* and run:

```
$ brew install mysql
```

On Linux you will probably have to install the necessary libraries first:

```
$ apt-get install libmysqlclient18 libmysqlclient-dev
```

Then install MySQL Server:

```
$ apt-get install mysql-client-5.5 mysql-server-5.5
```

On Windows, you can use MySQL Installer. Instructions can be found in the MySQL documentation (*http://bit.ly/mysql-installer*).

MySQL Installer simplifies the installation and updating process for a set of MySQL products. It allows the user to see which products have been installed, and configure, update, or remove them if needed. Through the installer it is also possible to install plug-ins, documentation, and tutorials; it includes a GUI and a command-line interface.

Once you've made sure MySQL is installed on your system and tested it is working with the command `mysql --version`, it is time to install the *mysql* gem for Rails, to allow our Rails app to interface with our database. Run:

```
$ gem install mysql
```

Now we are going to create a Rails app with MySQL support instead of SQLite3. Because we want to create an API-only application, we are going to use Rails::API. To install *rails-api*, run:

```
$ gem install rails-api
```

The application can then be generated by running:

```
$ rails-api new wikicat -d mysql
```

As before, the command will create our Rails application.

 Rails::API (*https://github.com/rails-api/rails-api*) generates a subset of a normal Rails application. It was designed specifically for creating API-only apps, where you usually don't need the entire Rails middleware.

Now that our application has been created, we have to initialize the database:

```
$ cd wikicat
$ rake db:create
```

rake db:create creates our development and test databases. The command is run only the first time the database is created. Subsequently we will instruct our application to run the specified database migrations. We'll discuss this in the next section.

Scaffolding the Models

Once our database has been prepared, we can start coding our application logic.

The categories table contains the following columns:

```
cat_id: <Integer>,
cat_title: <String>;,
cat_pages: <Integer>,
cat_subcats: <Integer>,
cat_files: <Integer>;
```

Each of these columns describes a property of a certain category. Let's take a look at these in order:

cat_id
    The unique category ID from Wikipedia

cat_title
    The actual category title, as in "Sports" or "Science"

cat_pages
    The number of pages belonging to that category

`cat_subcats`
> The number of subcategories belonging to that category

`cat_files`
> The number of files belonging to that category

We are going to generate the `Category` model accordingly:

```
$ rails generate model Category cat_id:integer cat_title:string\
  cat_pages:integer cat_subcats:integer cat_files:integer
```

The command will generate the `Category` model and a number of defaults:

```
invoke active_record
create db/migrate/20140821090455_create_categories.rb
create app/models/category.rb
invoke test_unit
create test/models/category_test.rb
create test/fixtures/categories.yml
```

 You can also simply use `rails g` instead of writing the entire command `rails generate`.

The first file to be generated is the migration file to create the categories table. Migrations are a feature provided by Active Record to evolve the database schema over time, in a consistent and easy way. The idea is that the developer doesn't have to write schema modification code in SQL, but can use Ruby syntax to describe the changes he wants to apply to the database or a single table.

The database schema initially has nothing in it; consequently, each time a migration is run, tables, columns, or single entries are added to or removed from the database. Active Record will then update the schema accordingly, and modify the *db/schema.rb* file to match the up-to-date structure.

Migrations are stored in the *db/migrate* folder and sorted by time of creation. A timestamp is added to the filename.

We can now open our first migration file to check how it looks:

```
# db/migrate/<timestamp>_create_categories.rb
class CreateCategories > ActiveRecord::Migration
  def change
    create_table :categories do |t|
      t.integer :cat_id
      t.string :cat_title
      t.integer :cat_pages
      t.integer :cat_subcats
      t.integer :cat_files
```

```
      t.timestamps
    end
  end
end
```

If we want to add more columns to our tables, we can generate a migration file. Or, as we have not applied our migration yet, we can just edit our *create_categories* migration file.

What we want to do is use the Wikipedia category ID as the primary ID, without generating another ID field. Also, we want to add the `created_at` and `updated_at` columns. We will therefore modify the migration file:

```
# db/migrate/<timestamp>_create_categories.rb
class CreateCategories > ActiveRecord::Migration
  def change
    create_table :categories, {:id =&gt; false} do |t|
      t.integer :cat_id
      t.string :cat_title
      t.integer :cat_pages
      t.integer :cat_subcats
      t.integer :cat_files
      t.date :created_at
      t.date :updated_at
      t.timestamps
    end
    execute "ALTER TABLE categories ADD PRIMARY KEY (cat_id);"
  end
end
```

Now we are going to create the `Link` model. We again start with the Wikipedia SQL dump to see what the `CategoryLinks` table looks like:

```
cl_from: <Integer>,
cl_to: <String>,
cl_sortkey: <VarBinary>,
cl_timestamp: <Date>,
cl_sortkey_prefix: <VarBinary>
cl_collation: <VarBinary>
cl_type: <String>
```

Again, each of these columns describes a property of a certain category link:

cl_from
> The page ID of the article where the link was placed.

cl_to
> The name (excluding namespace prefix) of the desired category. This is the actual category title, as in "Sports" or "Science."

`cl_sortkey`

> The title by which the page should be sorted in a category list. For a subcategory this is equivalent to the category title.

`cl_timestamp`

> The time at which that link was last updated in the table.

`cl_sortkey_prefix`

> This is either the empty string if a page is using the default sortkey (aka the sortkey is unspecified), or it is the human-readable version of `cl_sortkey`.

`cl_collation`

> What collation is in use.

`cl_type`

> The type of link: page/subcategory/file.

> In the Wikipedia SQL dump, columns are specified as `VARBINARY`. In MySQL the `BINARY` and `VARBINARY` types can be compared to `CHAR` and `VARCHAR`; the difference is that they contain binary strings instead of nonbinary strings. That is, a `BINARY` or `VARBINARY` type contains a byte string rather than a character string. Since byte strings have no character set, operations like sorting and comparison are based on the numeric values of the bytes in the string.
>
> In Rails, specifying a column as binary generates a BLOB column in MySQL. A BLOB is a binary large object that can hold a variable amount of data. BLOB values are treated by the database as byte strings, but they are a bit different from `VARBINARY` objects. Since they have no character set, for our simple API we will consider the two types equivalent, although you should know that they are allocated differently than any other MySQL column type. Please refer to the MySQL documentation (*http://bit.ly/mysql-blob*) for more information.

Starting from the SQL dump schema of the `categorylinks` table, we are going to generate the `Link` model:

```
$ rails generate model Link           \
          cl_from:integer             \
          cl_to:string                \
          cl_sortkey:binary           \
          cl_timestamp:date           \
          cl_sortkey_prefix:binary \
          cl_collation:binary         \
          cl_type:string
```

Let's take a look at our new migration file:

```
# db/migrate/<timestamp>_create_links.rb

class CreateLinks > ActiveRecord::Migration
  def change
    create_table :links do |t|
      t.integer :id
      t.integer :cl_from
      t.string :cl_to
      t.binary :cl_sortkey
      t.date :cl_timestamp
      t.binary :cl_sortkey_prefix
      t.binary :cl_collation
      t.string :cl_type
      t.timestamps
    end
  end
end
```

Again, we want to slightly modify the *create_links* migration file before applying it. We will edit the file as follows:

```
# db/migrate/<timestamp>_create_links.rb
class CreateLinks > ActiveRecord::Migration
  def change
    create_table :links, {:id =&gt; false} do |t|
      t.integer :cl_from
      t.string :cl_to
      t.binary :cl_sortkey
      t.date :cl_timestamp
      t.binary :cl_sortkey_prefix
      t.binary :cl_collation
      t.string :cl_type
      t.date :created_at
      t.date :updated_at
      t.timestamps
    end
    execute "ALTER TABLE links ADD PRIMARY KEY (cl_from);"
  end
end
```

We can now run the migrations:

```
$ rake db:migrate
```

At this point we have two choices. The first one would be to import the two SQL dumps from Wikipedia. This will take a while, and you probably just want to go ahead with coding the WikiCat API at this point.

If you want to go ahead with the MySQL dumps, though, you can download the pre-processed zipped files (*http://bit.ly/1XTkg4c*).

Then unzip the file and run:

```
$ mysqld &
$ mysql -u root -p wikicat_development <
  ~/Downloads/enwiki-latest-category.sql
$ mysql -u root -p wikicat_development <
  ~/Downloads/enwiki-latest-categorylinks.sql
```

> You can also find the actual Wikipedia dumps at *http://dumps.wiki-media.org/enwiki/latest/*.

Alternatively, if you don't want to wait several hours to have the whole Wikipedia dumps imported into your database, you can always populate it with *seeds.rb*.

> The file *db/seeds.rb* in the repository for this chapter (*https://github.com/hiromipaw/wikicat*) has been prepopulated with some category data and links so that you can quickly develop and test your API.

To populate the database this way, run the command:

```
$ rake db:seed
```

Coding Controllers and Serializers

Once our database has been set up and our models generated, we can start coding our controllers.

We are going to use ActiveModel::Serializers to encapsulate the JSON serialization of objects.

A common way to generate a JSON API in Rails is to add a `respond_to` block to the controller action so that we can see the JSON representation of the returned object.

Suppose, though, we would like to have total control over the returned JSON. We could do this by overriding the `as_json` method, or by passing some options through the controller.

The problem with both these approaches is that they will not provide the level of customization and simplicity that ActiveModel::Serializers delivers. So, we are going to use it in our application by adding it to the *Gemfile*:

```
source 'https://rubygems.org'
# Bundle edge Rails instead: gem 'rails', github: 'rails/rails'
gem 'rails', '4.1.4'
```

```
gem 'rails-api'
# Use mysql as the database for Active Record
gem 'mysql2'
# Serializer for JSON
gem 'active_model_serializers'
group :doc do
  # bundle exec rake doc:rails generates the API under doc/api.
  gem 'sdoc', '~> 0.4.0'
end
group :development do
  # Spring speeds up development by keeping your application
  # running in the background. Read more:
  # https://github.com/rails/spring
  gem 'spring'
end
```

and running Bundle to install it:

```
$ bundle install
```

We are now going to generate the serializer for our models by using the Serializers generator:

```
$ rails g serializer category
$ rails g serializer link
```

The generator will create a file in the folder *serializers/* under *app/*. Here we can specify which attributes we want to serialize in our JSON replies.

For our category serializer we would like to include the category title and the number of subcategories. We are therefore going to specify the attributes `cat_title` and `cat_subcats`:

```
# serializers/category_serializer.rb
class CategorySerializer < ActiveModel::Serializer
  attributes :title, :sub_categories
end
```

We will now start coding our controllers. This is a good point to think about how we would like our API to be served and what URI structure we are going to use to identify our resources.

From a Rails perspective we are going to provide an *api/* directory as our endpoint, followed by the API version, *v1*.

We are going to generate a category controller in the *api/v1* namespace with one action:

```
$ rails generate controller api/v1/category show
```

This will generate an empty controller with a single empty action called *show*. We can modify the controller to return the category requested through a parameter:

```
class Api::V1::CategoryController < ApplicationController
  respond_to :json
  def show
    category = params[:category] ? params[:category] : "sports"
    @category = Category.where(:cat_title =&gt;
                                category.capitalize).first
    render :json =&gt; @category,
    serializer: CategorySerializer,
    root: "category"
  end
end
```

Let us examine the controller bit by bit (not literally :).

First of all, we are instructing Rails to return only JSON by using the line `respond_to :json`.

Secondly, we are telling the controller that if the `category` param is not defined, the default category "sports" can be used.

Finally, we want the controller to return a category using the category serializer. We are also telling the serializer to use the string "category" as the root for the returned JSON.

Once the controller has been defined, we can define our routes. By default Rails fills the *config/routes.rb* file with some defaults and basic documentation on how to build routes for your application. Every time a controller is generated through the `rails generate` command, the routes file is modified with the default routes.

Therefore, we will go ahead and delete (or comment out, if you wish) all the defaults added to the routes file and replace them with the following:

```
Rails.application.routes.draw do
  namespace :api do
    namespace :v1 do
      get '/category/:category', :to => 'category#show'
    end
  end
end
```

The routes defined will instruct Rails to route the *show* action of the category controller within the *api/v1* namespace. Furthermore, the portion of the path defined after */category/* will be considered as the `category` parameter to pass the controller. Finally, it is time to test our serializer, controller, and routes:

```
$ curl http://0.0.0.0:3000/api/v1/category/science
```

If everything is going according to plan, we should receive the JSON string:

```
<p>{"category":{"cat_title":"SCIENCE","cat_subcats":34}}
```

We would like, though, to use different names in our JSON replies, and to add some text preprocessing.

We modify the serializer to force ISO-8859-1 and UTF-8 conversion and to replace any possible spaces left in the category titles with underscore characters.

Furthermore, we modify the attributes named cat_title and cat_subcats:

```
# serializers/category_serializer.rb
class CategorySerializer < ActiveModel::Serializer
  attributes :title, :sub_categories
  def title
    URI::encode(object.cat_title.force_encoding("ISO-8859-1")
        .encode("utf-8", replace: nil).downcase.tr(" ", "_"))
  end
  def sub_categories
    object.cat_subcats
  end
end
```

We can test again to see if the changes have been applied:

```
$ curl http://0.0.0.0:3000/api/v1/category/science
{"category":{"title":"science","sub_categories":34}}
```

Now that we can check single categories, we would like to display all subcategories of a given category passed as a parameter.

We are going to create a controller that will use the link serializer and build the category graph:

```
$ rails generate controller api/v1/graph show
```

Then we are going to modify it as follows:

```
class Api::V1::GraphController < ApplicationController
  respond_to :json
  def show
    cat = params[:category] || 'sports'
    @category = Category.where(:cat_title => cat.capitalize).first
    @links = Link.where(:cl_to => @category.cat_title,
                        :cl_type => "subcat")
    render :json => @links,
    each_serializer: LinkSerializer,
    root: @category.cat_title.downcase
  end
  private
  def graph_params
    params.require(:category).permit(:cl_to, :cl_type)
  end
end
```

As for the category controller, we are asking Rails to respond only with JSON. Then we define an *index* action where we retrieve a category and find all the corresponding subcategories. We render the JSON using the link serializer defined earlier. The category title is our root.

We also define a private function where we specify the permitted attributes for the Link model and the required category parameter.

Next, we modify the link serializer to rename the cl_sortkey attribute to sub_category. We also enforce UTF-8 and ISO-8859-1 encoding while removing whitespaces:

```
class LinkSerializer < ActiveModel::Serializer
  attributes :sub_category
  def sub_category
    URI::encode(object.cl_sortkey.force_encoding("ISO-8859-1")
        .encode("utf-8", replace: nil).downcase.tr(" ", "_"))
  end
end
```

Then we test:

```
$ curl http://0.0.0.0:3000/api/v1/graph/science
```

And if everything was set up correctly, we receive the graph JSON:

```
{
    "science": [{
        "sub_category": "_%0Ascientific_disciplines"
    }, {
        "sub_category": "_%0Ascientists"
    }, ...]
}
```

Testing

Now we are at the boring and tedious step of setting up an app: testing.

We want to make sure that our controllers will behave according to our design even if something changes in the future. So, we are going to write two simple tests to assure the default behavior for both controllers:

```
# test/controllers/api/v1/category_controller_test.rb
require 'test_helper'
class Api::V1::CategoryControllerTest < ActionController::TestCase
  test "should get show" do
    get :show, {'category' => 'science'}
    assert_response :success
    assert_equal "{\"category\":
                    {\"title\":\"science\",
                    \"sub_categories\":1}}",
                @response.body
  end
end
```

```
require 'test_helper'
class Api::V1::GraphControllerTest < ActionController::TestCase
  test "should get show" do
    get :show, {'category' => "sports"}
    assert_response :success
    assert_equal "{\"sports\":
                    [{\"sub_category\":
                      \"culture_and_sports_culture\"}]}",
                  @response.body
  end
end
```

Before running the tests we also need to prepare the fixtures. This is fake data that will populate our test database in order for the tests to work.

We are going to create two links and two categories. The two fixtures were already generated when we scaffolded the models, but we are going to modify both as follows:

```
# test/fixtures/links.yml
one:
  cl_from: 1
  cl_to: Sports
  cl_sortkey: CULTURE AND SPORTS CULTURE
  cl_timestamp: 2005-04-29 10:32:42
  cl_sortkey_prefix: Culture
  cl_collation: uppercase
  cl_type: subcat
two:
  cl_from: 2
  cl_to: Science
  cl_sortkey: SCIENTIFIC DISCIPLINES
  cl_timestamp: 2013-09-02 22:56:59
  cl_sortkey_prefix: Sci
  cl_collation: uppercase
  cl_type: subcat

# test/fixtures/categories.yml
one:
  cat_id: 1
  cat_title: Sports
  cat_pages: 1
  cat_subcats: 1
  cat_files: 1
two:
  cat_id: 2
  cat_title: Science
  cat_pages: 1
  cat_subcats: 1
  cat_files: 1
```

You can read more on fixtures in the Ruby on Rails documentation (*http://bit.ly/rails-fixtureset*).

We can then run the tests as usual:

```
$ rake test
```

 We haven't defined errors in the graph controller. What happens if the category isn't found?

You can find the solution in the WikiCat GitHub repository (*http://bit.ly/wikicat-github*).

Wrapping Up

In this chapter we learned how to create a first Rails application. In the next chapter we will explore how you can use Rails to build RESTful applications and, more specifically, how it is possible to reconcile CRUD with REST.

## CHAPTER 4

The REST of the World

REST is an architectural abstraction designed for distributed systems and the Web. Actions in REST map to URIs that identify resources. REST operates on resource representations that can differ from the data representations stored in the application database. A resource epresentation can be anything from a JSON string to the HTML returned when accessing a certain URL. The data object stored in a database record is something fundamentally different.

Life Is CRUD

Actions on database records are usually guided not by REST principles, but by CRUD. CRUD is an abbreviation of *Create, Read, Update, Delete*, the four basic functions of persistent storage.

Sometimes an additional function is considered: *Search*. In this case, CRUD is referred to as *SCRUD*.

 Wikipedia suggests that CRUD (*http://bit.ly/wiki-crud*) is rather a *backronym*. A backronym is a specially constructed acronym created to fit a specific word or concept. A famous backronym example is NASA's Combined Operational Load-Bearing External Resistance Treadmill (COLBERT), named after Stephen Colbert.

The actions CRUD refers to map to all of the major functions implemented in relational database applications. In fact, each letter maps to a standard SQL statement.

REST and CRUD are therefore two very different paradigms for two very different worlds.

REST is an architectural style for applications. REST resources can be the result of different database queries, and neither the client nor the REST server really needs to know how these queries are constructed or where the data comes from.

REST applications generally assume that they live in a REST world where everyone speaks their language, and therefore will delegate to some other component (known as *middleware*) the tasks of interfacing with a non-REST database and fetching the requested data. Figure 4-1 illustrates this paradigm.

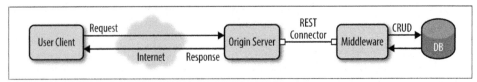

Figure 4-1. REST architectures interact with non-REST components or services through REST middleware acting as connector between the two worlds

RESTful Rails

The Rails router is responsible for redirecting incoming requests to controller actions.

The routing module provides URL rewriting in native Ruby. It recognizes URLs and dispatches them as defined in *config/routes.rb*. The routes file can therefore be considered as a map for your application requests. The map (or the router) tells each request where to go based on some predefined patterns.

The default resource routing in Rails allows you to declare all the basic routes for a certain controller with a single line of code. This means you do not have to declare all your routes separately for actions like *index*, *show*, *new*, *edit*, *create*, *update*, and *destroy*. The resourceful route will take care of that.

In Rails, *resourceful routes* provide the mapping between HTTP verbs and URLs and controller actions. These actions in turn map to CRUD operations in the database.

When a Rails application receives an HTTP request with a specific HTTP method such as GET, POST, PATCH, PUT, or DELETE, it asks the router to map it to a controller action. If the route is matched, Rails will dispatch that request.

An entry in the routes file of the form:

```
resources :categories
```

creates by default seven different application routes mapping to the categories controller, as shown in Table 4-1.

Table 4-1. Mapping of HTTP verbs and URLs to controller actions

HTTP verb	Path	Controller#Action	Result
GET	*/categories*	`categories#index`	Displays all categories
GET	*/categories/new*	`categories#new`	Returns an HTML form for creating a new category
POST	*/categories*	`categories#create`	Creates a new category
GET	*/categories/:id*	`categories#show`	Displays a specific category
GET	*/categories/:id/edit*	`categories#edit`	Returns an HTML form for editing a category
PATCH/PUT	*/categories/:id*	`categories#update`	Updates a specific category
DELETE	*/categories/:id*	`categories#destroy`	Deletes a specific category

Note that the mapping provided by the default resourceful route uses both HTTP verbs and URLs to match inbound requests. Therefore, four URLs correspond to seven different actions.

Some of the routes generated through the resourceful route mechanism are not always necessary. For example, an API application would not pass an HTML form to edit a resource; instead, it would use a PATCH/PUT request with the parameters that need to be modified. So, there are situations in which you might want to redefine routes according to your needs. It is important to generate only the routes that your application actually needs, to cut down on memory usage and speed up the routing process in your server.

You can define single routes by specifying the route and the action to be matched:

```
get '/categories/:id', :to => 'categories#show'
```

The HTTP helper methods GET, POST, PATCH, PUT, and DELETE can be used for routes that do not fit the default resourceful route.

If your route needs to respond to more than one HTTP method (or all methods), then using the :via option on match is preferable:

```
match 'categories/:id' => 'categories#show', via: [:get, :post]
```

This way, if you POST to */categories/:id*, it will route to the *create_category* action, while a GET on the same URL will route to the *show* action. It's as simple as that.

Rails routes are matched in the order they are specified. If you have a `resources :categories` above a `get 'categories/graph'` the *show* action's route for the *resources* line will be matched before the *get* line. You can move the *get* line above the *resources* line to match it first.

You can also use the :only and :except options to fine-tune the default Rails behavior of creating routes for the seven default actions (*index*, *show*, *new*, *create*, *edit*, *update*, and *destroy*). The :only option tells Rails to create only the specified routes:

```
resources :categories, only: [:index, :show]
```

The :except option specifies a route or list of routes that Rails should *not* create:

```
resources :categories, except: [:destroy]
```

 There is a lot more than meets the eye hidden in the Rails routing module. Refer to the Ruby on Rails documentation (*http://bit.ly/rails-routing*) and the Ruby on Rails Guides (*http://bit.ly/rguides-routing*) for more information.

Testing RESTful Routing in Rails

Routes in Rails can easily be tested to make sure that the mappings you write in *config/routes.rb* produce the results you expected.

Once routes have been created for your application you can visit *http://localhost:3000/rails/info/routes* in your browser while your server is running in the development environment to get a complete list of the available routes. You can also execute the following command in a terminal window:

```
$ rake routes
```

It will produce the same output.

Rails also offers three built-in assertions designed to make testing routes simpler:

- assert_generates
- assert_recognizes
- assert_routing

With assert_generates we can verify that a particular set of options generates a particular path. It can be used with default routes or custom routes:

```
assert_generates '/categories/1',
                 { controller: 'categories',
                   action: 'show', id: '1' }
assert_generates '/about', controller: 'pages', action: 'about'
```

With assert_recognizes we can verify that a given path is recognized and routed accordingly:

```
assert_recognizes({ controller: 'categories',
                    action: 'show', id: '1' }, '/categories/1')
```

Finally, `assert_routing` checks the route both ways—it tests that the path generates the options and that the options generate the path:

```
assert_routing({ path: 'categories', method: :post },
                { controller: 'categories', action: 'create' })
```

HTTP Semantics

HTTP verbs inherently have their own semantics, so it can become confusing if we try to map verbs in HTTP (and therefore REST applications) one-to-one to CRUD actions.

In general, CRUD actions are mapped to the following HTTP actions:

- Create = PUT/POST
- Read = GET
- Update = POST/PUT
- Delete = DELETE

So when do you use PUT, and when do you use POST? As we've seen, in Rails a *resource route* maps HTTP verbs and URLs to controller actions. Each action also maps to default CRUD actions. If you use resourceful routes, you will use POST to create resources and PUT to update them.

The mappings created with resourceful routes are RESTful. The problem arises when you are creating not-so-standard routes to handle specific controller actions.

This does not mean that CRUD and REST have no correlation whatsoever when things get complicated. It has been shown that CRUD clients can interact perfectly well with REST services; they just have different ideas on when it is appropriate to use PUT versus POST. In addition, you need to add some additional logic for the mapping to be considered a complete transformation from one space (REST and resources land) to the other (CRUD and the kingdom of persistent storage).

Generally speaking, Read maps to an HTTP GET request and Delete corresponds to an HTTP DELETE operation. What we are left with is PUT and POST and the Update and Create actions. The problem here is that in some cases Create means PUT, but in other cases it means POST, and in some cases Update means POST, while in others it means PUT.

More specifically, the problem lies in the definition of the POST and PUT methods in the HTTP protocol.

The HTTP/1.1 specification (*http://bit.ly/http1-1-spec*) states that the POST method "is used to request that the origin server accept the entity enclosed in the request as a new subordinate of the resource identified by the Request-URI in the Request-Line."

According to the spec, the POST method can be used to cover the following functions:

- Annotation of existing resources
- Posting a message to a bulletin board, newsgroup, mailing list, or similar group of articles
- Providing a block of data, such as the result of submitting a form, to a data-handling process
- Extending a database through an append operation

Conversely, the PUT method "requests that the enclosed entity be stored under the supplied Request-URI. If the Request-URI refers to an already existing resource, the enclosed entity SHOULD be considered as a modified version of the one residing on the origin server."

You can see why this is confusing—PUT and POST could almost be used interchangeably, and no one would notice.

As we have seen, Rails uses POST for creating resources and PUT to modify them in its default resourceful route. You can of course redefine the default routes, but the bottom line is that the difference between PUT and POST is quite subtle and in the end lies in the definition of *idempotency*.

HTTP/1.1 defines two types of methods: safe methods and idempotent methods. *Safe methods* are HTTP methods that do not modify resources. The specification warns developers of the established convention that the "GET and HEAD methods SHOULD NOT have the significance of taking an action other than retrieval" and states that these methods "ought to be considered 'safe'"—i.e., they do not modify the resources.

Idempotent methods are those that posses the property of "idempotence." An action is said to be idempotent if *n* repetitions of that action result in the same resource state as performing the action a single time.

The methods GET, HEAD, PUT, and DELETE are idempotent, as are the methods OPTIONS and TRACE (which should not have side effects).

PUT is idempotent, so if you PUT an object twice, it has no effect. This is a nice property, so use PUT when possible.

POST is not idempotent, but this doesn't mean it shouldn't be used for creating resources.

The magical rule of thumb is:

- If you are going to create a resource for which you already know the URL, it is better to use PUT: e.g., PUT `<resource>` /user/profile.

- If you are going to create a resource by sending some data to its resource controller, use POST instead and have the controller (or some other component) generate the corresponding URL for the newly created resource: e.g., POST `<resource>` `/categories/`.

The spec describes the difference between the two request types as follows:

> The fundamental difference between the POST and PUT requests is reflected in the different meaning of the Request-URI. The The URI in a POST request identifies the resource that will handle the enclosed entity. That resource might be a data-accepting process, a gateway to some other protocol, or a separate entity that accepts annotations. In contrast, the URI in a PUT request identifies the entity enclosed with the request—the user agent knows what URI is intended and the server MUST NOT apply that request to some other resource. If the server desires that the request be applied to a different URI, it MUST send a 301 (Moved Permanently) response; the user agent MAY then make its own decision regarding whether or not to redirect the request.

Note that it is possible for a sequence of several requests to be nonidempotent, even if all of the methods executed in that sequence are idempotent.

A sequence of actions is considered idempotent if execution of the entire sequence always yields a result that is not changed by a reexecution of all (or part) of that sequence. For example, we say that a sequence is nonidempotent if its result depends on a value that is later modified in the same sequence.

A sequence of actions that never has side effects on the server side is idempotent by definition (provided that no concurrent operations are being executed on the same set of resources).

We are now going to dive into the individual HTTP methods and what they do. Those of you who work with the HTTP protocol on a daily basis may want to skip this material. Otherwise, if you want to learn more about how HTTP methods are mapped to controller actions in Rails, keep reading.

GET

The GET method is used to retrieve information in the form of an entity identified by the Request-URI. The HTTP/1.1 specification also specifies that if the Request-URI refers to a process producing data, the data produced is what will be returned as the entity in the response, and not the source text of the process, unless the same text happens to also be the output of the process.

It may be possible to use a *conditional GET* if the request message includes an If-Modified-Since, If-Unmodified-Since, If-Match, If-None-Match, or If-Range header field. Conditional GETs provide a way for web servers to tell browsers that the response to a GET request hasn't changed since the last request and can be safely pulled from the browser cache. In this case the entity is transferred only under the conditions sent through the conditional header fields.

In Rails the conditional GET request works by using the HTTP_IF_NONE_MATCH and HTTP_IF_MODIFIED_SINCE headers. These pass back and forth both a unique content identifier and the timestamp of when the content was last changed. If the browser makes a request where the content identifier (etag) or last-modified timestamp matches the server's version, then the server only needs to send back an empty response with a "not modified" status. This allows the client to refresh cached entities without performing multiple requests.

We will see how these methods can be used in Rails when we look at how to implement caching and how to reduce unnecessary network usage.

HEAD

The HEAD method is identical to the GET method, except that with HEAD the server does not return a message body in the response. According to the spec, "The metainformation contained in the HTTP headers in response to a HEAD request SHOULD be identical to the information sent in response to a GET request." The HEAD method is therefore used to obtain metainformation about the entity without transferring the entity body.

It is possible to handle the HEAD method in Rails by using the head?() function:

```
# Is this a HEAD request?
# Equivalent to <tt>request.request_method_symbol == :head</tt>.
def head?
  HTTP_METHOD_LOOKUP[request_method] == :head
end
```

The response to a HEAD request can be cached, so the information it contains may be used to update a previously cached entity if the new values indicate that the cached entity has changed (i.e., if the values of the Content-Length, Content-MD5, ETag, or Last-Modified headers have changed).

POST

According to the HTTP specification, "The actual function performed by the POST method is determined by the server and is usually dependent on the Request-URI." The notion of subordinate resources is important for the POST method: the posted entity is subordinate to the Request-URI in the same way that a file is subordinate to the directory containing it.

If the POST method results in a resource being created on the origin server, it should return a 201 (Created) response. In this case the response should also contain an entity that describes the status of the request and refers to the new resource, as well as a Location header. This can be used to redirect the recipient to a location other than the Request-URI to complete the request or identify a new resource. In the case of a 201 (Created) response, it points to the location of the new resource created by the request. For 3xx responses, it should instead indicate the server's preferred URI for automatic redirection to the resource.

Responses to the POST method cannot be cached, unless they include the appropriate `Cache-Control` or `Expires` header fields. In this case, the 303 (See Other) response can be used to direct the user agent to retrieve a cacheable resource.

PUT

Through the PUT method, we can make a request to store the enclosed entity under the supplied Request-URI. If the Request-URI already exists, the entity enclosed in the request is considered a modified version of the existing one, and it replaces the version stored on the server. If the Request-URI does not point to an existing resource, a new resource with that URI is created.

When a new resource is created, the origin server must send a 201 (Created) response. When an existing resource is modified, the response sent to indicate successful completion of the request should be either 200 (OK) or 204 (No Content).

In the case that the resource could not be created or modified, the server should send an appropriate error response indicating the nature of the problem.

As with POST, responses to the PUT method are not cacheable.

DELETE

The DELETE method is used to request that the origin server delete the resource identified by the Request-URI.

With a DELETE request the client cannot be guaranteed that the operation has been carried out, even if the server returns a status code indicating that the action has been completed successfully. That said, the server should not indicate success unless it intends to either delete the resource or move it to an inaccessible location.

The server can send a 200 (OK) or 204 (No Content) response in the case of success, or a 202 (Accepted) response if the instruction has been accepted but the action has not yet been enacted.

Responses to the DELETE method are not cacheable.

Wrapping Up

In this chapter we have learned about the semantics of the HTTP methods, and how these can be used in different situations. We have also seen how HTTP methods can be mapped to Rails actions even when we are not using resourceful routes. In the next chapter we will start designing hypermedia APIs: you will learn how to reason about the application flow and to think about resources as you would think about web pages.

Designing APIs in RoR

In this chapter we will design a hypermedia API in RoR. We will first explore the principles of adaptable hypermedia interfaces and then see how to make resources explorable.

We will discuss the application flow that services should have, and we will talk about APIs in terms of actual interfaces instead of just sets of commands that you can learn by visiting a man page (or developer portal, in the case of web services).

Finally, we will make our Wikipedia categories API fully explorable.

Hypermedia and Adaptable APIs

In the API community, hypermedia is a hot topic capable of generating heated discussions. How should a hypermedia API be designed? What functionality should be implemented? What media types should be supported? Should new media types be defined? These are some of the questions that arise when talking about hypermedia APIs, and almost everyone seems to have different answers to them.

The whole concept of hypermedia is about making clients interact better with services, and making resources easily accessible and explorable.

Designing resources can be especially confusing, because the first question you need to answer is *what exactly is a resource anyway?*

Is a resource some table in a database? Is it something else? In reality a resource can be a bit of both. It can be a record in a database, but it can also contain information from other records, or from other databases or applications. A resource is essentially a gateway to some dataset.

Once we overcome the restriction of thinking about resources as records in a database, we can start thinking about resources as sets, or flows, or even better, streams of information.

If we think for a moment about the evolution of the Internet and the Web, we are witnessing the transformation of a complex system from a platform of interconnected computers to a platform of interconnected documents to a platform of interconnected data streams. This is what is intended by the "Web of Data": a platform built on the decisions that we have made in the past, mostly with the same or similar design objectives, that will provide new services with familiar paradigms.

When designing a hypermedia API we have to consider that users need to be able to act on these streams of information in a way that is both intuitive and permits them to freely use this flow of data to build other tools, applications, or services.

Making this possible—enabling developers to consume your stream of information and create new streams—needs to be your ultimate design goal when developing hypermedia services. So, hypermedia goes beyond making resources link to other resources; it is about making information available for consumption and explorable in an adaptable way that will still be valid a year from now, that will scale organically with demand, and that will evolve as the Web does, as new protocols and media types are introduced.

We have said that REST is essentially an abstraction of the Web, and building hypermedia applications or APIs isn't completely different from building web applications. The design processes and the underlying reasoning are essentially the same.

So what exactly is a RESTful API? And how do we make an API adaptable? To answer these questions we have to concentrate on two main aspects of REST and hypermedia. The first aspect is the uniformity of REST interfaces, and the second concerns hyperlinks between resources.

The uniformity of REST interfaces allows the usage of different types of identifiers in the same context, providing uniform semantics even when the access mechanism used may be different. As a matter of fact, we don't even have to be concerned with the access mechanism; we just need to ensure that our API replies consistently. The same principles permit us to introduce new types of resource identifiers without having to change the way existing identifiers work, while also allowing reuse of identifiers in a different context.

The uniformity principle enables us to develop and design different parts of a service independently from each other, while also providing a consistent way for these parts to communicate and exchange information.

The linked data model provides a way to interconnect data from various sources. Links provide the possibility to perform reasoning about resources, find contextual information, discover relationships, and associate data with real-world concepts.

Sometimes the semantic value of links is overlooked. One could argue that metadata and simple keywords could provide the same information, but while this may be true for some simple applications, links can certainly be used to provide more semantically accurate results.

Just imagine you're looking for a certain image using any image searching service (Google Images, Flickr, Instagram). If you just type a single keyword, the search results returned would reflect that keyword based on certain criteria, depending on the service: color, quality, popularity, number of views.

Now suppose you have an API application that returns you an image of a specific mountain with some JSON describing the image and its context:

```
"image":
{
  "title":"Matterhorn covered in snow",
  "timestamp": "Thu Oct 2 19:42:23 CEST 2014",
  "location":
  {
    "point":
    {
      "latitude":45.97638888888889,
      "longitude":7.65833333333333
    },
    "country":"Switzerland",
    "city":"Zermatt",
    "region":""Valais",
  },
  "links":
  {
    "self":
    {
      "href":"service.com/api/v1/users/user1794/albums
              /mountains/images/matterhorn_covered_in_snow.png",
      "method":"GET",
      "rel":"self"
    },
    "next":
    {
      "href":"service.com/api/v1/users/user1794/albums
              /mountains/images/matterhorn_from_the_slopes.png",
      "method":"GET",
      "rel":"next"
    },
    "wiki":
    {
      "href":"http://en.wikipedia.org/wiki/Matterhorn%20",
```

```
        "method":"GET",
        "rel":"wiki"
    }
  },
  "tags": ["mountain","snow","switzerland","skiing"],
  "data":"data:image/png;base64,<Data bit stream>"
}
```

Metadata containing only the tags used to describe the photo simply would not have been able to provide the same information. We would probably have known that it was a picture of the Matterhorn, but the semantic information provided by this simple API permits us to discover much more about the picture and its context.

The API also can be extended to include more information, like related searches or pictures by country or by city. And if designed properly the service can be developed organically by adding other interesting data and links that can be used by other services consuming our API.

You could for example decide to add an `album` field under `links` to point to the parent album. This can be easily done by simply adding a field in your JSON object:

```
"parent":
{
  "href":"service.com/api/v1/users/user1794/albums/mountains/",
  "method":"GET",
  "rel":"album"
}
```

What's more, developers wouldn't have to modify their applications. They could just continue using your API as before, and if they wanted they could integrate this new feature into their code.

REST Patterns

REST principles are extremely simple. So, a common question that comes up when talking about how to design APIs concerns the service and architecture complexity and where this can be hidden.

In reality the neat part of REST is that by combining relatively simple architectural elements is it possible to build entire systems with complex functions.

To begin with, in REST there are no objects or methods. We have resources instead. Of course, behind REST your system will contain objects, database records, and methods to modify and access these objects, but this doesn't concern REST.

REST is about resources and how their representations can be consumed. Although the resource is probably the most central element of REST, REST APIs do not define strict resource names or hierarchies of resources; neither do they strictly decouple client and server functionality.

REST APIs instead define a way to access resources and act on their representations. They require minimal knowledge about the actual implementation, impose minimum client-side dependencies, and make minimal assumptions about how they are going to be used, leaving a great deal of freedom in the user's hands. REST APIs are simple and permit developers to prototype simple or common use cases very quickly. They are self-describing and require only minimal documentation.

Creating Hypermedia Interfaces

Hypermedia is a fundamental component in the uniformity principle of REST interfaces. It allows clients to explore REST APIs by requesting a stream of data and following the hyperlinks included in this stream to retrieve other resources.

While REST is totally stateless, using hypermedia resource representations allows the client to manage state transitions. In fact, if an API defines a next field in the JSON response, the client could navigate to the next resource. This results in a navigation flow that could be considered similar to a user interface and which is the product of the interaction between the client and the server.

Hypermedia interfaces allow clients to maintain control over the application status and move state information away from the server while also allowing for more complex interactions (Figure 5-1). A hypermedia interface could be anything from a web app allowing a client to communicate with different devices to an application framework incorporating various idioms, data types, object models, and state information.

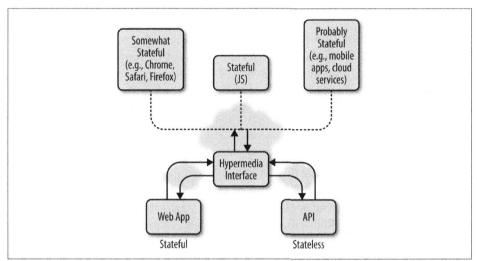

Figure 5-1. REST APIs and web apps can communicate via a hypermedia interface that can stream data in different formats to different devices

Resource-Oriented Thinking

Resource-oriented thinking represents a shift from entity–relationship and object-oriented design. The problem with resource-oriented thinking is that resources can be records in a database or models in our code, or a combination of the two.

Also, an important aspect of resource-oriented thinking is that the stream of data resulting from requesting a particular resource at a certain URI can be the product of the interactions of different services.

Let's think again of our image object in JSON. We might have obtained it by requesting a specific photo resource from a certain album on our favorite image sharing service. The information attached to the photo could have been obtained by that service making requests to a number of other services and applications that we might not even know about.

How do we start thinking about our applications in terms of resources, then? We have said that resources are in reality streams of data. So, we need to start designing our applications in terms of data and actions on data streams rather than on objects or entities.

Designing Explorable Resources

Designing explorable resources implies thinking about what data you want to serve and what actions on that data you want to provide.

If we go back again to the photo object example, you can see we have included a *next* and a *parent* link. We also have provided an external link, to the Wikipedia page for the object described in the picture.

We have specified a link field only for the photo object, and not, for example, for its keywords or its location information. Deciding what other resources or streams we want to link to a given resource is entirely a design choice. We could have decided to list pictures taken nearby, or external information regarding the country or the city fields. It all depends on what services we want our API to provide.

HATEOAS

HATEOAS (Hypermedia as the Engine of Application State) is a constraint of REST that distinguishes it from almost any other architectures. The core principle is that the client can interact with an application through hypermedia calls. The REST client does not need any prior knowledge of the particular implementation of the server. The server *dynamically* provides *links* for the client to explore the set of available resources.

Traditionally, web APIs have been designed as a simple way to get some data out of some service. By using hypermedia for their representation, APIs are instead transformed into application interfaces, used by software agents to discover and create information. If APIs are designed with this paradigm in mind, once the client hits the application entry point, it should be able to find its way around the application, in a similar manner to a human reader browsing the content of a website.

The application flow defines the way resource representations are accessed and acted upon. Therefore, thinking in terms of explorable resources is easier if we concentrate on the application flow we want our users to follow.

Each time the API is called, it will return an array of links that the user or software agent can follow to request more information about a call or to further interact with the application. The logic necessary to use the API doesn't need to be hardcoded in the client; it only needs to adhere to REST principles.

More importantly, the application can be designed to return only contextual links, so the client will only receive the information relating to a certain request.

The WikiCat Hypermedia API

We are now ready to extend our Wikipedia categories API into a fully hypermedia API.

Our objective is that a client visiting the API entry point will not need any information about the API itself to navigate it.

Our starting point is defining the application flow: i.e., *once a client hits the entry point of our application, what information would we like to present?*

The API we have built up to this point returns categories and their subcategories. It makes sense to show our top categories once we hit the API entry point. From there the client might navigate the category graph if it wishes, or just send some requests once it has learned how to use the API.

Wikipedia recognizes a list of major classification topics, used to organize the presentation of links to articles. This list of topics is included under the top category: *Main_topic_classifications.*

Another list of top-level categories is included under *Fundamental_categories.* This is based on a smaller number of initial thematic classifications.

You are free to experiment with the two top categories, and I have prepared the *seeds.rb* file to include both.

I believe, though, that it is more interesting to use the *Main_topic_classifications* category, simply because it contains a richer list of subcategories to be explored. Two of these, *Sports* and *Science,* have been included in the *seeds.rb* file so that you can explore the graph two levels deep.

We start by modifying the graph controller under *controllers/api/v1/graph_controller.* We want to make sure that the default category is *Main_topic_classifications.* Therefore, we change the following line in the *index* action:

```
category = params[:category] ? params[:category]
            : "Main_topic_classifications"
```

This says if a `category` parameter is provided, use it, and otherwise, use *Main_topic_classifications.*

Let's start the database and the server and verify it is working:

```
$ mysqld &
$ rails server
```

If everything is working correctly, we will see the JSON string describing the graph for the top category:

```
{
  "main_topic_classifications": [
  {
    "sub_category": "arts",
    ...
  }
]}
```

Once we have made sure that our gateway is working correctly, we can continue defining the other actions in the controller.

First, we'll modify the *show* action. This time we will also make sure to render errors properly:

```
def show
  cat = params[:category] || 'sports'
        : "Main_topic_classifications"
  @category = Category.where(:cat_title => cat.capitalize).first
  if @category
    @links = Link.where(:cl_to => @category.cat_title,
                        :cl_type => "subcat")

    render :json => @links, each_serializer: LinkSerializer,
                            root: @category.cat_title.downcase
  else
    render :json => {:error => {:text => "404 Not found",
                    :status => 404}}
  end
end
```

Now we'll modify the link serializer to display some more information. What we would like to achieve is displaying a category link pointing to the subcategory information with *self*, a *next* link pointing to the next linked category, and a *graph* link pointing to the same subcategory graph:

```ruby
class LinkSerializer < ActiveModel::Serializer
  attributes :sub_category, :links
  def sub_category
    URI::encode(object.cl_sortkey.force_encoding("ISO-8859-1")
    .encode("utf-8", replace: nil).downcase.tr(" ", "_"))
  end
  def links
    {:self => _self, :next => _next, :graph => graph}
  end
  def graph
    href = URI::encode("/api/v1/graph/
                        #{self.sub_category[/([^0A]*(.)$)/]}")
    {:href => href, :method => "GET", :rel => "graph"}
  end
  def _self
    href = URI::encode("/api/v1/category/
                        #{self.sub_category[/([^0A]*(.)$)/]}")
    {:href => href, :method => "GET", :rel => "self"}
  end
  def _next
    href = URI::encode("/api/v1/category/#{object.cl_to}")
    {:href => href, :method => "GET", :rel => "_next"}
  end
end
```

Note the difference between *self* and *object* in the serializer. Self refers to the serializer itself, while object refers to the link model.

You will notice that the link graph is a bit slow to load. To speed it up we would need to add an index on the `cl_sortkey` attribute in our links table. In order to create a new index we will generate a migration:

```
$ rails generate migration AddIndexToLinks cl_sortkey:index
invoke active_record
create db/migrate/20140908145510_add_index_to_links.rb
```

A file has just been created in the *db/migrate* folder. We can modify it in order to add another index field and speed up our queries to the links table:

```ruby
class AddIndexToLinks < ActiveRecord::Migration
  def change
    add_index :links, :cl_sortkey
  end
end
```

We can now test our graph API again and see if it works as expected:

```
http://0.0.0.0:3000/api/v1/graph/science.json
{"science":
  [
  {
    "sub_category":"scientific_disciplines",
    "links":
    {
      "self":
      {
        "href":"/api/v1/category/scientific_disciplines",
        "method":"GET",
        "rel":"_self"
      },
      "next":
      {
        "href":"/api/v1/category/Science",
        "method":"GET",
        "rel":"_next"
      },
      "graph":
      {
        "href":"/api/v1/graph/scientific_disciplines",
        "method":"GET",
        "rel":"graph"
      }
    }
  },
  { ... },
  ]
}
```

If you want, you can also create the *up* action in the graph controller to display the upstream graph from a category. We will use this in later chapters.

You can compare your solution with the one proposed in the next chapter, or check out the GitHub repository (*http://bit.ly/wikicat-github*) for the WikiCat API.

Now that we have obtained the explorable graph, we can make our categories explorable. Let's go ahead and modify the show method in the category controller. Our objective is displaying the *Main_topic_classifications* when no category param is provided:

```
def show
  category = params[:category] ? params[:category]
             : "Main_topic_classifications"
  @category = Category.where
             (:cat_title => category.capitalize).first
```

```
    if @category
      render :json => @category, serializer: CategorySerializer,
                                 root: "category"
    else
      render :json => {:error => {:text => "404 Not found",
                       :status => 404}}
    end
  end
end
```

Once we have modified the controller we can go ahead and modify the serializer. Our objective is to make the category resource explorable by linking to its graph:

```
class CategorySerializer < ActiveModel::Serializer
  attributes :title, :sub_categories, :_links
  def title
    URI::encode(object.cat_title.force_encoding("ISO-8859-1")
        .encode("utf-8", replace: nil).downcase.tr(" ", "_"))
  end
  def sub_categories
    object.cat_subcats
  end
  def _links
    {:self => _self, :graph => _graph}
  end
  def _graph
    href = URI::encode("/api/v1/graph/#{self.title}")
    {:href => href, :method => "GET", :rel => "graph"}
  end
  def _self
    href = URI::encode("/api/v1/category/#{self.title}")
    {:href => href, :method => "GET", :rel => "self"}
  end
end
```

If everything is working as expected we can test our category resource and receive the JSON object string:

```
http://0.0.0.0:3000/api/v1/category/science
{
  "category":
  {
    "title":"science",
    "sub_categories":34,
    "_links":
    {
      "self":
      {
        "href":"/api/v1/category/science",
        "method":"GET",
        "rel":"self"
      },
      "graph":
      {
```

```
      "href":"/api/v1/graph/science",
      "method":"GET",
      "rel":"graph"
    }
  }
 }
}
```

Perfect—our WikiCat API is now fully explorable! You can continue testing all the methods if you want, or you can read the other test cases that have been created for this app in the GitHub repository.

Wrapping Up

In this chapter we have sketched our first hypermedia API with Ruby on Rails. In the next chapter we will learn about asynchronous REST and what mechanisms we can use when the application server needs to perform some actions at a later time.

## CHAPTER 6

Asynchronous REST

Asynchronous operations might be one of the most complex aspects of RESTful architecture. Imagine performing a certain action on a resource that will take a considerable amount of time to finish. Should you leave the client to wait until the action has finished and you are able to return a meaningful HTTP code? In this chapter we will see what the best strategy is in situations like this one, and what codes your API should return when you want to tell the client that you will perform the operation at later time.

Asynchronous RESTful Operations

The HTTP protocol is synchronous. When an HTTP request is made to a server, the client expects an answer, whether it indicates success or failure (see Figure 6-1).

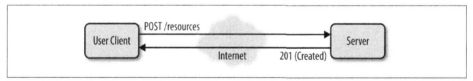

Figure 6-1. A simple REST request and response—the client has performed a POST request to a resource and the server has returned the 201 (Created) status code

Yet the fact that the server has returned an answer does not mean, per se, that the action or actions initiated by the request have to finish immediately. For example, you might request an operation that requires some time or resources to complete, and these might not be available at the moment the request is made.

This could very well be the case for a service that processes images or videos or audio files. In such a situation, the server usually accepts the request made by the client and agrees to perform the operation at a later stage.

This behavior differs slightly from creating or modifying a resource and returning a 201 code with a Created message or simply a 200. Therefore, we might be left asking ourselves the question: what code should the server return when agreeing to perform an action at a later time?

A common practice is to simply return a 202 HTTP code with an Accepted message (Figure 6-2). This tells the client that the request has been received and the server has accepted it, meaning there were no errors on the way when the request was passed. The server will also return a location that the client can retrieve to get the status of its request, among other things.

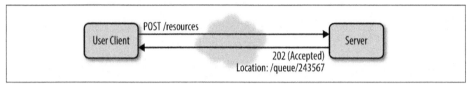

Figure 6-2. When a REST request is accepted to be performed later, the server sends a 202 (Accepted) status code and adds a location field so that the client can check the queue of processing resources

If the client retrieves the location returned to it, it might be able to perform different operations on the temporary resource, such as requesting that the operation be aborted (see Figure 6-3).

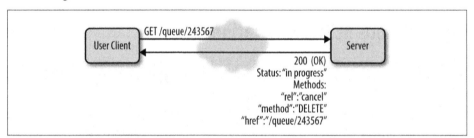

Figure 6-3. When the client retrieves the resource in the queue it will get its status and the list of actions that can be performed on the resource

When the server has finished processing, it will update the queue and let the client know the resource has moved to a different location. It will also return a 303 HTTP code with the message "See Other" and the location of the processed resource (see Figure 6-4).

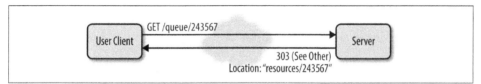

Figure 6-4. When the server has finished processing , it sends a 303 (See Other) status code with a location field specifying the permanent location of the resource

Asynchronous REST in Rails

Asynchronous REST is not difficult to understand in theory. We have seen what status code to return when a certain operation needs more time. But what happens in a Rails app when an operation needs to be performed later?

Rails Workers and Background Jobs

Operations that need to be completed later or in the background are usually performed by *workers*. Workers run processes that live outside of the application request/response cycle. These processes are usually called *background jobs*.

There are different solutions in Rails to manage background jobs. Here we will get started with Sidekiq (*http://sidekiq.org*), a multithreading library that lets us handle background jobs at the same time and in the same process.

We will create a service that receives an image and performs certain operations on it. The image is uploaded through an API call and stored on S3. We can generate our application as follows:

```
$ rails-api new localpic
```

Creating an Application Skeleton in Three Easy Steps

Let's start by editing the *Gemfile*:

```
source 'https://rubygems.org'
gem 'rails', '4.1.8'
gem 'rails-api'
gem 'spring', :group => :development

gem 'pg'
gem 'activerecord-postgis-adapter'

# Serializer for JSON

gem 'active_model_serializers'

gem 'refile', require: ['refile/rails', 'refile/image_processing']
```

```
# To upload images to S3 with refile we need:
gem 'aws-sdk'
gem 'aws-sdk-v1' # Can be used together with v2
                 # because of different namespaces.
gem 'mini_magick', '~> 3.7.0'

gem 'sidekiq'
gem 'ohm'
gem 'ohm-contrib'
```

And let's bundle:

```
$ bundle install
```

Now we will start sketching the `Picture` model and the pictures controller.

In the first step we create the model through the Rails generator:

```
$ rails-api g model picture title:string
```

In the second step we create the controller:

```
$ rails-api g controller api/v1/pictures index show create
  update delete
```

In the third step we will just edit the routes to reflect the actions that we have just
defined by adding the pictures resource:

```
namespace :api do
  namespace :v1 do
    resource :pictures do
        get 'index'
    end
  end
end
```

This sets up the skeleton for our RESTful resource, pictures.

Uploading Images Through an API Call

In order to be able to process images in the background, we will have to be able to
upload these images first.

We'll now sketch an image uploader API by using Refile (*https://github.com/refile/
refile*) and storing our files on S3.

To begin, we need an S3 account. Please refer to *http://aws.amazon.com/s3/* for
detailed instructions on how to create an account.

Then we will configure the Refile gem to upload files to S3. Refile is a file upload
library for Ruby (and Ruby on Rails) applications, designed to be simple and at the
same time very powerful.

To upload any files to S3 we need to provide to our Rails app information regarding our Amazon AWS keys. We can add this information to our *secrets.yml* file in */config*:

```
development:
  secret_key_base: <app_secret_key>
  s3_access_key_id:  <s3_access_key_id>
  s3_secret: <s3_secret>
  s3_bucket: localpic
  s3_region: eu-west-1

test:
  secret_key_base: <app_secret_key>
  s3_access_key_id: aws-key-id
  s3_secret: aws-secret
  s3_bucket: localpic
  s3_region: eu-west-1

# Do not keep production secrets in the repository,
# instead read values from the environment.

production:
  secret_key_base: <%= ENV["SECRET_KEY_BASE"] %>
  s3_access_key_id: aws-key-id
  s3_secret: aws-secret
  s3_bucket: localpic
  s3_region: eu-west-1
```

Remember not to upload your *secrets.yml* file to GitHub or any public repository. This is where you are storing your application secrets!

How to Exclude a File from a Git Repository

You can edit the *.gitignore* file to specify files and directories that Git needs to ignore.

For example, if you want to untrack *secrets.yml*, you just add it to *.gitignore*:

```
$ echo config/secrets.yml >> .gitignore
```

The Git documentation (*http://bit.ly/git-gitignore*) contains many more examples.

The *.gitignore* file is uploaded to your repository though, and sometimes you may want to exclude some files without adding them to your global *.gitignore*.

Imagine for example that you have a very personalized *.gitignore* that you do not want to track in the Git repository. In that case, it is better to add *.gitignore* to *.git/info/exclude*. This is a special local file that works just like *.gitignore* but is not tracked by Git.

Please refer to this article (*http://bit.ly/git-ignoring*) on ignoring Git files for more insight on the topic.

When the app is started, Rails runs an `initialize` method. All the class ancestors are traversed, looking for those responding to an `initializers` method. The ancestors are then sorted by name and run.

We are going to define initializers for the AWS gem and the Refile gem. Here we will include the configuration and credentials needed to interact with AWS, and the basic configuration needed to save our pictures on S3:

```ruby
# config/initializers/aws.rb

require 'aws-sdk'
Aws.config[:stub_responses] = true if Rails.env.test?
Aws.config[:credentials] = Aws::Credentials.new(
                           Rails.application.secrets.s3_access_key_id,
                           Rails.application.secrets.s3_secret)
Aws.config[:region] = Rails.application.secrets.s3_region
Aws.config[:log_level] = Rails.logger.level
Aws.config[:logger] = Rails.logger


# config/initializers/refile.rb
require 'aws-sdk-v1'
require "refile/backend/s3"

# Here we read the secrets from secrets.yml
aws = {
  access_key_id: Rails.application.secrets.s3_access_key_id,
  secret_access_key: Rails.application.secrets.s3_secret,
  bucket: Rails.application.secrets.s3_bucket,
}

Refile.cache = Refile::Backend::S3.new(prefix: "cache", **aws)
Refile.store = Refile::Backend::S3.new(prefix: "store", **aws)
```

Now we can prepare our `Picture` model to have an image attachment. We create a migration as follows:

```
$ rails generate migration add_image_to_pictures image_id:string
```

This will create a migration in *db/migrate*:

```ruby
class AddImageToPictures < ActiveRecord::Migration
  def change
    add_column :pictures, :image_id, :string
  end
end
```

We also have to specify in our `Picture` model that it has an attachment:

```ruby
class Picture < ActiveRecord::Base
  attachment :image

end
```

The last step is defining our pictures controller and all the actions that we need for our pictures resource.

We start by sketching an index, where we want the app API to return all the pictures created in the app. We use the same serializer mechanism we used earlier:

```
# GET /pictures.json
def index
  @pictures = Picture.all
  if @pictures
    render json: @pictures,
           each_serializer: PictureSerializer,
           root: "pictures"
  else
    @error = Error.new(text: "404 Not found",
                       status: 404,
                       url: request.url,
                       method: request.method)
    render json: @error.serializer
  end
end
```

We continue with a *show* and a *create* action:

```
# GET /pictures/1.json
def show
  if @picture
    render json: @picture,
           serializer: PictureSerializer,
           root: "picture"
  else
    @error = Error.new(text: "404 Not found",
                       status: 404,
                       url: request.url,
                       method: request.method)
    render json: @error.serializer
  end
end


# POST /pictures.json
def create
  @picture = Picture.new(picture_params)

  if @picture.save
    render json: @picture,
               serializer: PictureSerializer,
               meta: { status: 201,
                       message: "201 Created",
                       location: @picture
               },
               root: "picture"
```

```
    else
      @error = Error.new(text: "500 Server Error",
                         status: 500,
                         url: request.url,
                         method: request.method)
      render :json => @error.serializer
    end
  end
```

As you see, I have used an error serializer and a picture serializer. The idea is the same as described in the previous repository (*http://bit.ly/localpic*). I will not sketch all the serializers and error classes here. I encourage you to try yourself and then have a look at the full repository on GitHub.

 The full app repository for all the code in this chapter can be found on GitHub (*http://bit.ly/localpic*). You are encouraged to check the code there and see all the functionality in more detail.

If you want to try to upload a picture through an API call you can use the following curl command:

```
$ curl -F "picture[title]=unnamed" \
  -F "picture[image]=@./unnamed.jpg;type=image/jpeg" \
  http://0.0.0.0:3000/api/v1/pictures
```

Then you can check if the file has actually been uploaded to S3.

Creating Workers and a Jobs Queue

We are going to use Sidekiq to create and schedule our workers. Sidekiq worker classes are placed in *app/workers*. For our app, we are going to structure our workers in two distinct classes. We'll create a ServiceWorker, where we keep the general methods that we are going to use, and an ImageFilter worker to perform the actual filtering operations on the images.

We will start by sketching our ServiceWorker:

```
require 'rubygems'
require 'celluloid'

class ServiceWorker
  include Sidekiq::Worker

  class RequestError < StandardError; end
  class BadRequestError < RequestError; end
  class UnknownRequestError < RequestError; end

  protected
```

```
# This method will be responsible for downloading
# images to process from S3
def download(path)

end

# This method will be responsible for uploading
# processed images to S3
def upload(file, content_type, relative_path)

end

private

def setup_options_as_instance_variables(options)
  options.each do |k, v|
    instance_variable_set("@#{k}", v) unless v.nil?
  end
end
end
```

`instance_variable_set` is a method provided by the Ruby language. It is used to set the instance variable names by *symbol* to *object*. A symbol in Ruby is similar to a string, except strings are mutable, symbols are not. The variable did not have to exist prior to this call. This means that you will be able to call the variable as:

```
puts @variable
# 'bar'
```

I have also defined a `FileOperations` module in */lib* containing all the methods responsible for uploading and downloading files on S3. I am not going to sketch all the functionality here, but you can look at it in the repository for this chapter.

Now we are going to define the `ImageFilter` worker. This will be a simple worker class responsible for applying a sepia filter to an image:

```
class ImageFilter < ServiceWorker
  include ImageOperations

  sidekiq_options queue: :low

  sidekiq_options retry: 5
  sidekiq_retry_in { 3.minutes }

  sidekiq_retries_exhausted do |msg|
    logger.error "[worker][filter] Failed #{msg['class']}
                  with #{msg['args']}:
                  #{msg['error_message']}"
  end

  def perform(options)
    setup_options_as_instance_variables(options)
```

```
        logger.info "[id=#{@id}] FilterImages work started."
        process_filter
        perform_callbacks("filters/#{@id}")
    end

    private
        # Method responsible for applying a filter to an image.
        def process_filter
        end
end
```

Mocks and Stubs

Something that might not be completely clear when working with workers and asynchronous operations in general is how you go about testing them. In the next chapter you will find out all about testing, mocking, and stubbing.

Private and Protected Methods

When we define methods as private or protected in Ruby, it means we are changing their *visibility*. In other words, we are restricting the use of those methods.

Marking a method as private in Ruby means that you cannot access that method directly by calling it on an instance of a class. A private method can be called only from within the context of the calling object.

The difference between making a method private or protected is very subtle. When a method is protected, it may be also called by any instance of the defining class or its subclasses.

Private methods are never directly accessible from another object, even if the two objects are of the same class. Protected methods are instead accessible from objects of the same class or children.

Refer to the Wikibook "Ruby Programming" (*http://bit.ly/declaring-visibility*) to find out more about method visibility in Ruby.

Creating a Resource Queue

Now that we have defined the workers, we are going to create a temporary resource queue that we can call to see the status of a certain operation.

We will define a Filter model and controller to do this, and we will use the Ohm gem (*https://github.com/soveran/ohm*) to persist the queue in Redis.

Let's start by defining the `Filter` model:

```
require 'ohm'
require 'ohm/contrib'

class Filter < Ohm::Model
  include Ohm::DataTypes
  include Ohm::Versioned
  include Ohm::Timestamps

  # Here the class attributes are defined:
  attribute :filter_id
  attribute :message
  attribute :location
  attribute :status
  attribute :code

  # We use the filter_id as index on the class:
  index :filter_id

  # We define a simple serializer method:
  def serialize
    {
      filter: { id: filter_id, location: location },
      response: { message: message, code: code.to_i },
      status: status.to_i
    }
  end
end
```

Then we'll continue with the filter controller. The idea is to sketch actions that will allow a client to know the status of a filter operation and eventually cancel it. So, we will start with an *index* action:

```
def index
  @filters = Filter.all.to_a
  if @filters
    render json: @filters, status: 200
  else
    render json: filter_not_found, status: 404
  end

end
```

This is a simple action fetching all the filter operations in the queue, both finished and in processing.

We continue with a *show* action:

```
def show
  @filter = Filter.find(filter_id: params[:id]).first
  if @filter
    render json: @filter.serialize,
```

```
        status: @filter.serialize[:status]
    else
      render json: filter_not_found, status: 404
    end
  end
```

The filter *show* action follows the same logic that we used with the `Picture` model and controller. The concern *filter_operations.rb* contains all the logic that has been extrapolated out of the controller (for more on concerns, see "Defining the models" on page 116).

The `filter_not_found` method is defined in the concern following this logic:

```
def filter_not_found
  {
    response: {
      message: 'Not Found',
      code: 404
    },
    status: 404
  }
end
```

The next action that is defined in the filter controller is *create*:

```
def create
  if ImageFilter.perform_async(build_filter_params(params))
    @filter = create_filter(params)
    render json: @filter, status: @filter[:status]
  else
    render json: filter_error, status: 500
  end

end
```

The `create_filter` and `filter_error` methods are also designed in the concern:

```
def create_filter(params)
  filter = Filter.create(filter_id: params[:id],
                         message: 'Accepted',
                         location: "filters/#{params[:id]}",
                         code: 202, status: 202)
  if filter
    filter.serialize
  else
    filter_error
  end
end

def filter_error
  {
    response: {
      message: 'Internal Server Error',
```

```
        code: 500
    },
    status: 500
  }
end
```

The complete application can be found in the repository (*http://bit.ly/localpic*) for this chapter. I have decided not to sketch all the methods because I believe you might want to play with the code a little bit yourself before looking at the repository for the complete solution. I actually encourage you to do so. Hacking around a sample app is a great way to start applying new concepts and to try out what you have just learned.

Callbacks

A callback in the HTTP world is a GET or POST request that passes some argument to a certain web server, which returns a result or response.

Callbacks are used in asynchronous REST operations, like some of the tasks performed by the sample app that we have built in this chapter.

There is a difference between using callbacks and implementing a status queue. When you implement a status queue, it is the client's responsibility to check the queue periodically; the server will just expose the status of the operation or resource requested.

When callbacks are implemented instead, the client can request a certain operations that the server will execute at a later time. Then the client will expect the server to perform a request to a certain endpoint. That is a callback, and its effect will be to notify the client that the operation has finished with a certain result.

WebSockets

WebSockets is sometimes used instead of asynchronous RESTful requests; it is not a REST method. The WebSocket protocol is specifically used to provide a full-duplex communication channel over a single TCP connection. It does not use the HTTP protocol apart from the initial handshake, which is interpreted by the parties involved as an UPGRADE request.

An UPGRADE HTTP request uses the Upgrade header field: it is specifically used in the WebSocket domain to let the server know that the connection has switched to a different protocol.

The connection upgrade request must be made by the client. On the other side, if the server wants to enforce the upgrade to a newer or different protocol it may send a 426 (Upgrade Required) response.

The WebSocket protocol facilitates live content and the creation of real-time interaction between a browser client and a server. With the WebSocket protocol, the server can in fact send content to the browser without the client requesting it, in a standardized way. Messages between client and server can therefore be passed back and forth while the connection is kept open. This way the communication between server and client is really bidirectional (two-way).

Wrapping Up

In this chapter we have learned about asynchronous REST, Rails workers, and temporary resource queues persisted to Redis. In the next chapter we will concentrate on how to test RESTful services and APIs—what do you *mock* and what do you *stub*?

## CHAPTER 7

Testing RESTful Services

Testing RESTful services can be a difficult task that goes beyond just testing pieces of code. A service is in fact composed of different components, and in order to test its functionality, the interactions between these components need to be tested.

Most of the time, when testing techniques are introduced, we learn how to test if a given method actually returns the expected results for a given input or set of inputs.

Testing services requires instead that we test how our service interacts with Amazon AWS, or with external APIs, or with our own load balancer. This includes testing testing how all other services interacting with our APIs react to certain error codes or specific responses.

Testing in Rails

We learned in Chapter 2 that the Rails framework was built to allow test–driven development (TDD) from the beginning. Rails in fact creates a *test* folder as soon as a new Rails project is created. If you list the contents of this folder you will find that a different subfolder is created for each component of the application, so that tests can be structured accordingly:

```
$ ls test
controllers    fixtures    helpers        integration
mailers        models      test_helper.rb
```

Testing *models* in a Rails app usually means unit testing. With unit testing the smallest testable parts of your Rails application—the models, in this case—are tested individually and independently, to ensure that the defined methods work as expected.

Functional testing tests the controllers. The controllers handle the incoming requests and pass them to the various components of your service. When you are testing controller logic you are in fact testing the following:

- Was the request successful?
- Were the right HTTP code and message returned?
- In what case does the resource return an error?
- Which error does the resource return?
- If an action is initiated or a resource is requested, is the right response returned to the client?

Let's go back to our LocalPic application from the previous chapter. Imagine that we have a simple controller with an action that just returns the status of our service—i.e., if we request a certain resource and get a 200 response, we know the service is up and running.

This controller creates a status endpoint that can be used by monitoring services to periodically check on our LocalPic API. If our API goes offline for any reason, the monitoring service will send a notification.

Let's generate a simple status controller:

```
$ rails g controller api/status
```

And then the actual code:

```
class API::StatusController < ApplicationController
  def index
    render json: { alive: true }
  end
end
```

And the test for it:

```
require 'test_helper'
class API::StatusControllerTest < ActionController::TestCase
  test 'status should be fine' do
    get :index
    assert_response :success
    assert_equal '{"alive":true}', @response.body
  end
end
```

Of course this is a simple example, but the logic applied to test controllers follows the same pattern: *if we request a certain resource, do we receive the expected response?*

We'll continue by testing the actions on the pictures controller.

To test the *index* action we simply need to add the following test to the *pictures_controller_test.rb* file in *test/controllers*:

```
test "should get index" do
  get :index
  assert_response :success
end
```

Please note that this will only assert that the *index* action returns success. It will not assert what data the action actually produces.

Now we continue with the *show* action:

```
test "should get show" do
  get :show, id: 1
  assert_response :success
end
```

Note that in this action we are passing the id parameter. We therefore need to add it to our *pictures.yml* fixtures file.

We edit that file as follows:

```
one:
  id: 1
  title: "Test title"
```

Tests for the other controller actions can be found in the repository (*http://bit.ly/ localpic*) for the LocalPic application. I encourage you to try to write the tests yourself before looking at the repo for the solution. Writing tests is a great exercise to understand how our applications really work and to make sure that our code remains stable even when we change things.

Mocks, Stubs, Doubles, and Dummies

When you start testing RoR applications, and especially their interactions with different services, you will start hearing about "stubbing" and "mocking" certain things. But what exactly are mocks, and what are stubs? The difference is very subtle and often confusing.

Mocks Aren't Stubs

In 2007, Martin Fowler from ThoughtWorks published a famous blog post called "Mocks Aren't Stubs" (*http://bit.ly/mocks-stubs*).

A mock object is an unreal object that we create for testing purposes. We use this when we do not want to or cannot use real data in the test.

Mocks verify behavior. The mock object is told what to expect during the setup phase of the test. During the verification phase of the test, we ask the mock to *verify itself*.

You'll soon discover there are different terms to describe things that seem to overlap, at least in part. You'll hear about test doubles, dummies, fakes, stubs, and mocks.

Let's start from the beginning:

- *Double* is a general term to describe any not-real object used for the purpose of testing.
- *Dummy* objects are usually only used to fill parameter lists; they are not really used for actual testing.
- *Fake* objects can be used for testing as they possess some implementation of the actual objects they represent.
- *Stubs* are used to provide canned responses to calls made during the test but do not respond to anything outside of the test's scope. A good example of how and where we can use a stub is when we want to test how our application interacts with some external service, without having to call it directly. We stub the service so that it behaves exactly like it and answers to the same requests.
- *Mocks* are objects that are preprogrammed with certain expectations and follow the specifications of the real object.

Mocks are not like fixtures. Fixtures are only *fake database records*.

Testing RESTful Services

Testing RESTful services means integration testing. A service must interact with the outside environment through the APIs it exposes and the external APIs it integrates.

Now, in a perfect world, all services you decide to integrate—whether internal to your organization or external—would always expose the same APIs, or at least notify their users if they were about to change something with regard to what data they return or how to make certain requests.

In the real world, this is hardly the case.

Integration tests have to take this very important aspect into consideration. You've probably designed some portions of your application in a way that integrates perfectly with one or more services that you have chosen to or had to integrate. What happens if one day these services change, and some of your app's functionality does not work as expected?

A good idea to ensure that your integrations are stable is to test that each service is responding as expected. This means, in a continuous integration environment, that you write tests that are run every time your production environment is tested. This way you will be able to spot changes right away, hopefully before your users notice.

Imagine that you are integrating a payment service. You can write tests to ensure that you are always sending requests to the service in the right format. If something in the APIs changes, ideally your tests will notice it and raise an error or simply fail.

There are also tools that take care of things like this for you. These tools work like a pager for the APIs you want to monitor, and when something changes they send you a verification message.

Wrapping Up

In this chapter we took a quick look at testing, stubbing, and mocking RESTful services and APIs. We saw how we can test interactions between our app and the external services that will interact with our models and controllers. In the next chapter we will start talking about SOA practices applied to microservices and microapplications.

## CHAPTER 8

Microservices and Microapplications

In this chapter we are going to introduce some concepts regarding service-oriented architecture (SOA) and microservices architectures. We will develop a new API to discover possible thematic walks based on the user's location. To find the user's location we are going to build a different service that will return the user's geographical coordinates given her IP address. The same service will also return a list of geotagged Wikipedia articles that we can use as points of interest for our Citywalks API. We will deploy the new API on OpenShift, a Platform as a Service (PaaS) solution by RedHat, and we will access it from our local machine.

Basics of SOA and Distributed Systems Design

When we talk of service-oriented architecture, we really mean a set of design patterns, both for software systems and architectures. Here, "service" refers to a self-contained unit of functionality that provides one or more actions using defined protocols instead of APIs. A protocol describes how services pass and parse messages using descriptive metadata.

SOA patterns and paradigms have been designed for large distributed systems, where every computer runs a number of services, and each service can exchange information with any other service in the network. SOA is designed to make it relatively easy for computers connected over a network to cooperate, allowing, among other things, the physical distribution of each service across a network of interconnected computers.

SOA aims at building more flexible distributed systems, as opposed to monolithic architectures. By enabling the design of more loosely coupled services, SOA makes it easier to scale and maintain complex, large applications.

SOA services are an abstraction of actual business units performing a specific action or set of actions. SOA paradigms are therefore applied at different levels of the design process:

- Architecture
- Processes
- Governance

SOA patterns are closely linked to the business functions and processes of a set of technologies that span large distributed systems. SOA services are concerned mainly with the business value of a unit or interface. This concept is based on three important technical points:

- A service contains some business functionality. This can be a simple function like updating or retrieving customer data or something more complex, like placing an order for a certain product.
- The underlying infrastructure that distributes business processes between multiple services and systems is called the *enterprise service bus* (ESB).
- Because business processes are distributed over multiple physical machines, it is said that SOA systems are loosely coupled. This means that systems' interdependencies are reduced to allow independent development of different services.

SOA involves more than just the technical aspects of creating large distributed applications of interoperating services. SOA is in fact a business architectural set of patterns as much as it is a technological one.

On the other hand, there are certainly different analogies that we can trace between large distributed systems and open applications. These aspects, which are at the core of SOA design, can also be applied to RESTful development. Let's analyze these in order.

Legacies

Large distributed systems often have different legacy services, or just old units of code, in their architecture. Having to deal with legacies usually involves carefully adapting the structure of an existing system while dealing with old platforms and backward-compatibility issues. Sometimes SOA design is even considered a possible approach for the maintenance of a large system.

In such situations, following REST patterns is certainly a big advantage. RESTful services communicate with one another by exposing uniform interfaces. Legacies can thus easily be "hidden" behind a REST connector that can translate messages between the legacy system and the REST architecture.

Heterogeneity

Heterogeneity is the property of having diverse components in a system. Diversities are in a way unavoidable, no matter how hard you try: even in a monolithic and rather small application, as you try to scale that application it will reach a certain point where you will have to deal with diversity. Diversity can be seen as an emergent property of the process of scaling an application from blueprint design to production.

All large systems tend to become very heterogeneous, since different components and functions are developed with different purposes, at different times, with different technologies and programming languages (Figure 8-1). Scaling a system is hardly a harmonic process, although harmonization can help you in scaling your application.

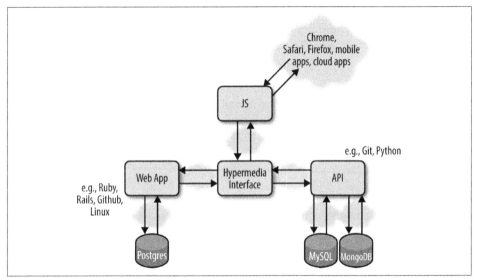

Figure 8-1. An example of a small application using different repositories, open source libraries, databases, programming languages, operating systems, and cloud platforms

Generally speaking any distributed system, complex application, or code base, once it has grown to a certain size, will reach a point where maintenance and iterative feature development become a problem.

This happens for a number of reasons, including:

- The difficulty of rewriting part of the software or system
- The learning curve for new developers to start contributing to the project

This suggests that when a system component gets to a certain size, it becomes very difficult to add new features quickly. Furthermore, you cannot fix bugs quickly, and you cannot throw it away easily when it becomes obsolete, because rewriting the existing functionality might require a big investment of time and money.

So, when you have an opportunity to avoid having to deal with or even design very large components, you should always do that.

SOA paradigms would suggest decoupling complex systems into self-contained units that serve fewer functions and can be developed independently over time. In SOA terms, this is considered an investment.

In RESTful development we can apply the same paradigms and design simple APIs that serve a limited number of functions and communicate with one another to exchange information and messages.

Complexity

Large distributed systems are often very complex. More importantly, they might be owned or maintained by different departments within an organization, or totally different companies. Integrating different systems may result in an added layer of complexity to overcome.

If each system, or application function, exposes a RESTful API, complexity can be resolved at the unit level and with almost total independence from the overall system design, as long as we ensure that the different units can continue communicating and exchanging information and messages.

Redundancy

Large systems all have a certain amount of redundancy. Some of this might just be accidental, but some might be intentional and managed, since not all data can be normalized and stored in a single place.

Integrating and consuming data that is spread across different heterogeneous systems is one of the problems shared by open applications that are sometimes operating on and sharing the same streams of data.

Microservices Paradigms

A *microservice* is a small, self-contained service, focused on doing one thing and doing it well. An example of a microservice is that of a *separate, independent* operating system process living on its own physical (or virtual) machine and performing a very specific function.

Microservices architectures are based on three main concepts:

- Microservices are independent operating system processes.
- Microservices are self-contained, highly decoupled processes.
- Microservices use language-agnostic APIs to communicate.

These three main aspects of microservices introduce a number of advantages. The main advantages of building a microservices-based architecture derive from the idea that everything is self-contained. This concept of self-containment is extended to the point that the actual functions that the service provides (and the code sustaining them) live in their own processes.

Also, because microservices use language-agnostic APIs to communicate with other services, a microservice can be technologically independent from the rest of the system, allowing the service designer to pick the most appropriate tools for each service instead of just adhering to an imposed standard.

Because of the independence of each unit, in a microservices environment new technologies are adopted more quickly. In a monolithic application scenario, each small change can severely impact the overall performance and stability of the system. In a microservices architecture, the risks and barriers of introducing new technologies are lowered, as the impact of a change in the system is contained at the single-microservice level. This allows for technological and architectural heterogeneity of the overall system design.

At the same time, with microservices architectures it is easier to isolate problems in the system, and the rest of the system can continue working independently. Microservices hence allow for more resilient and significantly more stable systems.

Microservices architectures are also easier to scale. Since each service can be developed independently and the system doesn't have to scale all together, we can scale on demand—i.e., scale different parts of our system at different moments.

The Evolutionary Approach

A microservices architecture is composed of a set of independent units or system processes performing independent functions and communicating via some language-independent API. While microservices are an exciting topic at the moment, we need to take a step back and focus on the fact that they are part of our applications' inner workings, both at the frontend and the backend level. This functionality of an application or service is hidden, or made transparent, to the end user. Ultimately, when a web or mobile application is accessed via the Web, the user does not now how many microservices are working behind it, nor what APIs are used or external services are called. In this sort of scenario it is important to maintain the overall vision of the aggregated system design.

Microservices introduce a number of benefits concerning the interdependency and flexibility of a system architecture. However, they also carry some complexity emerging from having a large set of movable parts, so there is a trade-off between small and smaller.

The biggest risk of microservices architectures is in fact losing control over a growing number of independent services and movable parts. Ironically, we could end up having the same problems as with big monolithic applications:

- Not knowing which part of the application is performing a certain function
- Not knowing which part of the application is failing
- Not knowing how to better scale certain functionality spread across a large number of small processes

A common approach when designing microservices applications is reasoning around business capabilities, or mere application logic.

This approach can be considered in a way evolutionary; your application actually evolves from having a set of core simple functions into offering more services.

So, the first step in the design process is identifying the set of core functions that the system will provide. Then, instead of addressing this set of problems by separating them across the application layers that will solve these problems, each problem is solved independently at all layers (i.e., data storage, backend, and frontend). Figure 8-2 illustrates this approach.

Thinking in Terms of Microapplications and Services

The idea of developing microapplications follows in the footsteps of microservices architecture design and SOA paradigms. A microapplication is an independent system solving a simple problem and sharing data with other applications and services through RESTful APIs.

Microapplications, like microservices, are self-contained and can be developed and scaled independently, while at the same time facilitating technological innovation.

An example of a microapplication is our Wikipedia categories API. The application returns through an API the category graph of a certain keyword. By itself it is not a complex application, but it could be coupled with a nice frontend layer to create interesting visualizations of the link graphs of the categories queried.

The categories API could also be part of one or more microapplications solving a different set of problems that might require some category knowledge. We could envisage any number of applications that require some sort of semantic knowledge of keywords to provide a better user experience. Using the categories API would free these applications from having to develop their own solutions—they could just integrate with our API and concentrate only on solving their own business problems.

This idea of building open platforms and enriching the Web with hypermedia APIs that can be easily accessed and integrated into a web of communicating applications follows in more than one way the idea of open source software.

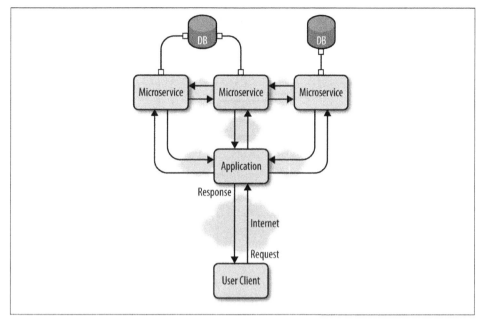

Figure 8-2. Microservices communicate using language-agnostic APIs and provide specific functions across all layers of an application architecture: data storage, backend, frontend

Certainly there are many different problems that haven't been tackled yet, but hyperdata, APIs, and the microapplications design patterns provide the basis to start developing very complex systems. While solving one simple problem at a time, you will notice that you will be creating a platform of independent services. By solving minimal classes of problems, each of these applications will be easier to design, develop, and scale. This approach also provides an unprecedented level of logical independence and facilitates a culture of quicker technological innovation.

The Thematic Walks API

The thematic walks API we will develop next is a service that searches for geographically tagged Wikipedia articles, filtered on categories. We will call it Citywalks. The user can query the API by providing geographical coordinates; otherwise, the user's IP address will be used to identify the geographical origin of the query.

The architecture of this service is composed of the Citywalks API, the Wikipin API, and the WikiCat API (see Figure 8-3). The WikiCat API is the example application developed throughout the previous chapters, while the Wikipin API is a service returning geolocated Wikipedia articles based on the provided geographical coordinates or the positioning of the user's IP address.

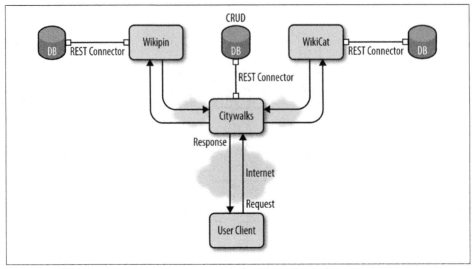

Figure 8-3. REST architecture for the Citywalks API—the Wikipin and WikiCat services for geographical points of interest and categories, respectively, are developed as independent services

The Wikipin API

Wikipin is an application that returns geolocated Wikipedia articles based on the provided location or on the requesting client's IP address.

Geolocated articles are provided from a database dump from Wikipedia, while the IP geolocation mechanism is based on MaxMind's IP geolocation databases.

> MaxMind's downloadable databases can be found at the MaxMind Developer Site (*http://bit.ly/maxmind-dl-db*).
>
> The Wikipedia georeferenced article dataset can be downloaded from the GeoNames database (*http://www.geonames.org/wikipe dia/*). The dataset is also available as a webservice (*http://bit.ly/ wikipedia-webservice*).
>
> Edited links to the dumps can be found at *http://bit.ly/wikipin*.

For this API application we are going to use *rails-api* with PostgreSQL and PostGIS. PostgreSQL (*http://www.postgresql.org/*) is a popular object-relational database management system (ORDBMS) focused specifically on extensibility and standards compliance. It implements the majority of SQL standards and syntax, which will allow us to import the Wikipedia database dumps easily. Because we want to learn how to develop a platform of independent applications, we'll take this opportunity to try a different DBMS. For this next application, we will use PostgreSQL.

For a list of companies currently using PostgreSQL, see *http://www.postgresql.org/about/users/*.

We are also going to use PostGIS (*http://postgis.net/*), for geographical queries. PostGIS is a spatial database extender for PostgreSQL: it adds support for geographic objects, enabling location queries to be run in SQL.

Installing PostgreSQL

You can install PostgreSQL and PostGIS from multiple sources, depending on the operating system used and your personal preferences.

Binaries to install PostgreSQL on different operating systems are available on the website (*http://www.postgresql.org/download/*).

If you are on Mac OS X, you can also use *brew* to install the package:

```
$ brew install postgres
```

Or you can use Postgres.app (*http://postgresapp.com/*). Postgres.app contains a full-featured PostgreSQL installation in a single package, while also providing an intuitive way to manage your database instances.

To install PostGIS, you can rely on this official list (*http://postgis.net/install/*) of binaries provided for different operating systems.

On Mac OS X, you can use *brew* directly:

```
$ brew install postgis
```

If you have used Postgres.app, PostGIS should be included.

Creating the app

Once our database and extensions have been installed, we can create our application API by running:

```
$ rails-api new wikipin
```

Since we are using PostgreSQL, we also have to install the Postgres (pg) gem for our system:

```
$ gem install pg
```

Our *Gemfile* for the Wikipin application will include it as well, together with a set of tools and extensions for spatial connection adapters in Active Record:

```
source 'https://rubygems.org'
gem 'rails', '4.1.4'
gem 'rails-api'
```

```
gem 'spring', :group => :development
gem 'pg' # PostgreSQL gem
# RGeo Active Record patched version
gem 'rgeo-activerecord',
:git => 'https://github.com/nopressurelabs/rgeo-activerecord',
:branch => 'master'
# Active record PostGIS adapter
gem 'activerecord-postgis-adapter'
# Serializer for JSON
gem 'active_model_serializers'
```

RGeo::ActiveRecord is an optional RGeo module that provides spatial extensions for Active Record. RGeo also provides a set of helpers for writing spatial Active Record adapters and location-aware applications.

We have also added the ActiveModel::Serializer gem (*http://bit.ly/active-model-serializer*) to the *Gemfile*. We will use this gem consistently to serialize JSON in our APIs project through out this book.

 Please note that I have patched RGeo::ActiveRecord to fix an issue where calling:

```
self.lonlat = Pin.rgeo_factory_for_column(:latlon)
.point(self.longitude, self.latitude)
```

fails to return a factory and returns a proc instead if no params were passed.

Both in the examples here and in the repository, I used this patched version of the adapter. You can either use my version or use the official adapter (which has been developed in the meantime) by calling it like this:

```
self.lonlat = Pin.rgeo_factory_for_column(:latlon, {})
.point(self.longitude, self.latitude)
```

Run bundle install to install the gems.

The last thing left to do before we start to code our application is to configure the database in *config/database.yml*.

This is a file used to specify our database configuration in YAML format (rhymes with *camel*). YAML is a human-readable data serialization format that draws ideas from different programming languages, and XML. YAML syntax was designed to be easily readable and easily mapped to data types common to most high-level languages.

The *database.yml* file is structured in such a way that you can specify some default options and then a set of fields for each different environment. Our default options will include some encoding and access information, but also other information like pool size and timeout.

The pool field sets the maximum number of simultaneous database connection slots available. We will leave this at 5 for the moment, but setting this number correctly is quite important to allow your application to scale when traffic increases or to solve concurrency issues.

The timeout field defines the number of seconds to block and wait for a connection before giving up and raising a timeout error. It is expressed in milliseconds (default 5,000, or 5 seconds).

The default configuration looks like this:

```
default: &default
encoding: utf-8
username: postgres
password: password5
pool: 5
timeout: 5000
su_username: postgres_su # a superuser for the database
su_password: # the superuser's password
```

You do not have to change the default username and password, but if you want to you can run the following command:

```
$ sudo -u postgres psql postgres
# \password postgres
Enter new password:
```

If you want to create a superuser, you have to run this command instead:

```
$ createuser --interactive postgres_su
Shall the new role be a superuser? (y/n) y
```

Next, set the development and test options as follows:

```
development: <<: *default
adapter: postgis
database: wikipin_db_dev
postgis_extension: postgis # default is postgis
schema_search_path: public,postgis
test:
adapter: postgis
<<: *default
database: wikipin_db_test
```

Generating the models

At this point we are going to generate our models for the geolocated articles and our IP block and location objects.

The IP block object describes the IP address block and contains some information regarding the origin city and country (see Figure 8-4).

```
                                   Table "public.blocks"
             Column              |            Type            |                Modifiers
--------------------------------+----------------------------+------------------------------------------------
 id                             | integer                    | not null default nextval('blocks_id_seq'::regclass)
 network_start_ip               | character varying(255)     |
 network_prefix_length          | integer                    |
 geoname_id                     | integer                    |
 registered_country_geoname_id  | integer                    |
 represented_country_geoname_id | integer                    |
 postal_code                    | character varying(255)     |
 latitude                       | numeric(7,4)               |
 longitude                      | numeric(7,4)               |
 is_anonymous_proxy             | boolean                    |
 is_satellite_provider          | boolean                    |
 created_at                     | timestamp without time zone|
 updated_at                     | timestamp without time zone|
 lonlat                         | geography(Point,4326)      |
Indexes:
    "blocks_pkey" PRIMARY KEY, btree (id)
    "index_blocks_on_geoname_id" btree (geoname_id)
```

Figure 8-4. IP block table schema

We are going to use the Rails generator to generate the model class and migrations:

```
$ rails generate model block \
  network_start_ip:string network_prefix_length:integer \
  geoname_id:integer registered_country_geoname_id:integer \
  represented_country_geoname_id:integer postal_code:integer \
  "latitude:decimal{7,4}" "longitude:decimal{7,4}" \
--fixture false
```

The location table describes a city and its geographical information (Figure 8-5). It is used so that we can obtain the actual city where an IP block is located. The `Location` model and table won't be used in this chapter.

```
                             Table "public.locations"
         Column          |            Type            |                Modifiers
------------------------+----------------------------+------------------------------------------------
 id                     | integer                    | not null default nextval('locations_id_seq'::regclass)
 geoname_id             | integer                    |
 continent_code         | character varying(255)     |
 continent_name         | character varying(255)     |
 country_iso_code       | character varying(255)     |
 country_name           | character varying(255)     |
 subdivision_iso_code   | character varying(255)     |
 subdivision_name       | character varying(255)     |
 city_name              | character varying(255)     |
 metro_code             | integer                    |
 time_zone              | character varying(255)     |
 created_at             | timestamp without time zone|
 updated_at             | timestamp without time zone|
 lonlat                 | geography(Point,4326)      |
Indexes:
    "locations_pkey" PRIMARY KEY, btree (id)
```

Figure 8-5. Location table schema

How would you use the `Location` model to further enhance the Wikipin API?

At this point we will generate the `Location` model and run the respective migrations:

```
$ rails generate model location \
  geoname_id:integer continent_code:string continent_name:string \
  country_iso_code:string country_name:string \
  subdivision_iso_code:string subdivision_name:string \
  city_name:string metro_code:integer time_zone:string \
  --fixture false
```

We will also need another model: the `Pin` model. From the database point of view, the pin table describes a geotagged Wikipedia article with its `url` corresponding to a Wikipedia page (Figure 8-6).

```
                           Table "public.pins"
    Column   |            Type            |                 Modifiers
-------------+----------------------------+--------------------------------------------
 id          | integer                    | not null default nextval('pins_id_seq'::regclass)
 longitude   | numeric(17,14)             |
 latitude    | numeric(17,14)             |
 title       | character varying(255)     |
 url         | character varying(255)     |
 created_at  | timestamp without time zone|
 updated_at  | timestamp without time zone|
 lonlat      | geography(Point,4326)      |
Indexes:
    "pins_pkey" PRIMARY KEY, btree (id)
```

Figure 8-6. Pin table schema

We are now going to generate the `Pin` model as follows:

```
$ rails generate model pin \
  id:integer "longitude:decimal{17,14}" "latitude:decimal{17,14}" \
  title:string url:string \
  --fixture false
```

Once our models have been created we can run the *rake* tasks necessary to generate our database and run the migrations:

```
$ rake db:create db:migrate
```

Let's familiarize ourselves a bit with our database by running a Postgres console and checking the results of our past actions:

```
$ psql
```

Once we are in the Postgres console, we can list all our databases:

```
\list
```

You should see the Wikipin development and test databases.

We can then connect to a specific database:

```
\c wikipin_db_dev
```

and list all the tables for the connected database:

```
\d
```

If we want to show a specific table we just have to run \d *<table_name>*:

```
\d blocks
```

Now we can copy the comma-separated values (CSV) dumps to our database:

```
COPY pins FROM '<full path>/wikipedia_articles_201107.csv'
    DELIMITER ',' CSV;
COPY blocks FROM '<full path>/GeoLite2-City-Blocks.csv'
    DELIMITER ',' CSV;
COPY locations FROM '<full path>/GeoLite2-City-Locations.csv'
    DELIMITER ',' CSV;
```

Defining the models

To be able to make geographical queries through PostGIS we need to define some factory logic that will set the location information for each record.

This is accomplished through the RGeo gem (*https://github.com/rgeo/rgeo*), which offers a flexible type system for geographical coordinates that can be quickly interpreted by analyzing the database columns containing these coordinates. For example, with RGeo it is possible to configure objects that exhibit certain properties based on their serialization, validation, coordinate system, or computation settings.

These settings are embodied in the RGeo factory, set within the model by calling set_rgeo_factory_for_column to use a particular combination of settings that Active Record uses for a specific column.

Most of the RGeo settings that we are going to define for the models will be shared methods and functionality. Because we do not want to repeat ourselves, we are going to introduce and use Rails concerns.

Concerns are parts of code that allow your application to be better organized, while keeping the models and controllers skinny without having to repeat shared snippets of code. Rails includes a *concerns* subfolder both in the *controllers* and the *models* folders.

We are therefore going to define the *GeoFactory* concern in *models/concerns/ geo_factory.rb*:

```
module GeoFactory
  extend ActiveSupport::Concern

  # The geo_factory function sets the actual latitude-longitude point
  # on the database column by using the values of latitude and
  # longitude.

  def geo_factory
```

```
    self.lonlat = self.class.rgeo_factory(self.longitude,
                  self.latitude)
  end

# We define our class methods

module ClassMethods
  def rgeo_factory(longitude, latitude)
    self.rgeo_factory_for_column(:latlon).point(longitude, latitude)
  end

  # We define a find_near function to search records in a
  # given radius

  def self.find_near(lon, lat, radius=0.5)
    factory = RGeo::Geographic.spherical_factory
    sw = factory.point(lon+radius, lat+radius)
    ne = factory.point(lon-radius, lat-radius)
    window = RGeo::Cartesian::BoundingBox
             .create_from_points(sw, ne).to_geometry
    self.where("lonlat && ?", window)
  end
end
```

There is a subtle difference between class and instance methods:

```
class Foo
  def self.bar
    puts 'class method'
  end
  def baz
    puts 'instance method'
  end
end

Foo.bar # => "class method"
Foo.baz # => NoMethodError: undefined method 'baz'
              for Foo:Class
Foo.new.baz # => instance method
Foo.new.bar # => NoMethodError: undefined method 'bar'
                  for #<Foo:0x1e820>
```

Now we are going to define the actual Block model:

```
class Block < ActiveRecord::Base
  # We include the concern
  include GeoFactory

  # The following line sets a geographic implementation
  # for the :lonlat column:
  set_rgeo_factory_for_column(:lonlat,
          RGeo::Geographic.spherical_factory(:srid => 4326))
```

```
# And that is actually it!
end
```

 SRID stands for Spatial Reference System Identifier: it represents a unique value used to unambiguously identify projected, unprojected, and local spatial coordinate system definitions. The actual value 4326 comes from the World Geodetic System (WGS) (*http:// bit.ly/wiki-wgs*), a standard used in cartography, geodesy, and navigation.

The same implementation is also used for the `Pin` and `Location` models.

Working on the controllers

In this section we are going to define the controllers for the pin and block resources.

We have seen how concerns help developers keep their models and controllers DRY, their application code organized, and their methods skinny. Therefore, we are also going to use concerns at the controller level.

First we are going to define the *FindBlock* concern in *controllers/concerns/ find_block.rb*. This concern is used to find the correct IP block on request, or given an `ip_address` parameter:

```
module FindBlock
  extend ActiveSupport::Concern

  # This snippet of code is executed when the concern is included,
  # but only for the get_block action.

  included do
    before_filter :find_block, only: :get_block
  end

  # Here we set the IP address of the request. If the ip_address
  # param is present we use this; otherwise we use the request
  # remote_ip.

  def set_ip
    if params[:ip_address]
      params[:ip_address]
    else
      request.remote_ip
    end
  end

  # Then we find the IP block corresponding to the IP address

  def find_block
```

```
  ip = set_ip

  # Here we do a bit of cosmetic work on the IP string because we
  # actually want to find the block, not the single IP address.
  # We remove the last part of the address (last octet)
  # and replace it with 0.

  @block = Block.where(:network_start_ip =>
                       "::ffff:#{ip.rpartition(".")[0]}.0").first

  end

# And that's it!
end
```

Working with Requests' IP Addresses

Please note that in a real-world application scenario, the remote IP address depends upon different network factors. Your Rails server might in fact receive a relative IP address depending on your network configuration.

To generate the block controller you can run:

```
$ rails g controller api/v1/block
```

Now we are going to define two actions in the controller. One will be a *show* action to just find and display the IP block by ID. The second will be used to find the block by IP address:

```
class Api::V1::BlocksController < ApplicationController

  # Include the concern

  include FindBlock

  # Use JSON

  respond_to :json

  # Find the block by ID.
  # If a block is found, render JSON through the serializer;
  # else render an error. We are going to define both the serializer
  # and the error object later.

  def show
    @block = Block.find(params[:id])
    if @block
      render :json => @block, serializer: BlockSerializer,
        root: "ip_block"
    else
```

```ruby
      @error = Error.new(:text => "404 Not found", :status => 404,
        :url => request.url, :method => request.method)
      render :json => @error.serializer
    end
  end

  # The block of this method is fetched through the concern.
  # If found it is serialized and rendered; otherwise an error is
  # returned.

  def get_block
    if @block
      render :json => @block, serializer: BlockSerializer,
        root: "ip_block"
    else
      @error = Error.new(:text => "404 Not found", :status => 404,
        :url => request.url, :method => request.method)
      render :json => @error.serializer
    end
  end

  # And that is it!
end
```

We will define the error object as a nonpersistent model. Since it is not persistent the error object will not use Active Record, although some "automagic" performed by Active Record might actually be useful for our goal:

```ruby
class Error

  # ActiveModel::Validations provides a full validation framework
  # to your objects; ActiveModel::Conversion handles default
  # conversions #to_model, #to_key, #to_param, and #to_partial_path;
  # and finally ActiveModel::Naming creates a model_name method on
  # your object.

  include ActiveModel::Validations
  include ActiveModel::Conversion
  extend ActiveModel::Naming

  # We need to define the set of attributes that can be accessed.
  # The method attr_accessor defines a named attribute for the
  # module and creates an instance variable (@name) and a
  # corresponding access method to read it.
  # It also creates a method called name= to set the attribute.

  attr_accessor :text, :status, :url, :method

  def _links
    {:url => request, :entry => entry}
  end
```

```ruby
  # This method serializes the request object

  def request
    href = URI::encode(url)
    {:href => href, :method => method, :rel => "request"}
  end

  # This method specifies a default entry point to return to
  # the client

  def entry
    href = URI::encode("/api/v1")
    {:href => href, :method => "GET", :rel => "entry point",
     :params => params}
  end

  # Here is how we display the params submitted through the query

  def params
    {:point => {:value => "{lon},{lat}", :optional => true},
     :title => {:value => "text", :optional => true}}
  end

  # The following method serializes the error object

  def serializer
    {:error => {:url => url, :text => text, :status => status,
     :method => method, :_links => _links }}
  end

  # Here the error object and its attributes are initialized

  def initialize(attributes = {})
    attributes.each do |name, value|
      send("#{name}=", value)
    end
  end

  # Here we just define the object as nonpersisted;
  # therefore we are not saving it to the database.

  def persisted?
    false
  end

# And that's it!
end
```

Now let's move on to the pin controller. First we need to define our concern to retrieve pins based on the user's IP address or on submitted geographical coordinates:

```ruby
module EntryFiltering
  extend ActiveSupport::Concern
```

```
# We want to perform only the entry_action for the index method

included do
  before_filter :entry_action, only: :index
end

# point is a string containing geographical coordinates in
# the form {logitude},{latitude}

def pins_by_point(point)
  point = point.split(',')
  @pins = Pin.find_near(point[0].to_f, point[1].to_f)
end

# If no coordinates are sent, we will try to locate the IP
# and retrieve pins close to the IP location

def pins_by_ip(ip)
  block = Block.where(:network_start_ip =>
                      "::ffff:#{ip.rpartition(".")[0]}.0").first
  if block
    Pin.find_near(block.longitude.to_f, block.latitude.to_f)
  end
end

# Finally, our entry_action fetches pins by IP if no
# point param is provided

def entry_action
  if params[:point]
    @pins = pins_by_point(params[:point])
  else
    @pins = pins_by_ip(request.remote_ip)
  end
end

# And that's it.
end
```

Finally we can define the pin controller, with an *index* action and a *show* action:

```
class Api::V1::PinsController < ApplicationController

include EntryFiltering
respond_to :json

# Here we display the pins fetched by location.
# If no pins are provided we send an error:

def index
  if @pins
    render :json => @pins, each_serializer: PinSerializer,
```

```
          root: "pins"
      else
        @error = Error.new(:text => "404 Not found",
          :status => 404, :url => request.url,
          :method => request.method)
        render :json => @error.serializer
      end
    end

    # Finally we find the pin by ID and return it serialized.
    # If no pin is found, we return an error:

    def show
      @pin = Pin.find(params[:id])
      if @pin
        render :json => @pin, serializer: PinSerializer, root: "pin"
      else
        @error = Error.new(:text => "404 Not found",
          :status => 404, :url => request.url,
          :method => request.method)
        render :json => @error.serializer
      end
    end

  # And that is it.
  end
```

You can go ahead and define the pin and block serializers. The full code is available in the Wikipin GitHub repository (*http://bit.ly/wikipin*).

The Citywalks API

The Citywalks API is a service that returns and creates geolocated routes within a certain location radius. It uses the Wikipin API to discover Wikipedia articles that are geolocated nearby and connects them in a possible route that the user can walk. Each article contains category information, so users could potentially create thematic walks related to specific categories. We will explore this aspect in the next chapter, when we will venture into creating a proper web application using the APIs that we have been developing up to this point.

The Citywalks API will be a *rails-api* application and will use MongoDB as a database. MongoDB (from "hu*mongous*") is an open source document database written in C++.

So what is a document database? A document database uses documents instead of tables. Documents are like objects, and they map nicely to programming language data types; also, embedded documents and arrays reduce the need for join operations, and using a dynamic schema makes polymorphism easier. A MongoDB deployment hosts a number of databases. A database holds a set of collections. A collection holds a set of documents. A MongoDB collection is similar to a SQL table. A document is a set of key/value pairs and can be compared to a record in a SQL table. We also said that documents have a dynamic schema. This means that documents in the same collection do not need to have the same set of fields or structure, and common fields in a collection's documents may hold different types of data.

 If you want to understand the difference between MongoDB and SQL terminology, check out the SQL to MongoDB Mapping Chart (*http://bit.ly/sql-to-mongo*).

The object document mapper (ODM) for MongoDB that we will use is *Mongoid* (pronounced *mann-goyd*).

 Mongoid (*http://mongoid.org*) is an ODM for MongoDB (*http://mongodb.org*) written in Ruby by Durran Jordan (*http://github.com/durran*). The philosophy of Mongoid is to provide a familiar API to Ruby developers who have been using Active Record or DataMapper, while leveraging the power of MongoDB's schemaless and performant document-based design, dynamic queries, and atomic modifier operations.

To create a Rails API application with Mongoid, we need to tell Rails to skip Active Record, since Mongoid will take its place:

```
$ rails-api new citywalks --skip-active-record
```

This will insert the following lines into *config/application.rb*:

```
require "active_model/railtie"
# require "active_record/railtie"
require "action_controller/railtie"
require "action_mailer/railtie"
require "action_view/railtie"
require "sprockets/railtie"
require "rails/test_unit/railtie"
```

Finally, we edit the *Gemfile*:

```
source 'https://rubygems.org'
gem 'rails', '4.1.4'

# Patched locally because of issue:
# https://github.com/rails-api/rails-api/issues/142

gem 'rails-api',
  :git => 'https://github.com/nopressurelabs/rails-api',
  :branch => 'master'
```

```
gem 'moped', github: 'mongoid/moped'
gem 'mongoid', '~> 4.0.0', github: 'mongoid/mongoid'
gem 'bson_ext'

gem 'spring', :group => :development

# Serializer for JSON
gem 'active_model_serializers'

# CORS
gem 'rack-cors', :require => 'rack/cors'
```

It is time to initialize our application. First we bundle:

```
$ bundle install
```

Then we run:

```
$ rake db:create
```

Rack CORS Middleware

Rack::Cors provides support for Cross-Origin Resource Sharing
(CORS) for Rack-compatible web applications.

The CORS spec (*http://www.w3.org/TR/cors/*) allows web applications to make cross-domain Ajax calls without using workarounds
such as JSONP.

Cross-Origin Resource Sharing is a mechanism defined by the
W3C, and it is used to enable client-side cross-origin requests. The
mechanism defines the specifications that enable an API to make
cross-origin requests to some resources. For instance, if an API is
used on *http://example.org* resources, a resource at *http://hello-
world.example* can opt in to using the mechanism (e.g., by specifying `Access-Control-Allow-Origin: http://example.org` as a
response header), which would allow that resource to be fetched
cross-origin from *http://example.org*.

Discovering the /lib Directory

The Citywalks API will use the WikiCat API to find categories about pins and the
Wikipin API to actually find pins nearby.

To fetch data from external sources we will have to write some logic that will make a
REST call fetch and parse some data. The code that we are going to need to do this is
not strictly related to our core app. It does not belong to our models or our controllers, nor does it extend them.

This code lives in the */lib* directory.

The first module that we are going to write is going to handle REST requests and responses, while also creating meaningful errors in case something goes wrong. Create a new document under */lib* called *restful.rb* and define it as follows:

```ruby
require 'net/http'
require 'json'

module Restful

  def send_request(end_point)
    request_url = URI.parse(URI.encode(end_point))
    log "Request URL: #{request_url}"
    res = Net::HTTP.get_response(request_url)
    unless res.kind_of? Net::HTTPSuccess
      raise Restful::RequestError, "HTTP Response: #{res.code} #{res.message}"
    end
    Response.new(res.body)
  end

  class RequestError < StandardError; end

  # Response object returned after REST call to service.

  class Response

    def initialize(json)
      @doc = JSON.parse(json)
    end

    # Return JSON object.
    def doc
      @doc
    end

    # Return true if response has an error.
    def has_error?
      !(error.nil? || error.empty?)
    end

    # Return error message.

    def error
      @doc.has_key? "error"
    end

    # Return error code.

    def error_code
      if @doc.has_key? "error"
        @doc["error"]["status"]
      end
    end
```

```
    end

    protected

    def log(s)
      if defined? RAILS_DEFAULT_LOGGER
        RAILS_DEFAULT_LOGGER.error(s)
      elsif defined? LOGGER
        LOGGER.error(s)
      else
        puts s
      end
    end
  end
end
```

Now we are going to define two similar modules: one for the Wikipin API and one for the WikiCat API.

We will start by creating a *wikicat.rb* file under */lib*, defined as follows:

```
require 'net/http'
require 'json'

module Wikicat
  # Here we define the API version and the endpoints
  # we are going to use

  CAT_VERSION = '1.0'
  CAT_SERVICE_URL = 'http://0.0.0.0:3000'
  PIN_SERVICE_URL = 'http://wikipin-nopressurelabs.rhcloud.com'

  # Given a pin's relative URL will get the pin's upper category graph

  def pin_upper(pin)
    get_pin = self.class.send_request("#{PIN_SERVICE_URL}#{pin}")
    cat = get_pin.doc["pin"]
    if cat
      sub_category = cat["title"]
      request_upper_graph(sub_category).doc[sub_category]
    end
  end

  # Given a pin's relative URL will get the pin's lower category graph

  def pin_lower(pin)
    get_pin = send_request("#{PIN_SERVICE_URL}#{pin}")
    cat = get_pin.doc["pin"]
    if cat
      sub_category = cat["title"]
      request_lower_graph(sub_category).doc[sub_category]
    end
  end
end
```

```
      # Fetch the actual upper category graph

      def request_upper_graph(category)
        self.class.send_request("#{CAT_SERVICE_URL}/api/v1/graph/up/
          #{category.gsub!(/\s/,'_')}")
      end

      # Fetch the actual lower category graph
      def request_lower_graph(category)
        self.class.send_request("#{CAT_SERVICE_URL}/api/v1/graph/
          #{category.gsub!(/\s/,'_')}")
      end
    end
```

Now we will create a *wikipin.rb* file under */lib*, defined as follows:

```
require 'net/http'
require 'json'

module Wikipin

  PIN_VERSION = '1.0'
  PIN_SERVICE_URL = 'http://wikipin-nopressurelabs.rhcloud.com'

  # Here we make the call to get the pins available for our
  # position.
  # We can either provide a point with latitude and longitude
  # or have the service locate us through our IP address.

  def request_pins(point=nil)
    # point = "lon,lat"
    if point
      send_request("#{PIN_SERVICE_URL}/api/v1/pins/?point=#{point}")
    else
      send_request("#{PIN_SERVICE_URL}/api/v1/pins")
    end
  end

  # Here we request the IP address block information
  def request_block(ip)
    send_request("#{PIN_SERVICE_URL}/api/v1/blocks?ip_address=#{ip}")
  end

  # Here we simply get the pin
  def get_pin(pin)
    send_request("#{PIN_SERVICE_URL}#{pin}")
  end
end
```

The */lib* directory is a great place to start testing code that you would like to extract
from the app, and eventually into a Ruby gem. Moving code there allows you to test it
in isolation. Also, this forces you to write the code as an independent class from your

app. Then, if you are satisfied with what you have obtained, you can easily extract it into an external gem.

Defining the Models

Now that we've defined the build logic, we can go back to our app to define our actual models.

The first model that we are going to need is a `Walk` model. We will start by creating a *walk.rb* file under *app/models*:

```
class Walk
  include Mongoid::Document
  include Mongoid::Timestamps::Created
  include ActiveModel::SerializerSupport

  # Remember the difference between extend and include?

  extend Wikipin
  extend Restful
  include Wikicat

  # These are the fields that the Walk model contains.

  field :title, type: String
  field :author, type: String
  field :pins, type: Array
  field :location, :type => Array
  field :categories, :type => Array

  index({ location: "2d" }, { min: -200, max: 200 })

  validates :pins, length: { minimum: 0, maximum: 10 }

end
```

Then we create the index in our database dynamically by just running:

```
$ rake db:mongoid:create_indexes
```

We also need to define a nonpersistent error object. It will be identical to the error object defined earlier in this chapter, so I will not repeat the same code (you can find the code in the repository).

Building the Controllers

The walks controller will allow us to perform all the CRUD operations on the walk resource. We want to be able to list all the walks, create walks, delete walks, and modify walks:

```ruby
class Api::V1::WalksController < ApplicationController
  respond_to :json

  # Here we include two concerns that will be defined later on
  # and will be used to create and locate walks.

  include WalkLocator
  include WalkCreator

  # before_action is a filter.
  # Filters are methods that are run before,
  # after, or "around" a controller action.
  # Filters are inherited, so if you set a filter on
  # ApplicationController, it will be run on every controller
  # in your application.

  before_action :set_walk, only: [:show, :edit, :update, :destroy]

  def index
    if @walks
      render :json => @walks.to_a, each_serializer: WalkSerializer,
        root: "walks"
    else
      @error = Error.new(:text => "404 Not found",
        :status => 404, :url => request.url,
        :method => request.method)
      render :json => @error.serializer
    end
  end

  # GET /walks/1
  # GET /walks/1.json
  def show
    if @walk
      render :json => @walk, serializer: WalkSerializer,
        root: "walk"
    else
      @error = Error.new(:text => "404 Not found",
        :status => 404, :url => request.url,
        :method => request.method)
      render :json => @error.serializer
    end
  end

  # GET /walks/1/edit
  def edit

  end

  # GET /walks/new
  def new
    @walk = Walk.new
```

```ruby
end

# POST /walks
# POST /walks.json
def create
  @walk = initialize_walk(walk_params)
  if @walk.save
    render :json => @walk, serializer: WalkSerializer,
    root: "walk"
  else
    render :json => @walk.errors
  end
end

# PATCH/PUT /walks/1
# PATCH/PUT /walks/1.json
def update
  if @walk.update(walk_params)
    render :json => @walk, serializer: WalkSerializer,
      root: "walk"
  else
    render :json => @walk.errors
  end
end

# DELETE /walks/1
# DELETE /walks/1.json
def destroy
  if @walk.destroy
    render :json => { :head => ok }
  else
    render :json => @walk.errors
  end
end

private

# Use callbacks to share common setup or constraints
# between actions.
def set_walk
  @walk = Walk.find(params[:id])
end

# Never trust parameters from the scary Internet;
# only allow the whitelist through.
def walk_params
  params.require(:walk).permit(:title,
                               :author,
                               :location,
                               :pins,
                               :categories)
```

```
    end
  end
```

Now we define the concerns that we have included in our controller. The first one will be used to locate walks:

```
module WalkLocator
  extend ActiveSupport::Concern

  included do
    before_filter :entry_action, only: [:index]
  end

  def walks_by_point(point)
    point = point.split(",")
    @walks = Walk.geo_near([ point[0].to_f, point[1].to_f ])
             .spherical
  end

  def walks_by_ip(ip)
    if ip = "127.0.0.1"
      walks_by_point("41.23,2.09")
    else
      block = Walk.request_block(ip).doc["ip_block"]
      if block
        longitude = block["point"].scan(/\((([^\)]+)\)/)/)
          .last.first.split(" ")[0]
        latitude = block["point"].scan(/\((([^\)]+)\)/)/)
          .last.first.split(" ")[1]
        Walk.geo_near([ longitude.to_f, latitude.to_f ]).spherical
      end
    end
  end

  def entry_action

    if params[:location]
      @walks = walks_by_point(params[:location])
    else
      @walks = walks_by_ip(request.remote_ip)
    end
  end
end
```

The second concern will be used to create walks:

```
module WalkCreator
  extend ActiveSupport::Concern

  def initialize_walk(params)
    params[:location] = set_location(params[:location])
    params[:pins] = params[:pins].split(",")
    Walk.new(params)
```

```
    end

  def set_location(location)
    if location
      location = location.split(",")
      [location[0].to_f, location[1].to_f]
    else
      block = retrieve_position(request.remote_ip)
      if block
        longitude = block["point"].scan(/\((([^\)]+)\)/)
          .last.first.split(" ")[0]
        latitude = block["point"].scan(/\((([^\)]+)\)/)
          .last.first.split(" ")[1]
        [longitude.to_f, latitude.to_f ]
      end
    end
  end

  def retrieve_position(ip)
    Walk.request_block(ip).doc["ip_block"]
  end
end
```

Now if everything is working as expected we will be able to make a POST request to our API and actually create a walk with some test pins:

```
$ curl --data "walk \
  [author]=<username>&walk[title]=first-walk& \
  walk[location]=2.09,41.23& \
  walk[pins]=/api/v1/pins/27,/api/v1/pins/28" \
  http://0.0.0.0:3001/api/v1/walks
```

Wrapping Up

In this chapter we explored the concepts of SOA, microservices, and microapplications. We have extended our multi-API platform and started connecting things together.

In the next chapter we will venture into frontend land. We will specifically see how we can map different data streams to the same application UI. We will also learn some Ember.js basics.

Mapping Data Streams onto an Application UI

In this chapter we are going to venture into aspects of frontend programming and user interface (UI) design. We are going to discover Ember.js, a JavaScript framework, and a different MVC pattern. This is almost a non-Rails chapter, in which we discover how data streamed from our APIs is integrated into a web application to build what is defined as the user experience (UX). The application that will be designed and built in this chapter will use the Citywalks API and display the user's walks on a map.

Wanderings in Frontend Land

Up to this moment we have been developing API-only applications. You may look at these apps as a sort of skeleton upon which different products can be built. Once you have some data streams, you can combine them in a way that others—users and services—can also consume and reuse.

Therefore, depending on what application you are working on, at a certain point you will need to venture into frontend programming.

Frontend development is defined as the development of those elements of an application that the user sees and directly interacts with. Ultimately users cannot directly interact with JSON; they will need visual elements to manipulate the information that the application is receiving from the different data points.

The widely held misconception about frontend development is that it mainly means creating the application's graphical interface—i.e., arranging the information containers and action elements in a way that the user will find both visually appealing and intuitive and pleasant to use.

As we have seen, a core concept of RESTful services is that each call is stateless. Either the server or the client will have to retain state information. Sometimes, though, managing state only on the server side becomes both difficult and expensive.

Before Ajax, most websites were mostly static documents, served from the server as a response to an HTTP page request and with a single HTTP response, which contained the full HTML document.

With websites evolving into web applications and becoming more complex, clients and servers now rely less on passing actual markup information and more on passing just data. In this scenario, JavaScript frameworks have become an important aspect of web application development.

There are a number of situations for which you should consider stateful web front-end development. Imagine for a minute that the user has sent a request to the server by clicking a button. Certainly, you could grey out the button or display a circling wheel while you wait for the server to confirm that the action has been performed. Now imagine that you know that 99% of the time when you click the button the request is going to complete successfully—you might feel more inclined to hide the button and show the result to the user right away, without waiting for the server to reply. This will ensure a smoother interaction with the app, and in the infrequent event that the request fails, you can always show an error message and restore the previous state in the UI.

Using a framework ensures that your application will behave similarly to a native application, even if it is on the Web.

Furthermore, a framework has a number of advantages over the use of jQuery libraries only. jQuery works well if you just want to add light interactivity to your app. If you start introducing more state information to your application, you have to store data in your document object model (DOM), usually in `data-*` attributes, which implies having to create a system to easily find and fetch those attributes based on where and when events were triggered.

Generally speaking, a software framework is a set of code libraries, tools, APIs, compilers, and support programs, creating a reusable software environment that provides particular functionality as part of a larger software platform. A software framework facilitates the development of software applications, products, and solutions.

There are a variety of JavaScript frameworks available, and choosing the best framework certainly depends on a number of different factors and your application's unique characteristics and goals.

In the following sections of this chapter we are going to introduce and use Rails templating options, although our goal is to handle the frontend of our application completely in JavaScript by venturing into Ember.js and one-page app development. I just felt that in a book about building APIs in Rails it was important to briefly touch on how we can combine everything in an application frontend.

In the words of the Ember.js core team, "Ember.js is a framework for creating ambitious web applications." What "ambitious" really means will be explored in the next sections.

Rendering and Templating in Rails

When a request reaches the Rails server it is handled by Action Pack (*http://bit.ly/rails-actionpack*) and split between the controller and view parts. The controller part is handled by the Action Controller module, while the view part is Action View's responsibility. More specifically, Action Controller will take care of communicating with the database and performing CRUD actions where necessary. Action View is responsible for compiling the responses and rendering them.

In a normal Ruby on Rails application for each controller there is an associated directory in *app/views*, where the template view files associated with that controller are located.

These files are used to render the view resulting from the performed controller action.

There is also a specific naming convention in Rails, where the views share their names with the associated controller actions. So, for example, an *index* controller action will be associated with an *index* view template, and so on.

Action View templates can be written in several ways. For example, if the template file has a *.erb* extension it will use a mixture of ERB (included in Ruby) and HTML. If the template file has a *.builder* extension, the Builder::XmlMarkup library is used instead.

Other common possibilities when it comes to templating are *Slim* and *Haml*.

Slim (*http://slim-lang.com/*) is a template language designed to reduce the template syntax by removing as much as possible from the standard HTML template without losing functionality or becoming cryptic.

Therefore, Slim doesn't use closing tags or other HTML elements. A *.slim* HTML template will look like this:

```
doctype html
html
  head
    title Slim Welcome!
    meta name="keywords" content="template language"
    meta name="author" content=author
    javascript: alert('Slim supports embedded JavaScript!')
  body
    h1 Slim markup examples
```

```
#content
  p This example shows you what a basic Slim file looks like.
```

Haml (*http://haml.info/*) is another templating option in Rails; its name is an acronym for HTML Abstraction Markup Language. The main idea behind Haml is *markup should be beautiful*, so template creation can be simplified and accelerated.

Haml aims at avoiding repetition by relying on indentation more than text to determine how and where elements and block of codes begin and end. Because Haml relies on indentation, the resulting templates are cleaner while also being easier to write, read, and maintain, since the XML and HTML document structure is naturally preserved.

A simple *.haml* HTML file will look like this:

```
%html
  %head
    %title Haml Welcome!
    %meta{:name => "keywords" :content => "template language"}
    %meta{:name => "author" :content => @author}
    :javascript:
      alert('Haml supports embedded JavaScript!')
  %body
  %h1 Haml markup examples
  #content
    %p
      This example shows you what a basic Haml file looks like.
```

Action View Documentation

Complete Action View documentation can be reviewed at the Ruby on Rails Guides (*http://bit.ly/rails-action-view*).

Ember.js: A Framework for Creating Ambitious Web Applications

Ember.js (*http://emberjs.com/*) is a highly opinionated JavaScript framework that will structure your application into logical abstraction layers and will force the development model to follow object-oriented paradigms as much as possible. Ember.js has a strong Model-View-Controller (MVC) architecture and promises to be built and designed for productivity and with developer ergonomics in mind.

The Ember.js MVC implementation enriches both the controller and the view layers of the application, while also introducing some extra concepts at each layer of the MVC architecture.

Personally, I am very opinionated about Ember.js, since I consider it the closest mapping to a JavaScript framework of Rails development logic. I also think it might be easier to learn and use if you come from a Ruby on Rails background. This is because Ember.js provides "Rails-like" defaults by convention for common coding patterns, intelligent memory management, built-in integration testing, and a client-side persistence solution called *ember-data*.

The framework was created by Yehuda Katz, a member of the jQuery, Ruby on Rails, and SproutCore core teams. To understand where Ember sits today in the development community, we have to look a bit at its past and its origins.

Ember.js came out of another JavaScript framework called SproutCore (*http://sprout core.com*). SproutCore is a JavaScript framework created with the objective of allowing developers to create web applications with a UX comparable to that of a native desktop app. While SproutCore is now released under the MIT license, it was first developed at Apple as the framework powering Apple's MobileMe web applications (now iCloud).

SproutCore was the first JS framework to push the MVC paradigm and take a widget-based approach to UI design. These concepts are now very popular, but back in 2007 they were really innovative.

The creator of SproutCore, Charles Jolley, left Apple in 2010 and started a company with Tom Dale and Yehuda Katz, who were also working on Rails and jQuery. Due to diverging opinions on the direction that SproutCore was taking, some core members of the project started Project Amber, a rewrite of SproutCore that, among other things, added Yehuda Katz's Handlebars library for templating. This new version of the framework was soon renamed to Ember.js due to a naming conflict with an existing JavaScript project.

Ember.js is maintained by a group of open source developers, independently of venture capital and giant corporations, as a true community project.

Announcing Amber.js

Yehuda Katz's blog post announcing Amber.js (*http://bit.ly/ announcing-amberjs*) gives historical insight into how and why Ember.js was created.

Designed for Application Development

The core idea behind Ember.js is to allow web applications to compete with native desktop apps in terms of complexity of user interaction, while still maintaining the agility of a web app.

Some of the patterns and techniques used in Ember.js are already established in native JavaScript and more generally in web development. Ember therefore borrows from the MVC paradigm and mixes in web-specific solutions aimed at making web apps more robust and lightweight.

There are a number of reasons to choose Ember.js above other frameworks (or not). My reasons for introducing Ember in this book were the following:

- Ember.js is an open source project, and there isn't a single, big corporation behind it.
- Some aspects of its logic, like the MVC pattern, make it easier to grasp if you come from Rails.
- It is currently being used in different projects in production, so people are starting to get excited about it.
- Like Rails, Ember follows strong conventions and is very opinionated.

TodoMVC

If you need help choosing a JavaScript framework, you might find it helpful to compare all of them in a simple application scenario: a Todo app. TodoMVC (*http://todomvc.com/*) is a project that offers the same Todo application implemented using MV* concepts in most of the popular JavaScript MV* frameworks of today.

MVC Paradigm of Frontend

Ember.js tries to combine the tools and concepts of native GUI frameworks with the very feature that makes the Web so powerful: the URL.

There are a few concepts that Ember.js introduces and that constitute the core structure of an Ember.js application:

Templates

An Ember.js template is written in the Handlebars templating language and describes the app's user interface. Each template is backed by a model, and the two are closely coupled. This means that the template automatically updates itself if the model changes.

Handlebars (*http://handlebarsjs.com*) is a library that allows you to create semantic templates easily and effectively.

Ember.js templates, in addition to plain HTML, can contain expressions, outlets, and components. An *expression* is something like a variable that allows us to include some information from the model in the HTML. An *outlet* is used instead to display some templates, depending on the route. A *component* is a custom HTML element.

Router
> The Ember.js router translates a URL into a series of nested templates. As the templates being shown to the user change, Ember automatically updates the URL in the browser's address bar. This means that if a user shares the URL with someone else, that person is assured of seeing the same content.

Components
> A component is a reusable control: a custom HTML tag whose behavior is implemented in JavaScript and whose appearance is described using Handlebars templates.

Models
> Models are objects that store persistent state; templates display the models to the user by turning them into HTML.

Route
> Routes are what tell the templates which models they should display.

Controllers
> Controllers are objects that store application state. A template can have both a controller and a model and can retrieve properties from both.

Rails MVC Versus Ember.js MVC

Both Rails and Ember.js use the MVC paradigm, yet there are some differences between the two implementations.

The Rails request lifecycle flows in the following order:

1. First, the Rails router receives an HTTP request from the browser or client application. This is passed to the designated controller that will handle it.
2. Then the controller receives the HTTP parameters, and instantiates the model(s) necessary for that action.
3. The model retrieves the requested objects from the database.
4. The controller passes the requested model(s) back to the view, which renders them.
5. The view generates a text response (e.g., in HTML, JSON, JavaScript format), and interpolates Ruby objects where needed.
6. The controller's response is returned to the router, and the router sends it to the client.

Figure 9-1 illustrates.

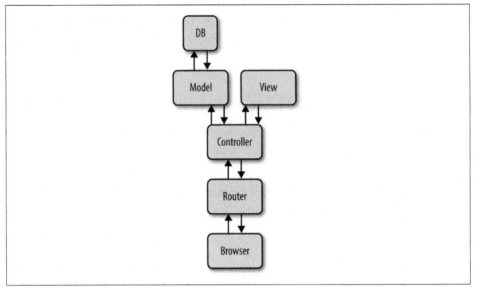

Figure 9-1. The MVC model in Rails

Ember.js instead uses what is called a *run loop*. This is where Ember's internals and most of the application code gets executed. Ember uses the run loop to batch, order, and reorder actions in the optimal way.

In the run loop tasks are scheduled in specific queues that have a certain priority and are processed and completed according to that priority order.

Please note that within the run loop when we refer to the model and controller, we are referring to the Ember.js concepts, not the Rails ones, and therefore we are talking about actions that happen in the browser.

In web browsers, some of the Ember run loop's concepts are natural. For example, web browsers already batch changes to the DOM, so Ember's approach of batching similar work allows for better pipelining and further optimization.

You might of course decide to run your own optimizations on a case-by-case basis, but with Ember.js you get classes of optimization for free that can be applied across the entire application.

The run loop is started either through an event triggering an action, or by visiting a URL directly (for example, by writing it in the browser's address bar).

The Ember.js run loop works in the following order:

1. The router answers a request from the browser, requests the necessary model data, and performs the controller action.
2. The router will now render the template for the requested resource.
3. The template will now get its properties from the controller. Since the template doesn't know where a property it displays is defined, the controller acts as a decorator for the model, providing that property, either by itself or through its model.

Figure 9-2 illustrates the Ember.js run loop.

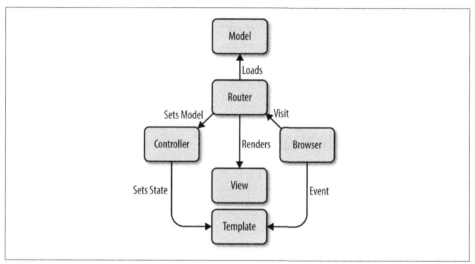

Figure 9-2. The MVC model in Ember.js

Work in Ember is scheduled in the form of function invocations on certain queues. These queues already have a priority assigned and are processed to completion in the following order:

```
["sync", "actions", "routerTransitions", "render", "afterRender",
 "destroy"]
```

The `sync` queue has the highest priority and the `destroy` queue the lowest. The "Understanding Ember.js" guide (*http://bit.ly/understanding-emberjs*) describes what happens in these queues as follows:

- The `sync` queue contains binding synchronization jobs.
- The `actions` queue is the general work queue and will typically contain scheduled tasks, e.g., promises.
- The `routerTransitions` queue contains transition jobs in the router.
- The `render` queue contains jobs meant for rendering; these will typically update the DOM.

- The `afterRender` queue contains jobs meant to be run after all previously scheduled render tasks are complete. This is often good for third-party DOM manipulation libraries, which should only be run after the entire DOM tree has been updated.
- The `destroy` queue contains jobs to finish the teardown of objects other jobs have scheduled to destroy.

According to the guide, the jobs in the queues are executed according to the following algorithm:

1. Let the highest priority queue with pending jobs be: `CURRENT_QUEUE`; if there are no queues with pending jobs the run loop is complete.
2. Let a new temporary queue be defined as `WORK_QUEUE`.
3. Move jobs from `CURRENT_QUEUE` into `WORK_QUEUE`.
4. Process all the jobs sequentially in `WORK_QUEUE`.
5. Return to Step 1.

Planning the Application

I have said that Ember.js has many aspects in common with Ruby on Rails. One of these is certainly that Ember.js favors convention over configuration.

Another similar feature that Ember.js possesses is its command-line utility, Ember CLI (*http://www.ember-cli.com/*).

Broccoli

Ember CLI's asset pipeline is provided by Broccoli (*http://bit.ly/ broccolijs*). Broccoli is a fast, reliable asset pipeline, supporting constant-time rebuilds and compact build definitions. It is comparable to the Rails asset pipeline in scope, although it runs on Node and is backend-agnostic.

Getting Started with Ember.js

Ember CLI provides a strong conventional project structure. It will allow us to quickly structure our Ember.js application while also maintaining a clear view of its architecture.

Before diving into Ember.js, though, we need to get our system ready.

Prerequisites

To run Ember CLI we need to install Node.js. This is used by Broccoli, and it's required because Ember uses the *npm* installer.

According to its website, "Node.js is a platform built on Chrome's JavaScript runtime for easily building fast, scalable network applications. Node.js uses an event-driven, non-blocking I/O model that makes it lightweight and efficient, perfect for data-intensive real-time applications that run across distributed devices."

To install Node.js please refer to its website (*http://nodejs.org*), or use your preferred package manager, such as *brew*.

After installing Node, verify that it is set up correctly by typing the following commands on the command line:

```
$ node --help
$ npm --help
```

Both should output the help text.

Once Node has been installed you can install Ember CLI globally with:

```
$ npm install -g ember-cli
```

This will give you access to the *ember* command-line runner.

You will also have to install the Bower package manager, in order to keep your front-end dependencies (including JQuery, Ember, and QUnit) up-to-date. This is accomplished by running:

```
$ npm install -g bower
```

By default in Ember CLI your integration tests will run on PhantomJS. You can install it via *npm* as well:

```
$ npm install -g phantomjs
```

We are now ready to create our first Ember.js application:

```
$ ember new walks
$ cd walks
$ ember server
```

Navigate to *http://localhost:4200* to see your new app in action. To test the app, navigate to *http://localhost:4200/tests*.

There are a number of packages that we need for this project. Packages are declared in the *bower.json* file, which is a sort of *Gemfile*.

Once the packages are specified, you can install them by running:

```
$ bower install
```

Our *bower.json* file contains the following packages:

```
{
  "name": "walks",
```

```
"dependencies": {
  "handlebars": "~1.3.0",
  "jquery": "^1.11.1",
  "ember": "1.7.0",
  "ember-data": "1.0.0-beta.10",
  "ember-resolver": "~0.1.7",
  "loader.js": "stefanpenner/loader.js#1.0.1",
  "ember-cli-shims": "stefanpenner/ember-cli-shims#0.0.3",
  "ember-cli-test-loader": "rwjblue/ember-cli-test-loader#0.0.4",
  "ember-load-initializers":
                          "stefanpenner/ember-load-initializers#0.0.2",
  "ember-qunit": "0.1.8",
  "ember-qunit-notifications": "0.0.4",
  "qunit": "~1.15.0",
  "ember-leaflet": "master",
  "leaflet-plugins": "1.0.1"
  }
}
```

Some of the packages specified are added by default by Ember CLI; others, like the
Leaflet plug-in, need to be added manually.

Modeling Data

With Ember.js we need to model the data that we are going to consume in our application. In a way this is very similar to defining a model in a Rails application.

We can generate a model with:

```
$ ember generate model walk
```

This will create a file named *walk.js* under *app/models*, while also generating test files
under *tests/units/models*.

A model is a class where the properties and behavior of the data that you present to
the user are defined. Models also define persistent data that is stored in a database.

To help us define our Ember.js model, we can go back to our Citywalks Rails application and see how our Walk model was defined:

```
class Walk
  include Mongoid::Document
  include Mongoid::Timestamps::Created
  include ActiveModel::SerializerSupport
  extend Wikipin
  extend Restful
  include Wikicat
  field :title, type: String
  field :author, type: String
  field :pins, type: Array
  field :location, :type => Array
  field :categories, :type => Array
```

```
    index({ location: "2d" }, { min: -200, max: 200 })
    validates :pins, length: { minimum: 0, maximum: 10 }
end
```

This can be almost literally translated into Ember.js:

```
import DS from 'ember-data';
export default DS.Model.extend({
    author: DS.attr('string'),
    categories: DS.attr('string'),
    title: DS.attr('string'),
    location: DS.attr('string'),
    points: DS.attr(),
    created_at: DS.attr('date')
});
```

 Ember Data

Ember Data (*http://bit.ly/ember-data*) is a library for managing models within Ember.js applications; it is included in Ember CLI by default.

Once we have defined the model, we define how the data is streamed into our applications. To do so we are going to edit *application.js* in *app/adapters*:

```
import DS from 'ember-data';
export default DS.ActiveModelAdapter.extend({
    namespace: 'api/v1',
    host: 'http://localhost:3001',
    corsWithCredentials: true
});
```

Here we define the namespace of our API and the host endpoint, and we specify to allow CORS.

The last step is defining our route files.

Routing in Ember.js

Ember.js applications are usually designed to be single-page apps. The idea of a single-page app is that the user doesn't have to navigate between different pages; instead, it is the application that is responsible for transitioning through many different states.

When you build a monolithic application in Rails or another framework, you are able to respond to certain questions regarding the state of the app by either querying the database or requesting the status from the server. It is Rails that specifically generates the HTML that the web application returns. Ember.js provides similar tools to answer questions about the status of the application while also being able to interact more deeply with the user.

Application states in Ember.js are represented by URLs. Route handlers are defined in Ember for each URL in the application. At each moment, one or more route handlers are active in an Ember application. An active handler changes either when the user has interacted with a view, therefore changing the URL via an action, or when the URL has been changed manually (for example, via the back or forward buttons in the browser).

Whenever the URL changes, the active route handler will render or update the template, update the controller to represent a model, or perform a redirect to a different URL.

We are now going to define the routes for our Walks application as follows:

```
import Ember from 'ember';
import config from './config/environment';

var Router = Ember.Router.extend({
  location: config.locationType
});

// Here is where we define the resource route and
// the path to the individual resource:

Router.map(function() {
    this.resource('walks', function() {
        this.resource('walk', { path: '/:walk_id' });
    });
});

export default Router;
```

Ember CLI helps you structure your route files by defining a *routes* folder at the beginning.

Here we define an *index.js* route file for the index of the application:

```
import Ember from "ember";
var IndexRoute = Ember.Route.extend({
  model: function() {
    return ['red', 'yellow', 'blue'];
  }
});

export default IndexRoute;
```

We have defined a static color array to be returned, just to try it out :). We will see how this can be included in our templates in the next section.

Next, we define a general *walk.js* route file:

```
# Here we define how we access the single walk object.
import Ember from 'ember';
export default Ember.Route.extend({
    model: function(params) {
        return this.store.find('walk', params.walk_id);
    }
});
```

The last route file that we are going to need is an *index.js* file within the *walks* folder. It is going to be defined as follows:

```
import Ember from 'ember';
export default Ember.Route.extend({
    model: function() {
        return this.store.findAll('walk');
    }
});
```

This simply tells our application to list all walks from our store.

Defining the Templates

Ember.js uses the `application` template as the default template that is rendered when the application starts.

Here we define where decorative content, like the header or footer, goes. Note that at least one `{{outlet}}` needs to be defined. `{{outlet}}` is the placeholder that the application router fills with the template for the URL.

The application template file is called *application.hbs*. In our case it's defined as follows:

```
<h2 id='title'>Welcome to Ember.js</h2>
# Here we define our application menu:
<ul>
    <li>{{link-to 'Home' 'index'}}</li>
    // You can just list all walks or have the API figure
    // out your location.
    // I have opted for sending a specific location to the API.
    <li>{{#link-to 'walks' (query-params location="41.23,2.09")}}
        Walks{{/link-to}}</li>
</ul>
<hr>
{{outlet}}
```

The next template that we are going to define is the *index.hbs* file within the *app/templates* folder. Here we will tell our app to display our colors in a bulleted list:

```
{{#each color in model}}
    <li>color: {{color}}</li>
{{/each}}
```

This is a very common expression in Ember.js: if you need to enumerate over a list of objects, Handlebars provides the {{#each}} helper.

The template inside of the {{#each}} block will be repeated once for each item in the array, with the item set to the color keyword.

The last template that we are going to need for our small project is the *index.hbs* template within the *templates/walks* folder. Here we define how we are going to display all the walks that we will retrieve:

```
<ul>
    {{#each walk in model}}
        <li>
            <p>Walk: {{walk.title}},</p>
            <p>Author: {{walk.author}}</p>
            <p>Location: {{walk.location}}</p>
            {{#each point in walk.points}}
                <p>pin: {{point.title}}</p>
                <p>{{point.point.latitude}},
                    {{point.point.longitude}}</p>
            {{/each}}
        </li>
    {{else}}
        <li>No walks found.</li>
    {{/each}}
</ul>
// We will understand what this means better in a few paragraphs
{{leaflet-map
  width="600px"
  height="400px"
  latitude="41.23"
  longitude="2.09"
  zoom=10
  walks=walksMarkers
}}
```

The last part of the template is a map to display our point of interest. We are going to use the Leaflet library and we are going to configure it in the next section. There we are going to discover some more interesting aspects of Ember.js, controllers and components.

Writing a Component

Components can be defined as custom HTML elements. Components in Ember follow the specification for HTML components as defined by the W3C.

The W3C is currently working on the Custom Elements specification (*http://bit.ly/custom-elements-spec*).

Ember's components implementation has been developed to adhere as closely as possible to the W3C specification, so when custom elements become widely available in browsers, it should be possible to migrate your Ember components to the W3C standard for use by other frameworks.

To understand components, you have to take a step back in the history of the Web. HTML was designed at a time when the browser was a simple document viewer. Developers looking to build great web apps need something more powerful than just HTML tags. Tags limit developers, since they are restricted to what has already been defined in the HTML specifications. Imagine, though, if you could define your own application-specific HTML tags, and then implement their behavior using JavaScript...

This is what Ember.js permits, by embracing HTML and adding powerful new features that make it easier to build web apps.

To highlight the power of components, we are going to use one to define our simple map. Running this command:

```
$ ember generate component leaflet-map
```

will generate a *leaflet-map.js* file within the *components* folder. We are going to edit it as follows:

```
import Ember from 'ember';
export default Ember.Component.extend({
  attributeBindings: ['style'],
  width: '800px',
  height: '400px',
  latitude: '41.23',
  longitude: '2.09',
  zoom: '5',
  walks: [],

  style: function() {
    return [
    'width:' + this.get('width'),
    'height:' + this.get('height')
    ].join(';');
  }.property('width', 'height'),

  didInsertElement: function() {
    var walks = this.get('walks');
    var center = [this.get('latitude'), this.get('longitude')];
    var zoom  = this.get('zoom');
    var map = L.map(this.get('element'));
```

```
      this.set('map', map);

      // set the view to a given place and zoom
      map.setView(center, zoom);

      // add an OpenStreetMap tile layer
      L.tileLayer('http://{s}.tile.osm.org/{z}/{x}/{y}.png', {
        attribution: '&copy; <a href="http://osm.org/copyright">
        OpenStreetMap</a> contributors'
      }).addTo(map);

      walks.forEach(function (walk, ind){

        var markers = [];

        walk._data.points.forEach(function (point, index){
          // add a marker in the given location, attach some
          // pop-up content to it, and open the pop-up
          L.marker(point.point.latitude,point.point.longitude)
          .addTo(map)
          .bindPopup(point.point.title)
          .openPopup();
        });
      });

    },

    willRemoveElement: function() {
      var map = this.get('map');
      if (map) { map.remove(); }
    }
  });
```

We are also going to define an extension to the walks controller. Running this command:

```
$ ember generate controller walks
```

will create an *index.js* file within *controllers/walks*:

```
import Ember from 'ember';
export default Ember.ArrayController.extend({
  walksMarkers: function() {
    var markers = this.filter(function(walk) {
      return walk.get('points');
    });
    return markers;
  }.property('@each.markers')
});
```

Exploring Walks Through Categories

Now we can start to think about creating walks and categorizing them.

Here is where our WikiCat API could be useful. We could retrieve our top categories, or the category graph of a given category (like *shopping* or *arts*), and start exploring walks in the graph.

What we would like, then, is a way to query our walks table with a set of tags. This is easily accomplished in MongoDB and through Mongoid with the following query:

```
Walk.in(categories: ["Science", "Sports"])
```

We can include this in the walks controller, or create an endpoint to return categorized walks.

Wrapping Up

In this chapter we learned about EmberJS and saw how it is possible to map different data streams to the same application UI. In the next chapter we will learn about API management and deployment and we will see our APIs live on the Web.

Deploying an API

In this chapter we are going to see what options we have when it comes to deploying our API. Do we need an API management service? What services do we need to be provisioned and managed by third parties, and what can we develop in house? We will see how to deploy one of our APIs to OpenShift, a PaaS solution that can be used to deploy and host applications in the public cloud if you are not ready to invest in infrastructure. We will also familiarize ourselves with concepts like reverse proxies and we will practice with technologies like Ngnix.

How Is an API Deployed?

A RESTful API ultimately lives on the Web, or on a communication network where different parties can expose and consume data streams.

There are different aspects that need to be considered when deploying on the public cloud. For example, would an API management solution help you deploy your API? Or should you consider deploying with infrastructure developed and maintained in house? Which services are you ready to maintain yourself, and which would you like to have provisioned and managed by some third-party service?

There isn't a general rule of thumb on how to decide which services you'd like to have managed externally and which you'd like to manage and develop in house. Generally speaking, everything that you develop yourself will go through the same design and development stages that your main product has gone through. So, the real question here is: do we have the resources and time to develop and maintain it ourselves?

Most of the time it is more economically viable to externalize the services that are not directly part of your core product or business, especially if your product is a one-person show. This way you can keep your focus on developing your main product without having to worry about the rest.

API Management

API management platforms offer a set of services and built-in strategies that you can use as guiding principles when working with developers and creating an application ecosystem.

There are different areas where an API management platform can help in your product development. These are:

- Design
- Documentation
- Analytics
- Access
- Scalability

Design

API management platforms can offer the possibility to write an API mockup in a short time. You model the endpoints and what data should be returned, then share it with other stakeholders and let them use it for a test flight.

You are not writing any code yet; you are just defining what your API should do, and you are using the API management service infrastructure to test whether your assumptions actually make sense.

You can automatically create and run mock servers, tests, validations, proxies, and code samples in your language bindings. This way, once you start coding your actual product you can be sure you are going in the direction you intended.

Prototyping your API in a test environment can really speed up the design and development stages. Plus, since you've already planned how your API will be used by possible applications, once you start implementing you are already iterating.

An alternative to an API management platform in this case is to use one of the open source tools that are available and adjust it to your needs.

Two useful tools available at the time of writing are API Blueprint and APITools.

API Blueprint (*http://apiblueprint.org/*) is a tool for documenting and mocking your APIs at the time of design. It facilitates cooperation among various teams and stakeholders when planning an API product, but can also be used during your whole API lifecycle.

APITools (*https://github.com/APItools/monitor*) is a hosted proxy service that can be used to wrap API calls and modify their data flows before sending everything to your application.

Documentation

Great documentation is paramount when exposing an API, either to your company or to the public on the Internet. Well-written documentation takes a lot of effort and time, but it is the key element to excite developers about your product. If developers are going to invest time and money in applications that will use your service, they need to be convinced that your API can be an important and useful component for their projects.

API management systems can expose a list of tools to create quality documentation right from your code or your method definitions. Also, they can be linked directly to your code base, so every time you push a change your documentation can be immediately updated.

The alternative once again is to use configurable open source libraries for the same purpose. You won't have to reinvent the wheel, but you will be responsible for updating your documentation if something changes in your code base, and for keeping your dependencies up to date.

> apiDoc (*http://apidocjs.com/*) is one useful tool that creates documentation from API descriptions in your source code.

Analytics

API management platforms can also offer complete analytics solutions to monitor your API traffic. Which developers are making the most requests? Which methods are called the most? These questions can be answered easily if the platform you are using has built-in reporting and analytics services.

A management platform can also provide something more than just usage data. For example, it could offer the possibility to reach out to developers if some specific event happens, or reach out to customers that aren't actively using your service.

Of course, you can achieve the same results if you choose to actively and personally monitor your server calls. Especially regarding analytics, the open source community offers a vast range of tools and software that can easily fit your specific use case.

> One option here is Sensu (*http://sensuapp.org/*), an open source monitoring framework providing an agent, message bus, and event processor. It provides a platform to build upon, enabling developers and operations teams to compose comprehensive telemetry and monitoring systems to meet unique business requirements.

Access

Access and key provisioning is probably the one aspect of deploying an API where a management platform delivers most of its value. A platform may in fact offer key provisioning, traffic, lifecycle, and security management capabilities from a simple dashboard.

This means that with your API you only have to authorize a single application, the management platform, which will be responsible for provisioning API keys and handling the authorization process for all your developers and, eventually, their customers.

Another advantage of using a management platform is that you do not need to support a number of authentication and authorization standards to make sure your customers can easily integrate your product into their infrastructures. You are free to choose the methods you prefer, and you can let the management platform worry about the rest.

Alternatively, you can provide authentication and authorization within your Rails application.

Scalability

An API management solution will certainly help you to scale your service, simply because it will take care of some of the design, development, and maintenance work that managing an app ecosystem requires.

The management platform is already designed to scale with your users and traffic, especially if it also offers to host your API. In this case you only have to concentrate on developing your core product, and you can forget about operations and management hassles.

PaaS Solutions

Platform as a Service (PaaS) is a category of cloud computing services providing both a computing platform and a solution stack as a service. There are different service models in the various cloud computing solutions. PaaS is only one possibility; many providers also offer Infrastructure as a Service (IaaS) and Software as a Service (SaaS) solutions. PaaS solutions provide a bit of both, since you can easily create an application using a set of tools and libraries from the PaaS provider, while also hosting it on their infrastructure.

You can also easily control software deployment and configuration settings, while the PaaS provides the networks, servers, storage, and other services that are required to host your app.

The main advantage of PaaS solutions is that they facilitate the deployment of applications or services without the added cost and complexity of buying and managing the underlying hardware and software and provisioning hosting capabilities. The initial cost is low, and it grows incrementally as your service usage increases. PaaS solutions are self-service and have best practices built in; they facilitate and support resource sharing, automated deployment, management services, lifecycle management, and reuse.

We are going to use a PaaS solution to host one of our APIs: the Wikipin API. In particular, we are going to use OpenShift (*http://www.openshift.com*) by Red Hat, since it is an open source solution that can also be installed on premises if desired.

Deploying the Wikipin API on OpenShift

OpenShift is Red Hat's PaaS, and it comes in three different versions: OpenShift Origin, OpenShift Online, and OpenShift Enterprise.

OpenShift Origin (*https://github.com/openshift/origin*) is the free and open source version of OpenShift, as well as the upstream project for the other two versions. All changes committed, both from Red Hat and from external contributors, go through the public repository. OpenShift Origin is not offered as PaaS, but is intended to be installed on your own infrastructure. We are not going to cover the installation steps required to get OpenShift up and running on premises; instead, we will be covering the steps needed to get up and running on OpenShift PaaS.

The OpenShift Origin repository is packed and released as a new version of OpenShift Online every three weeks or so (the length of a sprint). OpenShift Online is hosted on Amazon Web Services (AWS), but to use it you just need to create an account with OpenShift. All the DevOps work, including updating the OS and managing networks, is covered by the OpenShift operations team, so that you are free to focus on your application.

The last version of OpenShift is OpenShift Enterprise. This version allows you to take a complete PaaS solution and run it anywhere you wish. It is packaged with Red Hat Enterprise Linux and is fully supported by Red Hat; it's intended for customers who are looking for stability and a production-ready solution out of the box.

OpenShift uses some specific terminology for its environment. I will briefly explain it here, but I recommend that you have a look at the documentation.

A *gear* on OpenShift is the server container where your application is hosted. OpenShift currently offers three types of gears, depending on your needs.

A *cartridge* is a sort of plug-in that you install to enable certain functionality. Cartridges can be used to enable a certain database or your language of choice.

Applications on OpenShift expose only HTTP port 80, HTTPS port 443, and SSH port 22. Beta WebSocket support is also provided.

 A great resource on OpenShift is Katy Miller and Steve Pousty's *Getting Started with OpenShift: A Guide for Impatient Beginners* (O'Reilly).

In order to work with OpenShift you also need to be a little familiar with *git* and *ssh*.

Git is a free and open source distributed version control system; it is what you will use to push and deploy your code to OpenShift. There are a multitude of introductory documents about Git; one that I can recommend is Al Shaw's "Get Started with Git" (*http://bit.ly/shaw-git*).

Secure Shell (SSH) is a cryptographic network protocol for secure data communication. I will assume a basic knowledge of the two technologies. A great starting point to learn ssh is *SSH, The Secure Shell: The Definitive Guide* (*http://bit.ly/secure-shell-tdg*) by Daniel J. Barrett and Richard E. Silverman.

Preliminary Steps

Before getting started deploying your application, you'll need to create an OpenShift account and install the rhc command-line tools.

You can sign up for an OpenShift account at *http://bit.ly/openshift-signup*.

Instructions on how to install the *rhc* tools can be found at *http://bit.ly/openshift-tools*.

 If you use rbenv for managing Ruby, you also need to run `rbenv rehash`.

Check that *rhc* has been installed correctly by typing:

```
$ rhc
Usage: rhc [--help] [--version] [--debug] <command> [<args>]
Command line interface for OpenShift.
```

If you want to see all the cartridges available, just type:

```
$ rhc cartridges
```

Meet Jenkins

Jenkins is an open source continuous integration tool written in Java, allowing developers to run their tests automagically every time they push to a branch.

Before actually meeting Jenkins and discovering what it can do for you, we will first take a step back and praise the practice of continuous integration and continuous deployment.

When developing a large project, integrating new features can become a long and painful process if not done properly. Continuous integration tries to solve this problem.

The term continuous integration (CI) was first introduced by Martin Fowler in 2000, in his famous blog post about his experience of applying CI at ThoughtWorks (*http://bit.ly/ci-thoughtworks*).

CI is in practice just about a workflow that encourages teams to integrate their code several times a day to avoid integration conflicts, while also being able to deploy features and fixes at the same rate. Continuous integration is, therefore, the practice of testing each change made to your code base automatically, in a test-driven development environment, as early as possible.

So what is Jenkins, and what can it do for you? Jenkins is an application used to monitor and execute repeated jobs, like building a software project or a simple cron job. It is particularly focused on the following two tasks:

- Building and testing software projects continuously, providing an easy-to-use CI system
- Monitoring the execution of jobs that are run externally (even on remote machines) like cron jobs

Jenkins can easily be run on OpenShift as a standalone application. To create a Jenkins application on OpenShift, run:

```
$ rhc app create jenkins jenkins-1
```

You need to write down the administrator username and password that are created and returned by *rhc*. These will be needed to administer Jenkins.

Once a Jenkins application has been created, you can access the user interface at *https://jenkins-<namespace>.rhcloud.com*.

You can also enable Jenkins for a previously created application. From your OpenShift dashboard, go to Applications, click on the application you want to edit, then click on "Enable Jenkins" under "Continuous Integration" (see Figure 10-1).

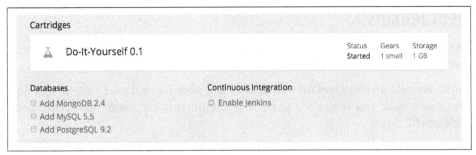

Figure 10-1. Enabling Jenkins on OpenShift

You can perform all management tasks on Jenkins from its web interface. The basic Jenkins workflow will follow these simple steps:

- As you commit and push new code to a repo, Jenkins runs a full series of tests.
- With OpenShift, if the tests and build are successful, the new code gets deployed. In case of failure, the old code continues to run with no downtime related to the push.

Users can always go to the web interface to check the persistent build history maintained by Jenkins about their projects and builds, as seen in Figure 10-2. Through the web interface they can also trigger and customize builds, manage resources and plugins, and interact with many other features.

So, when your code is pushed, the build/test/deploy sequence in Jenkins is triggered. Jenkins uses a scheduling process that involves creating a temporary builder for the application. A node (also known as a slave) is created on the Jenkins side, and a corresponding builder application is created in OpenShift. If the node/builder already exist at scheduling time, the existing builder will be used and the build will fire immediately.

Note that on OpenShift the node and builder application will consume one gear each. Nodes and builder applications are automatically deleted and the corresponding gears are freed after 15 idle minutes.

You can also use Jenkins running on OpenShift to execute the tests of an application stored in a GitHub repository. To do so, you have to create a new item and choose "Build a free-style software project." Then fill in the GitHub information for your project, as shown in Figures 10-3 and 10-4.

Figure 10-2. Jenkins web interface running on OpenShift

In your Jenkins project configuration, you will also need to specify information about the build environment (the version of Ruby that you want to test your project against, if you want to use an rbenv- or RVM-managed environment, and what gems—for example, *bundler, rake, mysql*—are preinstalled) and the build itself. This may include what command you want to execute at build time (e.g., `bundle install`) and which *rake* task you want to run (e.g., *test*).

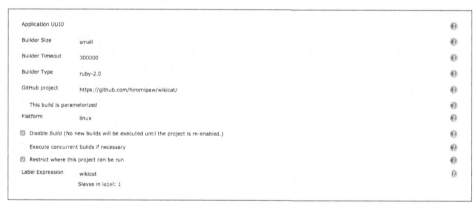

Figure 10-3. Add your GitHub repository URL

To troubleshoot errors that you might encounter while building/testing/deploying with Jenkins, you might want to look at applications logs showing compilation and test failures. These are available via the Jenkins web UI under the corresponding node's build history and will usually help you find the problem.

Figure 10-4. Add your GitHub repository information

Wrapping Up

In this chapter we have seen how an API is deployed and how to start developing an API platform. In the next chapter we will learn how to manage an API or application ecosystem and what complexities you should start considering even in your minimum viable product.

Managing an App Ecosystem

Once a number of developers start using your API through their applications, you will notice that a community of interacting parties will start growing around your product. Applications and developers in your community might develop different or converging interests regarding your product, and a set of relationships will form that you will need to manage directly or indirectly. In this chapter we will analyze these relationships and explore what you can do to maximize the satisfaction of your direct and indirect customers. We will focus particularly on how data can help you manage your relationship with your customers and developer community.

API Management

Your API and the applications that are using it, no matter how many or few these may be, have created a community of interacting parties. This community is often compared to an ecosystem.

In ecology, an ecosystem is a biological community of interacting organisms and their physical environment. If we translate this concept to a system of developers, applications, and APIs, we can start to see the analogies with the natural world. In an app ecosystem, the parties forming it interact to form different relationships with various purposes: they exchange data streams and communicate with one another and, perhaps, the rest of the world. Figure 11-1 illustrates this idea.

When you start managing a complex application ecosystem, you have already built a successful API that other developers have started using and integrating into their projects. So first of all, take a moment to congratulate yourself on this achievement.

Once you have congratulated yourself, and maybe your team or organization, you can start analyzing the intricate network of relationships that you will have to build and therefore manage with the developers that are using your service.

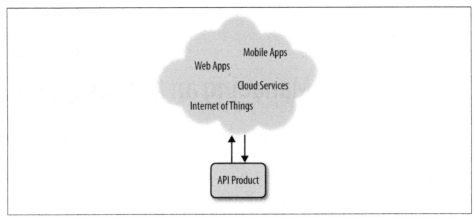

Figure 11-1. An ecosystem where an API feeds different applications and services

As an example, let's consider our Citywalks API, which uses the WikiCat and Wikipin APIs to create thematic walks. The Citywalks API also has a customer, the Walks app, which displays walks on maps.

This is a three-level relationship where a certain API feeds another service, which then feeds different parties. The end result of this is an intricate network of relationships. Such a network could eventually evolve into a kind of mesh of APIs and apps, where some APIs feed other applications, to the point where, by adopting open protocols, each node in the network shares data with the others (see Figure 11-2).

 A mesh network is a network topology in which each node (called a mesh node) relays data for the network. The nodes cooperate to distribute data throughout the network. For more information, see the Wikipedia article on mesh networking (*http://bit.ly/wiki-mesh-networking*).

APIs Are Not Consumer Products

There is a small mental leap that you need to make when starting to develop an API, and that is recognizing that an API is not a consumer product (at least, not yet)—but it could feed a large number of different products with its data.

It is true that many products have APIs that are used to drive more users to their platforms, but per se an API is not a consumer product. It is an interface that is meant to be used by developers to build applications.

These applications may have anywhere from a few hundred to millions of users, but these will not be your direct customers. Ultimately, your API's customers are the applications consuming it, which in turn will have users of their own.

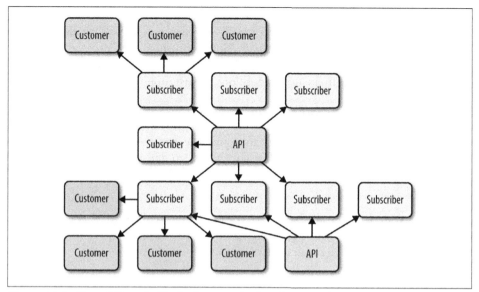

Figure 11-2. Your API probably feeds a set of subscribers, or developers; each of them will have a number of customers

There are a number of key features of a successful application ecosystem. These are:

A developer portal
> Generally speaking, a developer portal is a web app providing different tools and services to your developer community. These typically include API documentation, community forums, key provisioning, and general tools and suggestions to facilitate integration and support your community.

Testing and quality assurance
> A standard procedure to test applications and to assure quality is extremely important for both parties involved in the integration process.
>
> With a testing procedure in place, the API provider can ensure that all applications adhere to its terms of service and quality standards and that no malicious activity can be performed by the applications. Also, you can make sure that you catch any issues before the app's users do. Consider this a stress, quality, and security test for your API as well as for the new developer's app.

Application management
> Application management programs provide all the techniques and procedures needed to deploy an application and deliver optimal performance and operations, including best practices for app versioning and onboarding.

Advertising services

Some business models use advertisements to ensure a stable cash flow; others rely on external ad networks to help developers promote their projects. Advertising services therefore help both the service providers and their subscribers to effectively reach new users, drive adoptions, or just monetize their products.

User management

User management services constitute an important feature of any app ecosystem. There is in fact more to manage than just the end users of your developers' projects: there are also roles within your platform and permissions to be managed to ensure that developer groups can operate efficiently.

Analytics

Analytics services are all those features that support data-driven decisions for your developers and your platform. These include monitoring, optimizing, and continuously enhancing your ecosystem.

Managing Your Community's Happiness

We have said that managing an application ecosystem means managing different players on our platforms. At the highest level, we have the developers trying to integrate our services into their products. At lower levels, we have the application's end users. Their satisfaction, at least partially, depends on our API, including its ability to scale to meet traffic demands and its availability.

We will start by introducing how to bootstrap a developer program. We will then explore how to measure application and API quality, and finally we will talk about user happiness.

Developer Programs

A developer program is a set of features and tools you provide to help developers get started creating projects with your API.

A developer program usually includes your API documentation and a suite of case studies to help developers produce their first "hello world" call with your API. These could involve just fetching a resource or posting a simple update. It is up to you to create interesting case studies.

There are different ways to create good documentation, and a number of tools are available to help. Some of these are often included in API management platforms and do some of the heavy lifting for you. In other simpler cases you may just want to go with a simple open source library. Some libraries even allow you to write documentation descriptions directly in your code and test cases.

In the previous chapter I mentioned apiDoc (*http://apidocjs.com*), a Node package that generates documentation for you right from your code. We will now see how to use it effectively to get started with a simple API project.

Getting started with apiDoc

Installing apiDoc is as easy as running:

```
$ npm install apidoc -g
```

 To run *npm* you need Node.js installed. You can download an installer for your system from the Node website (*http://nodejs.org/download/*).

Once apiDoc has been installed, you can easily add a bit of documentation to your code. For example, let's say we would like to document the blocks API methods of the Wikipin API:

```
=begin
  @api {get} /blocks/:id Show Block
  @apiName ShowBlock
  @apiGroup Block
  @apiParam {Number} id Blocks unique ID.
=end
```

Then we would have to run the apidoc command from our application folder in a terminal window to obtain the HTML documentation:

```
wikipin user$ apidoc -o doc/
```

This will generate everything in the *doc/* folder.

If you then want to specify some more information regarding your API, you can create an *apidoc.json* file with the following information:

```
{
  "name": "WikiPin API",
  "version": "1.0.0",
  "description": "apiDoc inherit example"
}
```

To apply the changes, run the previous command again:

```
wikipin user$ apidoc -o doc/
```

Then navigate to the *doc/* folder to see your documentation in HTML format.

apiDoc is an easy tool that can really help you in generating explorable documentation for your API methods. You can also use it to sketch your methods before you actually code them and share the schematic of your API with other members of your team.

Creating a developer community

Writing useful and clean documentation is not the only important aspect of creating a developer program. Giving your developers tools to easily integrate with your service and access to support resources is also paramount.

Just think of how many times you have struggled yourself trying to understand some piece of documentation or trying to figure out if your code had a bug or it was something in the API you were trying to import. You really need to allow developers to come to you and ask questions, while also providing a place where they can discuss their experiences and share snippets of their code.

There are certainly different ways to do so. Some products or companies set up Stack Overflow categories (like Facebook (*http://bit.ly/stackoverflow-fb*), for example). Others prefer to have a forum on their developer portal where people can ask questions, or a GitHub issues page. What is important is that you provide a place where developers can come and ask for help or showcase their projects. This is a simple way to attract fellow developers and drive attention to your API product, and eventually also to your main product.

App and API Quality

There are a number of issues that arise once external applications start integrating your services. Firstly, you need to check if the way developers are using your API product adheres to your terms of service or usage agreement. While it is certainly a good thing that you have opened up your service to the web population, you need to make sure that you can provide a certain level of quality and reliability, and that you profit from the endeavor.

The terms of service set the boundaries for the number and types of operations that developers can perform with your API. Terms of service and developer agreements are written in legal jargon, but they also set some very technical limits that allow your product or business to be scaled gracefully.

A simple example is the situation where you are scaling your service according to the number of applications using it. In this case, you might decide to set a maximum number of API call per minute/hour/day. In fact, if you know that you will be able to provide a certain service for a certain number of applications as long as they do not make more than a certain number of API calls per hour, you will also know how to allocate resources proportionally to the actual number of active applications.

Another aspect of app quality management that you might want to consider is providing automated testing. Application testing is important for a number of reasons.

Firstly, it allows you to make sure that developers are using your API methods according to the terms of service. Secondly, it enables you to search for common bugs in integrating your service. Thirdly, you might have built a number of test cases that will ensure that the developer's app will work reliably on a number of platforms.

As part of your app or service testing framework, you can implement security policies. This simplifies the developer's operations and makes sure that every application or API in your ecosystem will adhere to certain principles that you are comfortable with.

User Happiness

User happiness management involves using a set of procedures and tools to ensure that you and your developers can provide the desired level of satisfaction.

The first step here is understanding that you might not directly have end users. You might in fact be in a situation in which you are providing a service to a third party, and this party has its own user base.

A possible different scenario would instead be the situation in which you are providing a certain API to third-party developers, but their applications will be accessed through your main platform or product. In this case the end users of their apps will also be your product's users.

In both cases you will have to manage different levels of relationships. On the one side, you need to ensure that developers are happy to create projects with your API; on the other side, you need to make sure that the end users are satisfied with the service they are ultimately using. Having a clear picture of how users interact with your APIs can help you to support developers and ensure the quality of their apps and APIs. Also, you can use the information you extract from your data to make intelligent decisions.

Data Management and Analytics

When managing an ecosystem of apps, APIs, developers, and users, you have a multitude of data sources that you might want to keep under control for various reasons.

For example, you might have a monitoring and analytics program in place that you can draw upon to make data-driven decisions. Questions like "How much traffic are our services producing?" and "How many requests are we receiving per second?" can be easily answered by carefully monitoring your backend and endpoints.

Also, once you can provide informative answers to questions like these, you can plan for the future. How many machines should you provision next month/year? To make these kinds of decisions, you will need accurate data.

Depending on your business models, you may need data for a variety of purposes.

One such purpose could be monetizing your API. In this scenario, your developers might pay you a certain amount to use your API, depending on the terms of their service contracts. These fees might be calculated on a pay-per-use basis, or on a tiered basis. Either way, you will need to know data like the number of requests per developer or application, and general usage statistics.

Another reason why you may want to build a strong reporting infrastructure is for marketing. You might want to suggest products or services through your API, or you might want to provide the possibility for your developers to advertise through your API. In such scenarios, you might want to collect end user data.

Another possible reason would be for providing statistics to the end users. A possible scenario where this could be important is one in which the developers creating apps on your platforms are also your business partners and are selling some services on your behalf.

Business intelligence, statistics, and reporting are all legitimate reasons to justify an investment in data management and analytics to capture event data. Event data can really be anything: signups, upgrades, impressions, purchases, errors, shares—these represent those constant little interactions that happen all day, every day, in any application.

Wrapping Up

In this chapter we have seen how to manage an API ecosystem and what complexities need to be considered from the beginning. In the next chapter we will see how to consume different data streams and integrate external APIs into our application.

Consuming Data Streams: Integrating External APIs in Your Application

In this chapter we are going to integrate two external APIs into our Walks application. We are going to see how integrating external services is somewhat similar to integrating an internal API. There are some issues regarding the way we consume and offer external content that need to be considered, however.

Creating a Weather Service

Imagine that our Walks application could be enriched with a weather forecast, or that our Citywalks API could also suggest that users pack an umbrella or sunscreen before leaving the house. If you are thinking what I am thinking right now, you would agree that this would be a nice feature to have.

The problem with this is that you actually need a simple weather forecasting service to implement it—yet you may want to code a way to get weather forecasts in your app yourself. The ideal solution would be a third-party service that you could talk to to get a weather forecast for a particular city or location.

Luckily for us, there are a number of APIs that offer this service on the Web. Most of these also allow your app to make a certain number of calls per day for free, which is our ideal situation since we are just starting with a test project.

I have chosen to use the OpenWeatherMap (*http://openweathermap.org*) project, since it adopts an approach to its business and service that is inspired by OpenStreetMap and Wikipedia and involves making its information available to everybody to use. OpenWeatherMap collects data from weather stations and forecasts from meteorological services and research laboratories, combining long-term and short-term forecasts with real-time data from weather stations. It processes all of this data and immediately updates the current weather and forecasts in its API.

Of course, you are free to integrate another service if you find something else that you like more. Please note that in this case the JSON returned will probably require different parsing, but in the end you should be able to easily adapt the code in the repository. As usual, you are encouraged to fork and modify what you see fit.

If This Then Something

To be able to provide weather recommendations through the Citywalks API we will need to create a new endpoint. We are going to call this *suggestions*. When a user calls the suggestions endpoint, this will consult the OpenWeatherMap API; if the percentage of cloud cover is predicted to be over 40% it will suggest some videos from YouTube, and otherwise it will return places of interest in the area. Figure 12-1 illustrates this configuration.

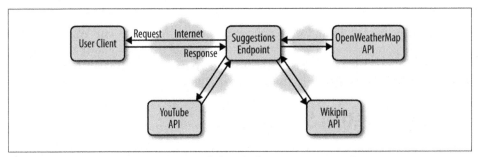

Figure 12-1. The Citywalks API extended with the suggestions endpoint

To search YouTube videos, the user can pass a `category` parameter. If the user doesn't pass the `category` param, the API will search for Radiohead videos.

To begin, we are going to create a new controller in *api/v1/*:

```
class Api::V1::SuggestionController < ApplicationController
  respond_to :json

  include MakeSuggestion

  def index
    if @suggestions
      render :json => @suggestions.to_json
    else
      @error = Error.new(:text => "404 Not found",
                         :status => 404,
                         :url => request.url,
                         :method => request.method)
      render :json => @error.serializer
```

```
    end
  end

end
```

MakeSuggestion is the concern that is going to handle part of the logic behind the suggestion controller. Therefore, we need to create a file in *controllers/concerns* called *make_suggestion.rb*. First we need to define an entry action that takes place as soon as we hit the endpoint:

```
def entry_action
  @suggestions = []
  if params[:location]
    location = params[:location].split(',')
    @suggestions << make_forecast(location[0],location[1])
  else
    @suggestions << suggestions_by_ip
  end
end
```

Then we define the make_forecast function:

```
def make_forecast(latitude, longitude)
  forecast = get_weather(latitude,longitude)
  if forecast[:forecast].doc["clouds"]["all"] > 40
    request_youtube_videos(params[:category] || "Radiohead")
  else
    request_pins("#{longitude},#{latitude}")
  end
end
```

Both the get_weather and request_youtube_videos methods will be defined in their respective modules.

The last method that we will need to define is suggestions_by_ip. This method will simply find out the request IP and corresponding location before calling the make_forecast method:

```
def suggestions_by_ip
  if ip == "127.0.0.1"
    get_weather("41.23","2.09")
  else
    block = Walk.request_block(ip).doc["ip_block"]
    if block
      longitude = block["point"].scan(/\((([^\)]+)\)/)
                    .last.first.split(" ")[0]
      latitude = block["point"].scan(/\((([^\)]+)\)/)
                    .last.first.split(" ")[1]
      make_forecast(latitude, longitude)
    end
  end
end
```

If you want to understand why the forecast variable was defined like that, you can have a look at the JSON returned by the OpenWeatherMap API. This command:

```
$ curl http://api.openweathermap.org/data/2.5/
  weather?lat=35&lon=139
```

returns:

```
{"coord":
   {"lon":139,"lat":35},
    "sys":{
       "message":0.0339,
       "country":"JP",
       "sunrise":1422136041,
       "sunset":1422173111},
       "weather":[
          {"id":803,
           "main":"Clouds",
           "description":"broken clouds",
           "icon":"04n"}
       ],
       "base":"cmc stations",
       "main":{
          "temp":272.266,
          "temp_min":272.266,
          "temp_max":272.266,
          "pressure":993.96,
          "sea_level":1039.54,
          "grnd_level":993.96,
          "humidity":100
       },
       "wind":{"speed":1.66,"deg":310.004},
       "clouds":{"all":76},
       "dt":1422223009,
       "id":1851632,
       "name":"Shuzenji",
       "cod":200
    }
```

Now we can create the modules that we need in the *lib/* folder. We start with the Weather module by creating a file called *weather.rb*:

```ruby
module Weather

  WEATHER_URL = "http://api.openweathermap.org/data/2.5/weather?"

  def get_weather(lat, lon)
    forecast = {
```

```
        forecast: send_request("#{WEATHER_URL}lat=#{lat}&lon=#{lon}")
      }
    end

  end
```

WEATHER_URL defines our endpoint on the OpenWeatherMap API; then we just define a method to call the API and pass latitude and longitude information.

The Youtube module is going to be a little bit more complicated to define. This is because to be able to use the YouTube Data API, our application must have authorization credentials. The Google Developers Console (*http://bit.ly/google-dev-cons*) supports different types of authentication methods that need to be configured for your project.

Start by visiting the Google Developers Console and selecting or creating a new project. In the sidebar on the left, select "APIs & auth." In the list of APIs, make sure the status is "ON" for the YouTube Data API v3.

Again in the sidebar on the left, select "Credentials." The API supports two types of credentials. Create whichever credentials are appropriate for your project.

If you choose OAuth 2.0, your application must send an OAuth 2.0 token with any request that accesses private user data. Your application sends a client ID and, possibly, a client secret to obtain a token. You can generate OAuth 2.0 credentials for web applications, service accounts, or installed applications.

If you choose to authenticate with API keys, you will use a developer key to authenticate your request. We will use this method. The key identifies your project and provides API access, quotas, and reports.

If the key type you need does not already exist, create an API key by selecting "Create New Key" and then selecting the appropriate key type, which in our case is a server key. Then enter the additional data required for that key type: in our case, the list of IPs that are allowed to use that key. If you are running your application in your local machine, this list will probably need to include only:

- 0.0.0.0
- 127.0.0.1

Otherwise, you will need the IP of the server where your app is running.

Once you have finished configuring your app in the Developers Console, you can start writing the module:

```
require "net/http"
require "json"
require "google/api_client"
require "trollop"
```

```ruby
module Youtube

  DEVELOPER_KEY = <Your Developer Key>
  YOUTUBE_API_SERVICE_NAME = "youtube"
  YOUTUBE_API_VERSION = "v3"

  def get_service
    client = Google::APIClient.new(
    :key => DEVELOPER_KEY,
    :authorization => nil,
    :application_name => <Your Application Name>,
    :application_version => '1.0.0'
    )
    youtube = client.discovered_api(YOUTUBE_API_SERVICE_NAME,
                                    YOUTUBE_API_VERSION)

    return client, youtube
  end

  def wrap_search_results(videos, channels, playlists)
    search_results = {
      videos: videos,
      channels: channels,
      playlists: playlists
    }
  end

  def wrap_json(search_result)
    result = {
      title: search_result.snippet.title,
      description: search_result.snippet.description,
      url: make_video_url(search_result)
    }
  end

  def make_video_url(search_result)
    case search_result.id.kind
    when 'youtube#video'
      "https://www.youtube.com/watch?
          v=#{search_result.id.videoId}"
    when 'youtube#channel'
      "https://www.youtube.com/channel/
          #{search_result.id.channelId}"
    when 'youtube#playlist'
      "https://www.youtube.com/playlist?
          list=#{search_result.id.playlistId}"
    end
  end

  def request_youtube_videos(query)
    opts = Trollop::options do
      opt :q, 'Search term', :type => String, :default => query
```

```
      opt :max_results, 'Max results', :type => :int,
          :default => 25
    end

    client, youtube = get_service
    begin
      # Call the search.list method to retrieve results matching the specified
      # query term.
      search_response = client.execute!(
      :api_method => youtube.search.list,
      :parameters => {
        :part => 'snippet',
        :q => opts[:q],
        :maxResults => opts[:max_results]
      }
      )

      videos = []
      channels = []
      playlists = []

      # Add each result to the appropriate list, and then display the lists of
      # matching videos, channels, and playlists.
      search_response.data.items.each do |search_result|
        case search_result.id.kind
        when 'youtube#video'
          videos << wrap_json(search_result)
        when 'youtube#channel'
          channels << wrap_json(search_result)
        when 'youtube#playlist'
          playlists << wrap_json(search_result)
        end
      end

      wrap_search_results(videos, channels, playlists)

    rescue Google::APIClient::TransmissionError => e
      puts e.result.body
    end

  end
end
```

Now we can call our new endpoint:

```
$ curl http://0.0.0.0:3001/api/v1/suggestion?location=41.23,2.09
```

You can try different locations to see how the results change with the cloud coverage.

Adhering to the Terms of Service

Every API defines some terms of service stating what users can do and what they cannot do with the service offered. You will have to consider the terms of the services you decide to integrate to better understand if the APIs you have decided to use are a good fit for your purposes.

When you review different services you might find that some APIs are a good fit technically, but will not scale as your app starts growing and serving more users. Some other APIs might instead provide very few limits in terms of traffic or the number of requests that you can send them, but restrict how you use the information provided.

While you're thinking about the terms of service of the APIs integrated into your app, you should also be thinking about how to develop your own terms of service for when you publish your API. The terms of service are a way to tell your users that you are offering your API under specific conditions. If those conditions are not met, you can decide to stop users from using your service.

This is particularly important if you are offering subscriptions to use your service. When the users subscribe, they agree to a contract, and the terms of service can also be part of this contract.

Thinking about your terms of service might also help you define your business model. For example, you might have published your API under some conditions for a certain amount of time. If you now recognize that you might offer a different kind of service, with the same infrastructure, you might as well offer it as an additional plan for your users to subscribe to. This is a typical scenario when you start developing an application that users can subscribe to for free, and then you have to figure out a way to scale this into a business and make money out of it.

In cases like this it sometimes makes sense to offer a pay-per-use plan or a paid subscription offering some additional features to the free plan.

Ramen Profitable

If you are thinking about setting up a startup and considering ways to get funded, you might find there are periods in which you have to live off your savings because your business isn't profitable yet.

Paul Graham wrote some years ago about the notion of being "ramen profitable," (*http://bit.ly/ramen-profitable*) or just profitable enough to survive and for founders to have time to develop the business.

Asynchronous REST

Up to this moment we have relied on the concept that every time we make a request to the server we are able to receive an answer almost immediately (allowing for small communication delays between the client and the server). This unfortunately isn't always the case.

Consider a situation where your users need to create resources, and these operations might take a considerable amount of time to complete. This could be the case when there is some image processing, for example, that happens in your backend. If you let the client wait for the request to finish, this might time out and return an error instead.

In cases like this you could have your API return a 202 (Accepted) response. This will tell the client that the request has been accepted for processing, but the processing has not been completed yet. When the server returns a 202 response, the client doesn't know exactly what will happen to its request, since there is no facility for status returns from asynchronous operations such as this. The request is not guaranteed to eventually be acted upon, as it may be disallowed when processing actually takes place. Therefore, you can also return a `Location: /resources/xxxxxx` field in your response telling the client where to ask for the actual status of the request.

For more on HTTP responses, see "HTTP Semantics" on page 61.

When the resource has finally been created and the request has completed, this temporary resource can return a 303 (See Other) response and the URI to the definitive resource.

To create a temporary resource, you might consider writing a model in your application that is not persisted to your database. Although you do not need to persist data to your database, the client might have to query the server, possibly more than once, to know the status of the requested resource and to ensure that the action being processed in the backend has actually completed.

In situations like this you might consider writing your object to a Redis instance. Redis is a key/value cache and store, released under the open source BSD license. It is also referred to as a data structure server since keys can contain strings, hashes, lists, sets, sorted sets, bitmaps, and hyperloglogs. In our case Redis will function as a normal database, storing our temporary resources for the time we need them.

To install Redis you will have to download and compile the source. A complete installation guide can be found at *http://redis.io/topics/quickstart*.

Under OS X with Homebrew you can just run:

```
$ brew install redis
```

We will use an object-hash mapping library for Redis called *Ohm* (*https://github.com/soveran/ohm*). Ohm comes packed in a gem for Ruby on Rails. You can install it by adding the following to your *Gemfile*:

```
gem 'ohm'
gem 'ohm-contrib'
```

We are now going to define our temporary resource model under *app/models*:

```
require 'ohm'
require 'ohm/contrib'
class Process < Ohm::Model
  include Ohm::Versioned
  attribute :process_id
  attribute :message
  attribute :location
  attribute :status
  attribute :code
  index :temp_id

  Ohm.redis = Redis.new(ENV['REDIS_URL'])

  def serialize
    { process: {
        id: process_id,
        location: location
      },
      response: {
        message: message,
        code: code.to_i
      },
      status: status.to_i
    }
  end
end
```

and define a processes controller in *api/v1*:

```
class API::V1::ProcessesController < ApplicationController
  include ProcessOperations
  def show
    @process = Process.find(process_id: params[:id]).first
    if @process
      render json: @process.serialize,
             status: @process.serialize[:status]
    else
      render json: process_not_found, status: 404
```

```
      end
    end

  def create
    if long_action_to_be_performed
      @process = create_process(params)
      render json: @process, status: @process[:status]
    else
      render json: process_error, status: 500
    end
  end
end
```

The *show* action fetches the process and displays its status. The *create* action triggers the long_action_to_be_performed method and creates our temporary process to track it.

We are not going to define the method long_action_to_be_performed since it can be a worker triggered or a service.

We are instead going to define the ProcessOperations module:

```
module ProcessOperations
  extend ActiveSupport::Concern
  def create_process(params)
    process = Process.create(process_id: params[:id],
                 message: "Accepted",
                 location: "processes/#{params[:id]}",
                 code: 202, status: 202)
    if process
      process.serialize
    else
      process_error
    end
  end
  def process_error
    error = {
      response: {
        message: "Internal Server Error",
        code: 500
      },
      status: 500
    }
  end
  def process_not_found
    error = {
      response: {
        message: "Not Found",
        code: 404
      },
      status: 404
    }
```

```
      end
    end
```

The `ProcessOperations` module creates the process and returns structured errors when called.

Finally, we are going to define the routes for the new model and controller we've introduced:

```
namespace :api do
  namespace :v1, format: :json do
    post 'processes/create', to: 'processes#create'
    get  'processes/:id',    to: 'processes#show'
  end
end
```

The asynchronous REST implementation shown here implies that the client will use polling to query the temporary resource until a 303 response is returned. The client itself can also implement some logic to perform the polling after a certain amount of time. Another option would be to implement web hooks on the server side and trigger an HTTP callback notifying the client that the resource is ready.

Wrapping Up

In this chapter we discussed how to integrate external data streams into our application. In the next chapter we will see how this leads us to design and develop products independently from the devices where they will be run. This approach to software development can be considered valid for web, mobile, or even IoT applications.

Device-Independent Development

When you develop a web app you are in fact developing an application expected to run on a number of different devices, which will interact with it in a way that will feel both web-like and native at the same time. When you access Gmail or Twitter or Facebook, you are still accessing a website and interacting with it in a way that resembles the way you would surf a website, even though it feels like a software application with an interface and functionality that do not really follow the typical website model. Furthermore, the Web is not accessed only by personal computers. There are mobile devices and tablets of all species and form factors surfing and exploring apps and websites, and there are also other kinds of devices and hardware platforms that just consume data. In this chapter we will see how you can easily integrate these classes of devices and have your application not only cover the mobile app space, but also serve customers in the IoT field.

Web Development Is a Broad Term

Web development has evolved considerably over the last few years. In the beginning, we were used to interacting with static websites, but as websites grew in complexity we started to get used to pages that were more like applications than simply browseable text documents.

When you are developing for the Web, you are developing for a multitude of devices that will need to access the same application seamlessly. There are different advantages to developing rich graphical applications that are able to work cross-platform on the Web, rather than native applications. Native applications need to be developed for each and every target device, and often in different languages. On the other hand, the Web is already cross-platform by design. Any device that can access the Internet and has a browser can access your application.

Web applications feel and act more like native applications than simply hypertext or old-fashioned static websites. By the term *native application*, we mean a software program that exposes a graphical user interface (GUI). In a GUI, users can manipulate graphical elements, as opposed to just interacting with the application through text commands. Web applications are therefore evolving into complex graphical applications that can also use hyperlinks to navigate to and communicate with resources on the Web.

The great advantage of the Web as a communication platform is the possibility to easily find resources through URLs. URLs can be easily shared and bookmarked, and this key feature makes web applications superior collaboration tools.

We can think of web applications as interfaces to complex systems, comprising a number of different APIs and feeding different interfaces on a variety of devices (not just personal computers). We can also use web frameworks to develop applications not only for the Web, but for a variety of platforms.

Developing for Mobile

Developing for mobile, handheld devices means developing for platforms that might have different energy constraints, lower and different resolutions, diverse operating systems, and different browsers used to access the Web. In such a scenario, making a "mobile application" can actually mean three different things: you can either develop a native application in the language of the platform you choose, or develop an HTML app that can be used cross-platform, or develop a hybrid application. A hybrid application will use some aspects specific to the platform where it will be running, while also implementing part of its logic in HTML.

Usually native applications make better use of the platform-specific features and HTML apps do feel a bit clumsier, but things are evolving rapidly, and more often than not you might ponder the two options and find equal benefits in both of them.

The benefit of developing in HTML directly is that you will be able to reuse the majority of your code on different devices, while if you develop a native app you will be able to make the most of the device-specific settings and system characteristics.

There are also a variety of solutions and frameworks that will allow you to write your app in a language that you already know, like JavaScript, HTML5, or Ruby, and translate it for you into a native application.

Finally, different platforms are already moving toward native HTML development environments. Firefox OS, an open source mobile operating system developed by Mozilla, is one of these.

Build native applications in a language you already know

Learning yet another language and becoming proficient with it is a challenge that we are not always willing to accept. This is especially true when we are already overloaded with developing and running a product on our own. In such a situation, we might consider developing in a framework that will do the hard work of translating the app to the native device language for us.

We have a few options to do this in Ruby already, such as the following:

RubyMotion (http://www.rubymotion.com/)
> A toolchain that lets you quickly develop and test native apps for iPhone, iPad, Mac, and Android (beta) using Ruby.

MobiRuby (http://mobiruby.org)
> A wrapper for mruby (*https://github.com/mruby/mruby/*), which is a minimalistic implementation of Ruby. It is maintained and developed by the chief designer of Ruby, Matz (*http://bit.ly/wiki-matz*).

You can also choose a framework that lets you develop in HTML5 or JavaScript, like:

PhoneGap (http://phonegap.com)
> An open source framework for quickly building cross-platform mobile apps using HTML5, JavaScript, and CSS.

Titanium by Appcelerator (http://www.appcelerator.com/developers/)
> A development environment for creating native applications across different mobile devices and OSes including iOS, Android, and BlackBerry, as well as hybrid and HTML5 apps. It includes an open source SDK, an Eclipse-based IDE, an MVC framework, and Cloud Services to integrate a mobile backend.

Streaming Data into a Firefox OS App

Firefox OS is the operating system designed for mobile devices developed by Mozilla and the Firefox community. It is designed to use HTML5 entirely and comply with open web standards.

The interesting aspect of Firefox OS for web developers is that the entire user interface is a web app capable of displaying and launching other web apps. Therefore, you can easily develop and modify Firefox OS apps and user interfaces using your knowledge of HTML, CSS, and JavaScript. This means that you get direct enhanced access to the mobile device hardware and services, like you would if you were to build a native app on Android or iOS.

Firefox OS is based on a Linux kernel booting into a Gecko-based runtime. Gecko is the rendering engine on Firefox OS used to display web content.

Gecko

Gecko (*http://bit.ly/mozilla-gecko*) is the layout engine developed by Mozilla and used in different Mozilla projects. Its original name was NGLayout, but that was changed along the road. Gecko's function is to read web content, such as HTML, CSS, XUL, and JavaScript, and render or print it. In XUL-based applications Gecko is used to render the application's user interface as well.

At the UI layer of Firefox OS we find Gaia, which is responsible for drawing everything that appears on the screen after the OS starts up and for handling the fundamental functions of the phone such as settings, calls, SMSes, taking and storing photos, etc.

Gaia is entirely written in HTML, CSS, and JavaScript. It interfaces with the underlying operating system and the device hardware through web APIs implemented by Gecko.

Gaia is designed to run on Firefox OS devices, but it can be implemented on other operating systems and web browsers; however, its functionalities might depend on the capabilities of the browser and device in use.

Gaia

Gaia (*http://bit.ly/mozilla-gaia*) is the user interface application for Firefox OS devices, designed as a web application running on top of the Firefox OS software stack.

Firefox has also developed the Firefox Marketplace, a channel for publishing web applications and making them discoverable by users of Firefox OS, Firefox for Android, and Firefox for Desktop.

Mozilla marketplace was built with the goal of bringing openness, freedom, and user choice to the world of mobile apps. At the same time it also provides a platform to publish applications across different devices. Figure 13-1 illustrates the process of publishing an app to the marketplace.

An installable open web app is just a normal web application or website, built using familiar web technologies like HTML, CSS, and JavaScript. The difference resides in a set of additional feature that are made available on the Firefox platform.

Therefore, your starting point to create an open web app is just to build a web application with the technologies that you are already familiar with. To identify this as an installable web app, you add a *manifest.webapp* file to the web app root directory.

The manifest defines a set of properties of the app, such as its name, icons, and localization information. Most importantly, the manifest also defines the permissions the app needs to access device APIs to use features like the camera, device storage, Bluetooth, and SMS.

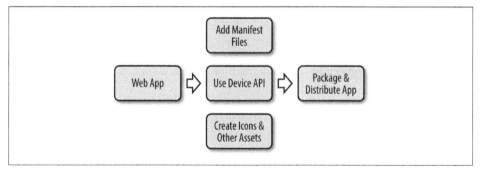

Figure 13-1. The process of publishing an open web app to the Firefox Marketplace

At this point, you might want to modify your web app and add additional functionality that makes use of the device APIs for which you have requested access in the manifest. For example, if you would like your app to be able to use the phone's camera, you will need to add code to enable that.

Finally, you need to create the assets needed by your app, such as icons and images; then you can package and distribute it on the Firefox Marketplace.

Your app can be published to the Firefox Marketplace in a variety of ways. You have the choice to say if your app is a simple self-published hosted app (in which case you'll have to write your own install functionality), or a packaged app distributed via the Firefox Marketplace (which handles the install functionality for you).

As this quick overview illustrates, Firefox OS is the perfect platform to start supporting mobile devices and quickly prototype a simple application.

Developing an Internet of Things App

The Internet of Things (IoT) is the interconnection of embedded computing devices and/or networks within the existing Internet infrastructure. It includes a variety of devices and networks of devices, from smart thermostats to biochips, and therefore IoT applications span a range of different protocols and domains. The fact that many IoT devices are embedded platforms implies a number of constraints and challenges involving minimizing the environmental and energy impact of such platforms, building adaptable and flexible products, taking telecommunication technologies into the physical world, and more. IoT devices often use short-range low-power WiFi for Internet connectivity, or carry solar cells to save battery power or to be energy independent. Yet this doesn't mean that IoT devices cannot connect to the Web. Depending on the device specification and on the application scope, an IoT device or a network of IoT nodes can also be a node in a web app, or run a web app itself. This simple concept has been called the Web of Things (WoT), a term that refers to the idea of fully incorporating everyday physical objects into the World Wide Web by giving them a RESTful API. Devices like the Arduino or Raspberry Pi, for example, are perfectly capable of running a web server while also interfacing with various environmental sensors.

Rails on the Raspberry Pi

The Raspberry Pi (*https://www.raspberrypi.org/*) feels like the perfect device to install a Ruby on Rails server on so you can start to experiment a bit with the kinds of applications that we have been building throughout this book.

The Raspberry Pi, as shown in Figure 13-2, is a low-cost minicomputer (starting at about $40), about the size of a credit card. It can be plugged into an external monitor or a TV, and is capable of performing an incredible variety of tasks. This is because a Raspberry Pi is capable of being programmed to do anything a desktop computer can do; it is also very portable and can easily interact with the outside world through sensors. Therefore, the Raspberry Pi has been used in a wide range of projects, from music machines to weather stations, from TV media centers to home automation projects, from arcade video games consoles to mini web servers.

Raspberry Space

If you thought the limit of the Raspberry Pi was the sky, think again (*http://www.raspberrypi.org/tag/space/*).

If you have bought a new Raspberry Pi (even a model B+), your standard system, Raspbian, comes with a system Ruby (1.9.3p194) installed. This means you need to update.

Figure 13-2. A Raspberry Pi kit

We will use *rbenv* to install Ruby, and since the Raspberry Pi comes with *git* pre-installed it won't be too complicated. In a terminal window, run:

```
$ git clone https://github.com/sstephenson/rbenv.git ~/.rbenv
```

Then export the *rbenv* folder to your *PATH*:

```
$ echo 'export PATH="$HOME/.rbenv/bin:$PATH"' >> ~/.bashrc
```

And finally, run:

```
$ echo 'eval "$(rbenv init -)"' >> ~/.bashrc
```

The last (optional) step is to install *ruby-build*:

```
$ git clone https://github.com/sstephenson/ruby-build.git \
  ~/.rbenv/plugins/ruby-build
```

As mentioned when we set up our environment in Chapter 2, *ruby-build* is an rbenv plug-in. It provides the `rbenv install` command needed to compile and install different versions of Ruby on Unix-like systems.

If you want precise control over Ruby version installation, you can use *ruby-build* without rbenv; or, if you just want to stick with the system's Ruby version, you can use rbenv without *ruby-build*.

At this point we will have to install some dependencies that we need to successfully run a Ruby on Rails application. The first step is to update our system packages:

```
$ sudo apt-get update
```

Then we can start installing the needed libraries:

```
$ sudo apt-get install autoconf bison build-essential
$ sudo apt-get install libssl-dev libyaml-dev libreadline6
$ sudo apt-get install libreadline6-dev zlib1g zlib1g-dev
$ sudo apt-get install -y openssl libreadline6-dev git-core
$ sudo apt-get install zlib1g libssl-dev
$ sudo apt-get install -y libyaml-dev libsqlite3-dev sqlite3
$ sudo apt-get install -y libxml2-dev libxslt-dev
$ sudo apt-get install -y autoconf automake libtool bison
$ sudo apt-get install install ruby-dev
```

We are now ready to install Ruby:

```
$ rbenv install 2.1.5
$ rbenv global 2.1.5
```

Please note that this process might take a long time to finish.

With rbenv it is a good practice to run `rehash` after installing every new command-line tool on your machine:

```
$ rbenv rehash
```

This ensures that the new commands are properly shimmed and available in the environment (see "rbenv" on page 17 for details).

At this point we want to tell the Raspberry Pi not to install documentation for any of the gems we require. This option is particularly useful since the Raspberry Pi works with limited processing resources and disk space. We can do this by running the following command:

```
$ echo 'gem: --no-ri --no-rdoc' >> ~/.gemrc
```

Also, Rails needs a JavaScript runtime available. We will install both *ExecJS* and *Node.js*.

ExecJS (*http://bit.ly/execjs*) is a gem that allows you to run JavaScript code from Ruby. It chooses the best runtime available to evaluate your program, then returns the result to you as a Ruby object.

Node.js (*http://nodejs.org*) is a platform built on top of Google Chrome's JavaScript runtime (*http://code.google.com/p/v8/*) that is designed to facilitate the development of scalable, lean network applications in JavaScript. Its event-driven, nonblocking I/O model makes Node.js both lightweight and efficient, ideal for data-intensive real-time applications that run across distributed devices.

To install both of them we will run:

```
$ gem install execjs
$ sudo apt-get install nodejs
```

Now, we can finally install Rails:

```
$ gem install rails
$ rbenv rehash
```

With that done, we can now pull our repository from Git and start to set up our application.

Creating the Raspboard App

The idea here is to create a dashboard that can pull information from different sources and display it in an informative way. To achieve this we will use Dashing (*http://dashing.io/*), a Sinatra-based framework that lets you build dashboards designed to be consumed on a TV screen.

Sinatra is basically a framework like Rails, with a focus on being small, flexible, and minimalistic. Unlike Rails, it does not follow the Model-View-Controller pattern.

Sinatra

Sinatra (*http://www.sinatrarb.com/*) is an alternative to Ruby on Rails that is small, lightweight, and minimalistic. It's a free and open source web application library written in Ruby, dependent on the Rack web server interface. The framework can be used to quickly create web apps in Ruby with minimal effort.

We'll run the dashboard on our Raspberry Pi, and the APIs that we have built up to now in Rails will be used to feed the dashboard.

Dashing can be installed as a gem from the command line:

```
$ gem install dashing
```

Once installed, you can create a new Dashing app as follows:

```
$ dashing new raspboard
```

Then *cd* into your new app directory:

```
$ cd raspboard
```

And bundle:

```
$ bundle
```

To start the Dashing server, just type:

```
$ dashing start
```

Then point your browser at *http://localhost:3030* and enjoy your new board.

A new Dashing project comes with some sample widgets and sample dashboards that you can customize. The directory structure of a Dashing application is as follows:

assets
This folder contains the image and font files, and JavaScript/CoffeeScript libraries. Dashing uses Sprockets for asset packaging.

dashboards
This folder contains one *.erb* file for each dashboard, which contains the layout for the widgets.

jobs
This is where Ruby jobs for fetching data are stored (e.g., for calling third-party APIs like YouTube, Twitter, or our Wikipin application).

lib
This folder holds optional Ruby files.

public

The *public* folder is where you put any static files that your app serves. This is where you would keep the app favicon or a custom 404 page.

widgets

This folder contains all the *.html*, *.css*, and *.coffee* files for individual widgets.

Sprockets

In the words of its creator, Sam Stephenson, "Sprockets is a Ruby library for compiling and serving web assets. It features declarative dependency management for JavaScript and CSS assets, as well as a powerful preprocessor pipeline that allows you to write assets in languages like CoffeeScript, Sass, SCSS, and LESS."

More info on Sprockets can be found at *http://bit.ly/rack-sprockets*.

Our objective in this section is to create a Dashing board and add a weather widget. We will begin by modifying the sample board (you can check out the Dashing demo online (*http://dashingdemo.herokuapp.com/sample*)).

The first step is to create a module that can interact with our Weather API service. We will create it in the *lib/* folder and call it *weather.rb*:

```
require 'net/http'
require 'json'
module Weather
  WEATHER_URL = "http://api.openweathermap.org/data/2.5/weather?"
  def get_weather(lat, lon)
  forecast = {
    forecast: send_request("#{WEATHER_URL}lat=#{lat}&lon=#{lon}")
  }
  end
end
```

To send the request to our weather service we will make use of our `Restful` module from Chapter 8. You can copy it from there (see "Discovering the /lib Directory" on page 121) as it is going to stay the same. We will also use the `Wikipin` module to retrieve our location and eventually places of interest around us. You can copy that from Chapter 8 as well. Rest assured that the complete Raspboard GitHub repository will contain all the libraries used in this project.

Now we need to create a weather job that will fetch the weather information we need. We will create it under the *jobs/* directory and again call it *weather.rb*:

```
# To begin with we include all the modules we need
include Restful
include Weather
include Wikipin
```

```
# Here for simplicity we hardcode a default location.
# In this case these are the coordinates for Barcelona, Spain:
LOCATION = "41.23,2.09"

# The following method finds your location through your IP
def suggestions_by_ip
  if ip == "127.0.0.1"
    get_weather("41.23","2.09")
  else
    block = Walk.request_block(ip).doc["ip_block"]
    if block
      longitude = block["point"].scan(/\((([^\)]+)\))/).last.first.split(" ")[0]
      latitude = block["point"].scan(/\((([^\)]+)\))/).last.first.split(" ")[1]
      make_forecast(latitude, longitude)
    end
  end
end

def make_forecast(latitude, longitude)
  forecast = get_weather(latitude,longitude)
end

# This is the actual scheduler. You do not need to actually
# run it every 1m.

SCHEDULER.every '1m', :first_in => 0 do |job|
  location = LOCATION.split(',')

  if location
    @forecast = make_forecast(location[0],location[1])
  else
    @forecast = suggestions_by_ip
  end

  # Here is where we define the fields in our data object.
  # We will use these later.
  if @forecast
    send_event('weather', {
      name: @forecast[:forecast].doc["name"],
      country: @forecast[:forecast].doc["sys"]["country"],
      coord: @forecast[:forecast].doc["coord"],
      code: @forecast[:forecast].doc["weather"][0]["id"]
    })
  end
```

Once we have created our job we can create our actual widget. This will be composed of three files in the *widgets* folder. We will call this *weather*:

```
widgets/
|  weather/
|  |
|  |  weather.coffee # The JavaScript file handling the events
```

```
|   | weather.html   # The HTML template
|   | weather.scss   # The CSS stylesheet
```

The JavaScript file handling the events is going to be quite simple in this case:

```
class Dashing.Weather extends Dashing.Widget
  ready: ->
  # This is fired when the widget is done being rendered.
  # We do not need to implement this.

  onData: (data) ->
  if data
    # Here is where we use the code from the data object to display
    # a weather icon.
    # One thing you need to do is modify the CSS class so that the
    # weather code returned from the API of your choice will match
    # the weather icon.
    $('i.climacon').attr 'class', "climacon wi wi-night-#{data.code}"
```

Next is the HTML template for the widget:

```
<i class="climacon wi"></i>
<h1 class="name" data-bind="name"></h1>
<h3 class="country" data-bind="country"></h3>
<p class="updated-at" data-bind="updatedAtMessage"></p>
```

And finally the CSS stylesheet, written using Sass:

```
// -------------------------------
// -------------------------------
// Sass declarations
// -------------------------------
//-------------------------------

$background-color: #9c4274;
$title-color: rgba(255, 255, 255, 0.7);
$moreinfo-color: rgba(255, 255, 255, 0.3);
$weather-background: rgba(255, 255, 255, 0.2);

// -------------------------------
// -------------------------------
// Widget-weather styles
// -------------------------------
// -------------------------------
.widget-weather {
  background-color: $weather-background;

  i.wi {
    color: #fff; font-size: 500%;
  }

  .title {
    color: $title-color;
  }
```

```
.more-info {
  color: $moreinfo-color;
}

.updated-at {
  color: rgba(255, 255, 255, 0.7);
}
}
```

We will also include Weather Icons to have a nice weather widget. You can download the set, with CSS included, from *http://bit.ly/weather-icons*.

To use the CSS stylesheet included in Weather Icons, we will have to modify the way it loads external assets, like the actual font files:

```
@font-face {
  font-family: 'weathericons';
  src: url('../assets/weathericons-regular-webfont.eot');
  src: url('../assets/weathericons-regular-webfont.eot?#iefix')
        format('embedded-opentype'),
        url('../assets/weathericons-regular-webfont.woff')
        format('woff'),
        url('../assets/weathericons-regular-webfont.ttf')
        format('truetype'),
        url('../assets/weathericons-regular-webfont.svg
            #weathericons-regular-webfontRg')
        format('svg');
  font-weight: normal;
  font-style: normal;
}
```

With our Dashing app, once our assets are compiled these will be located not in the *fonts* folder, but in the *assets* folder.

You can now start modifying the CSS so that the weather code matches with icons in the Weather Icons set. For example, for a clear day you could use:

```
.wi-day-800:before {
  content: "\f00d";
}
```

Figure 13-3 shows our final result.

It is certainly possible to extend our boards to include more useful information. The GitHub repository already includes a widget suggesting YouTube videos. You can try to integrate the API from the last chapter to suggest Radiohead videos to watch if the weather is bad, or a place to visit otherwise.

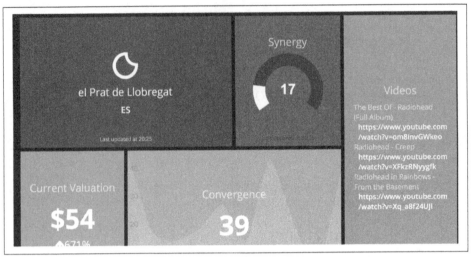

Figure 13-3. The Raspberry Pi dashboard project (final screenshot)

 The Raspboard GitHub repository can be accessed at http://bit.ly/ raspboard.

Wrapping Up

In this chapter we have seen how we can design and develop device-independent applications, and how this approach to software development can be extended to different platforms. In the next chapter we will talk about analytics and how you can monitor and keep control over different data sources in your application.

Data Analytics

Analytics is an often-overlooked aspect of developing applications or services in general. Yet, when you are offering a service or providing a platform for people to interact with, it is extremely important that you know exactly what is happening on it. Who is performing which actions, what calls are being made, which calls are most expensive, which are consuming most of your resources—these are all questions that a solid analytics system will be able to answer, by making data, logs, and events meaningful.

In this chapter we are going to learn how to recognize important events and actions on our platform, identify key metrics, and keep track of them. We will also meet some tools that can be effectively used to easily build your own analytics platform.

Data Comes from Everywhere

Users and applications are constantly generating an enormous amount of data. Once your applications or APIs start living on the Web, or are being consumed by a number of other services or users, you will have to start struggling through logs and user-generated events. The problem with these streams of data is that they are actually extremely valuable at a macro level, but probably difficult to interpret individually.

Think for example of a simple log entry for a timeout. If you spotted it, you could interpret it as a simple warning of a certain error that happens every now and again in your application.

Now imagine that you could easily correlate that timeout message with certain events happening in one or some of your services. You would be able to identify patterns, and perhaps find out that a certain user is accessing expensive methods or performing resource-consuming actions.

Building a strong analytics service will help you:

- Scale your systems and infrastructure where and when this is needed the most.
- Improve overall service availability and maintainability for your infrastructure, applications, and networks.
- Diagnose all your environments from one application.

Being able to rapidly search, filter, and visualize actions and events can significantly reduce the time required for root cause analysis, by providing insights into how your web application is being used and how it performs, so that you can focus your optimization efforts where they are needed.

Tools combining analytics, log management, and event tracking will parse all requests in the application's logs, create events on specific actions, create time series of various important metrics, and also send all the information gathered to a database so you can build up and keep historical data.

There are different services and tools available if you wish to develop an analytics platform. Some of these are open source, and you just need to install them. Others are provided as SaaS solutions that you can easily integrate into your application with an API.

What solution you should adopt depends, as usual, on a number of factors. Your decision would specifically result from how you answer the following questions:

- Can you maintain your analytics platform or would you like to focus only on developing your product?
- Can you maintain the analytics infrastructure (application server), or would you prefer not to worry about this aspect?
- Can you dedicate some time or resources to defining the events you would like to track, or would you prefer to work with a predefined set of events?
- Do you want to keep your event data, or do you not mind hosting it elsewhere?

Once you have decided to either build your own solution or use a framework or third-party service that handles some of the work for you, you can start planning your analytics and reporting architecture.

Monolithic Versus Microapplication Architectures

In a monolithic application all your data will be stored in one database, so to have meaningful insights into that data you will just have to query that database and retrieve the information you need. It is common practice, though, not to run the reporting application out of the same database as the main application. Instead, you duplicate the application database completely, to keep the reporting and the production environment separate (see Figure 14-1).

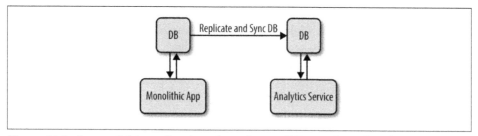

Figure 14-1. A monolithic application where the app DB is replicated in the reporting DB

There are a number of problems that such an architectural choice could bring. Firstly, your reporting application will run on "old" data. Typically the reporting database is updated at certain intervals, so you are never working on real-time data. Secondly, every time the databases need to be completely replicated or even updated, some stress will be generated on both systems. Thirdly, the reporting application might need data to be structured differently than your production environment, so you might end up having to duplicate some of the data, or store all the data plus some other information. You might then start to lose control of the extra data on the reporting database. Imagine when you need to track different events; you might end up without historical data about those events being directly available. In such a situation you might have to run expensive queries on your production database to find the data you actually need and have it available to your reporting service.

There is also a fourth issue that you might easily encounter when creating an external reporting system. If you would like your users to have access to some reporting data, they will have to go through the system. Therefore, you will either have to call it from your main application or have them access your reporting service through a different application. You can already see how this architecture in many ways encourages replication and complexity.

In a microapplication architecture, data is instead stored in a number of different databases and is shared through RESTful APIs. In this environment it makes sense that when an interesting event is triggered, the services or applications concerned make requests to the analytics service themselves.

Therefore, it is not up to the analytics and reporting service to run the queries on each database to pull the data. Each service or application instead "pushes" the data to the analytics service, through REST API calls, whenever an interesting event is triggered.

Interesting events are configured at the single application and service level, but all the statistics and reporting logic remains with the analytics service.

A microapplication approach will also allow you to easily integrate reporting tools and third-party services into your infrastructure through the analytics microservice. The analytics service is itself another application sharing and offering data in the architecture (see Figure 14-2). Therefore, if your users will need to access reporting information or logs, you will just have to map the appropriate API calls. Also, if you are missing historical data, you will not have to stress your entire system: only the application containing the data you need will have to sync with the analytics service.

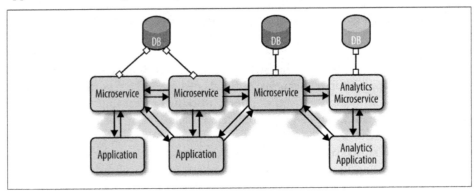

Figure 14-2. A microapplication architecture, where analytics is just another service in the platform

With this approach you can also decide if you would like some events to be sent to your reporting app as they happen. Here is what happens in this case:

1. An event is triggered in an application or service.
2. Data is sent with a REST call.
3. The analytics service processes the event.

Alternatively, the events may be scheduled to be sent at a later time. In this case it is often said that data is *pumped* to the reporting service at regular intervals. The workflow is then:

1. An event is triggered.
2. The event is scheduled to be sent in the next pump.
3. The pump is sent to the analytics service.
4. The analytics service processes the batch of events that it has just received.

In the next sections we are going to see what tools we have available at the moment and how we can configure events in our application.

Monitor, Optimize, and Enhance

Monitoring a system in production can become a complex task when the system is composed of a multitude of small services and applications.

With monolithic applications the ultimate source of errors is always the application itself, but in a microapplication environment any system component could be a source of potential problems; therefore, each microservice and microapplication needs to be monitored.

In addition, in a microservices application several third-party services are probably integrated within the application to solve additional issues. These calls need to be monitored as well.

One of the first objections against a microservices-oriented architecture is that you have to analyze multiple log sources in order to debug an issue. While it is true that microapplications and microservices certainly introduce more complexity when it comes to monitoring, it is also true that since the system is clearly split into logical units performing simple actions, it is possible to clearly understand which actions we need to monitor.

So, while microapplication systems can generate an enormous amount of log data that could easily become unmanageable, with the right tools in place we can easily isolate issues to the microservice or microapp level, without having to debug an entire monolithic application code base.

If we analyzed the architecture of a hypothetical monolithic app, we would find the same components as in a microservices architecture. These components wouldn't be services on their own, but instead would be libraries or classes in the app. Also, some functions in the app could be scattered across several classes, and each of these classes could integrate different libraries. In such a situation, finding the culprit behind a slow call would probably be quite difficult. Of course, each approach has its pros and cons, but it is clear that using efficient statistics and correctly configuring reporting systems will make a microservices architecture easier to debug, by cutting maintenance complexity and isolating issues to a single service.

To understand how a microservices architecture should be monitored, we should think in terms of the single logical units first. Each microservice would ideally correspond to a logical unit, performing a single action.

Let's go back to the Citywalks API. This application integrates two other APIs, the WikiCat API and the Wikipin API (Figure 14-3). In such a scenario, to begin with, we would probably want to monitor that our calls to all the APIs we are integrating are not timing out.

There are a number of indicators of how your Rails application is performing that you should monitor. We will take a look at these in order. In general, there are two simple rules when it comes to monitoring: *if you can measure it you can improve it*, and *if you want to improve it you need to measure it first*.

Application Logs

You can start analyzing a Rails application via its log files. Logs are stored by the Rails server in the */log* directory, where each runtime environment has its separate log file.

Logs monitor application errors and general runtime messages and warnings, depending on your configuration.

Rails uses the standard Ruby logger to log information, but you can substitute another logger if you wish (such as Log4r) by specifying the alternative logger in your *environment.rb* or any environment file:

```
Rails.logger = Logger.new(STDOUT)
Rails.logger = Log4r::Logger.new("Application Log")
```

 Log4r (*http://bit.ly/log4r*) is a logging library for Ruby applications.

When a certain action or error is logged, it gets printed to the corresponding log file (so long as the log level of the message is equal to or higher than the configured log level of the app). By default, each log is created under *Rails.root/log/* and the log file name is *<environment_name>.log*.

The standard Rails logger offers five log levels: :debug, :info, :warn, :error, and :fatal, corresponding to the log level numbers from 0 to 4, respectively. To change the default log level, use:

```
config.log_level = :debug # In any environment initializer, or
Rails.logger.level = 0    # at any time in your code
```

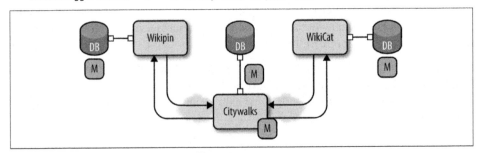

Figure 14-3. Monitoring the Citywalks API

The default Rails log level is `info` in production mode and `debug` in development and test modes.

To write in the current log, use the appropriate `logger.(debug|info|warn|error|fatal)` method from within a controller, model, or mailer:

```
logger.debug "Resource attributes hash: #{@resource.attributes.inspect}"
logger.info "Processing the request..."
logger.fatal "Terminating application, raised unrecoverable error!!!"
```

Adding extra logging messages makes it easy to monitor unexpected or unusual behavior in your application. If you decide to produce extra logging messages, though, be sure to adjust the logging levels accordingly to avoid filling your production logs with noise.

Monitor Request Response Times

By monitoring requests, you can find out which methods are slowing down your application and therefore taking more time to load, among other things. In a microservices architecture composed of multiple services, the question is where you should monitor such metrics.

In microservices architectures it is common, as the number of services grows, to set up a middleware for all your APIs to communicate. A middleware is really like a proxy, where all requests, external and internal, are routed to the appropriate service or application.

We are going to introduce the notion of middleware in the next chapter, where we will also see how to configure an Nginx server for different APIs to communicate. For the moment, we will consider a middleware as a proxy routing all our calls to the various services and applications in our architecture. In a scenario where all calls are routed by a central service (the middleware), a common solution is to monitor call performance on the middleware itself.

There are different solutions to use as middleware, but common choices are Nginx (*http://nginx.org*) and HAProxy (*http://www.haproxy.org/*). Both possess a number of features allowing control over various statistics.

The `ngx_http_status_module` module of Nginx provides access to various status information, including:

- The total number of client connections
- The total number of accepted client connections
- The total number of dropped client connections
- The current number of active client connections
- The current number of idle client connections
- The current time in milliseconds since the epoch

- The total number of client requests
- The current number of client requests

If you are using several virtual servers, you might configure these in *zones*. A zone is a shared memory area where all information common to all servers in that zone—for example, sticky session information—is contained.

For each zone, it makes sense to check the following metrics:

- The number of client requests that are currently being processed
- The total number of client requests received from clients
- The total number of responses sent to clients
- The number of responses with status codes 1xx, 2xx, 3xx, 4xx, and 5xx
- The total number of bytes received from clients
- The total number of bytes sent to clients

In general, a good way to approach configuring response alerts is to understand what kind of baseline traffic your application experiences and trigger events around possible exceptional activities.

A common pattern is triggering an alert if the traffic data collected over a precise interval is significantly higher than expected, indicating a sudden traffic spike, or if the values are suddenly significantly lower, which might be indicating a problem preventing users from reaching your app.

Once you start having consistent information, you can benchmark your server to identify the traffic levels that start to slow down the server and the levels that make the server completely overloaded and therefore unusable. These values will also serve as a good upper limit that you can use to trigger customized alert and warning messages.

Monitor Processes

As part of your deployment process you should also keep your server processes and tasks running smoothly, without consuming too many resources.

There has been a long-running discussion in the Rails community about how Ruby on Rails does multithreading, how efficient this is (or isn't), and whether it consumes too many of our server resources.

Consider two Ruby threads: thread A is waiting and does not need to use the CPU, while thread B is waiting but does need to use the CPU. Ruby specifically switches to another thread when it needs to block for I/O. That is, whenever a Ruby thread needs to wait and it is not using the CPU, like with thread A, Ruby allows for another waiting thread to take over the CPU—so in this case, thread B takes over the CPU, while A waits.

This means that in the unlikely situation that one of your web requests uses the CPU for 30% of the time and waits for I/O the rest of the time, you can ideally serve three requests in parallel, almost maximizing usage of your CPU resources. Figure 14-4 illustrates this scenario.

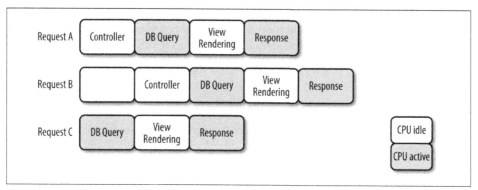

Figure 14-4. Simple multithreading in Ruby

Nevertheless, you might consider using a monitoring framework to monitor your server's performance.

God (*http://godrb.com/*) is a monitoring framework completely written in Ruby. God performs actions such as keeping processes up or restarting processes when resource utilization exceeds your desired specifications. It is possible to configure many different kinds of conditions to have your processes restarted when memory or CPU usage is too high, when disk usage is above a threshold, when a process returns an HTTP error code on a specific URL, and more.

In addition, you can write your own custom conditions and use them in your configuration files. And because the config file is written in actual Ruby code, you can use Ruby language syntax to define conditions in your configuration, thus eliminating duplication. Many different lifecycle controls are available, alongside a sophisticated and extensible notification system.

To understand how God works, let's imagine writing a simple process:

```
loop do
  puts 'Hello'
  sleep 1
end
```

Let's save it as *server.rb*.

Now we can write a God config file to monitor our process. We'll call it *monitor.god*:

```
God.watch do |w|
  w.name = "god-monitor"
  w.start = "ruby /full/path/to/server.rb"
```

```
      w.keepalive
    end
```

This is the bare minimum God configuration, declaring a `God.watch` block (a *watch* represents a process that you want to watch and control). At minimum, for each watch you must provide a unique name and a command that tells God how to start the process. The `keepalive` declaration tells God to keep the process alive. If it's not running when God starts, it will be started, and if it dies it will be restarted.

For more configuration possibilities, see the God website (*http://godrb.com/*).

Threads (in Ruby): Enough Already

Although it's now a bit old, I recommend this great blog post from Yehuda Katz (*http://bit.ly/katz-threads*) about threads in Ruby.

Monitor Your Server Diagnostics

Monitoring a server is about making sure that the system is healthy. This applies for your web server, your middleware server, and your database server.

Depending on the configuration and the tasks the server executes, there are a number of metrics that may need to be monitored. Memory usage and access to I/O are only some of these. You might also want to monitor average CPU utilization across all CPUs or cores, as well as on a per-CPU or per-core basis. You can set alerts to let you know when CPU utilization reaches a certain level or when your application is overloading your server memory. You might also want to keep control of how many times the server was unavailable or has restarted in the last time interval.

A list of common metrics to monitor includes:

- Uptime
- Active users
- Server time
- Average CPU usage
- Memory usage
- Resource usage

Let's look at each of these in turn. The `uptime` command:

```
$ uptime
```

gives a one-line display indicating the current time, how long the system has been running, how many users are currently logged on, and the system load averages for the past 1, 5, and 15 minutes.

You can see which users are currently running processes on your system by running the following:

```
$ ps aux | awk '{ print $1 }' | sed '1 d' | sort | uniq
```

This uses the ps command, with a few filters: we get rid of everything except the first column of output (the usernames), remove the header, sort the output, and eliminate duplicate lines, displaying only the users list.

You could also filter out all system users and only show the names of regular users (and/or the root user) with active processes:

```
$ ps aux | awk '{ print $1 }' | sed '1 d' | sort |
  uniq | perl -e 'for (<>) { chomp; $u = ( getpwnam($_) )[2];
  print $_, "\n" if ( ( $u >= 1000 || $u == 0 ) &&
  ( $_ =~ /[[:alpha:]]/ && $_ ne "nobody" ) ) }'
```

This would probably output just your system name and the root user.

To see the server's local time and date, use:

```
$ date
```

What if you would like to know the number of CPUs available in your system? You can check it on your instance by running the following command:

```
$ grep processor /proc/cpuinfo | wc -l
```

To see how much memory your server is using you can use the free command, which displays RAM details in *nix machines:

```
$ free

        total      used       free     shared    buffers    cached
Mem:   7513644    7115076     398568    52424     381372    1134788
-/+ buffers/cache:     5598916    1914728
Swap:  50331640   6500400    43831240
```

The first line gives details about memory: total RAM, used RAM, free RAM, shared RAM, RAM used for buffers, and RAM used for caching content. Line 2 indicates the actual total RAM used (including by buffers and the cache) and actual total RAM available, while line 3 indicates the total swap memory available as well as how much is used and how much is free.

Resources usage

Using the top command you can get an overview in real time of which processes are using most of the system resources on your server:

```
$ top
```

Figure 14-5 shows some sample output.

```
top - 06:02:08 up 32 days, 21:03,  0 users,  load average: 8.98, 6.93, 5.63
Tasks:  19 total,   1 running,  18 sleeping,   0 stopped,   0 zombie
Cpu(s): 47.7%us, 51.4%sy,  0.2%ni,  0.0%id,  0.2%wa,  0.0%hi,  0.5%si,  0.0%st
Mem:   7513644k total,  7444516k used,    69128k free,   269700k buffers
Swap: 50331640k total,  6542868k used, 43788772k free,  1126472k cached

  PID USER      PR  NI  VIRT  RES  SHR S %CPU %MEM    TIME+  COMMAND
112850 1925     20   0 12808 1108  872 R  1.3  0.0   0:01.00 top
 23353 1925     20   0  196m 1404 1332 S  0.0  0.0   0:02.54 postgres
 23354 1925     20   0  127m 1660 1236 S  0.0  0.0   0:13.69 logshifter
 23371 1925     20   0  196m  552  492 S  0.0  0.0   0:00.67 postgres
 23372 1925     20   0  196m  584  520 S  0.0  0.0   0:35.77 postgres
 23373 1925     20   0  196m  504  456 S  0.0  0.0   0:33.49 postgres
 25839 1925     20   0  105m 2128 2064 S  0.0  0.0   2:43.47 httpd
 25840 1925     20   0  255m 1696 1236 S  0.0  0.0   0:14.28 logshifter
 25872 1925     20   0  4076  368  344 S  0.0  0.0   0:00.00 tee
 25873 1925     20   0  4076  372  344 S  0.0  0.0   0:00.13 tee
 25874 1925     20   0  206m 1184 1108 S  0.0  0.0   0:00.12 PassengerWatchd
 25877 1925     20   0  815m 2356 1904 S  0.0  0.0  73:03.67 PassengerHelper
 25882 1925     20   0  207m 1320 1280 S  0.0  0.0   0:08.23 PassengerLoggin
112206 1925     20   0  102m 2784  828 S  0.0  0.0   0:00.01 sshd
112252 1925     20   0  104m 2220 1456 S  0.0  0.0   0:00.31 bash
142705 1925     20   0  480m  23m 5320 S  0.0  0.3   0:04.71 ruby
295017 1925     20   0  197m 5092 3664 S  0.0  0.1   0:00.02 postgres
369026 1925     20   0  105m 1808 1236 S  0.0  0.0   0:02.30 httpd
446632 1925     20   0  105m 1840 1268 S  0.0  0.0   0:01.50 httpd
```

Figure 14-5. System statistics with top

The first line of *top* output gives the load and uptime values, followed by the number of users and the load average. The next lines summarize the task list (which will depend on what operations your server is performing at the moment), the load on the CPUs, and memory and disk swap statistics.

In *top* you can also customize the output in order to filter the processes. If you type n and then the number of processes you want to look at—for example, 5—you will see only the top 5 processes.

If you press Shift-M (for "memory"), you can order the processes by memory consumption.

If you want to check the CPU usage—more specifically, what processes are using the CPU and how much—you proceed by choosing which field (column) to study by pressing Shift-O (the letter O, not the number 0). To concentrate on CPU usage, press k—note in Figure 14-6 how the asterisk (*) moves next to the "k: %CPU" row, indicating the CPU field has been selected—and then press Enter.

Return to the processes page, and you will see that the %CPU column is the ordered field. From the interface page (Shift-O) you can choose to monitor different metrics to know exactly what is happening on your server. Also, as *top* by default automatically updates every 3 seconds, it gives a real-time overview of the status of your server.

```
Current Sort Field:  K   for window 1:Def
Select sort field via field letter, type any other key to return []

    a: PID     = Process Id                              strict ASCII collating sequence.
    b: PPID    = Parent Process Pid                      (shame on you if WCHAN is chosen)
    c: RUSER   = Real user name
    d: UID     = User Id
    e: USER    = User Name
    f: GROUP   = Group Name
    g: TTY     = Controlling Tty
    h: PR      = Priority
    i: NI      = Nice value
    j: P       = Last used cpu (SMP)
  * K: %CPU    = CPU usage
    l: TIME    = CPU Time
    m: TIME+   = CPU Time, hundredths
    n: %MEM    = Memory usage (RES)
    o: VIRT    = Virtual Image (kb)
    p: SWAP    = Swapped size (kb)
    q: RES     = Resident size (kb)
    r: CODE    = Code size (kb)
    s: DATA    = Data+Stack size (kb)
    t: SHR     = Shared Mem size (kb)
    u: nFLT    = Page Fault count
    v: nDRT    = Dirty Pages count
    w: S       = Process Status
    x: COMMAND = Command name/line
    y: WCHAN   = Sleeping in Function
    z: Flags   = Task Flags <sched.h>

  Note1:
    If a selected sort field can't be
    shown due to screen width or your
    field order, the '<' and '>' keys
    will be unavailable until a field
    within viewable range is chosen.

  Note2:
    Field sorting uses internal values,
    not those in column display.  Thus,
    the TTY & WCHAN fields will violate
```

Figure 14-6. The top settings interface shows what processes are available for inspection; the columns show a letter, the column code, and a summary of that code

Comprehensive Monitoring Solutions

There are different comprehensive monitoring solutions that you might consider integrating into your Rails application. A monitoring application usually takes the results of whatever checks, scripts, and programs that you might have put in place and run across your systems and, when certain conditions are met, passes the information across, sends alert messages, or just updates some values, depending on your configuration.

The solution that I am going to introduce is *Sensu*, an open source monitoring framework available at *http://sensuapp.org*.

 Sensu is a monitoring framework that aims to be "simple, malleable, and scalable." It is released under the MIT license and its core repository is available on GitHub (*https://github.com/sensu/sensu*).

Sensu uses *checks* to monitor services or measure the status of resources. Checks are basically scripts executed on servers running the Sensu client. These scripts output data to STDOUT or STDERR and produce an exit status code to indicate a state (0 for OK, 1 for WARNING, 2 for CRITICAL, 3 or greater for UNKNOWN or CUSTOM).

Sensu uses *handlers* for taking action on event data. Handlers are scripts that perform actions like sending email or SMS messages, generating alerts, or adding metrics to external stores like Graphite.

Sensu is written in Ruby using EventMachine (*http://bit.ly/event-machine*), an event-processing library for Ruby, and can be easily configured in JSON. It has great test coverage with continuous integration via Travis CI (*http://bit.ly/travis-ci-github*) and it was designed with a message-oriented architecture, using RabbitMQ (*http://www.rabbitmq.com/*) and JSON payloads.

Service Applications for Monitoring Ruby on Rails Apps

I have introduced Sensu because it is an open source framework that is also written in Ruby. Of course, there are different commercial options on the market that you might consider:

- New Relic (*http://newrelic.com/*) is a platform for data analytics that delivers much more than just application performance.
- Skylight (*https://www.skylight.io/*) is a profiler specifically for Ruby on Rails applications, written in Rails and Ember.
- Airbrake (*https://airbrake.io/*) instead helps you monitor errors and exceptions.

Actions and Events

There is a subtle relationship between data and events. Generally speaking an event is a data point resulting from something that has simply happened, and where different information has been recorded. An event can be the result of a user action, or of a state change in your system.

Events are a unifying paradigm crossing different fields of study, and how you define events in your service will inherently depend on the kind of problem that your business or application is trying to solve.

Events that we will consider valuable to record are those that we are interested in. Other types of events still occur, but we may decide to ignore them.

Doing Data Science

Data science, or more generally simply reasoning about data, can really make a difference in a number of situations. To get started with data science you don't need to have a degree in statistics, but some learning and research might be required, especially at the beginning. Lectures from the Harvard Extension School's Data Science class (CS109) (*http://bit.ly/harvard-cs109*) are freely available online and are a good starting point.

Imagine that you have deployed an application suggesting videos based on certain information about the user. Imagine now that you also wish to offer the user an interesting new video every time she logs in.

In order to recommend something that your users will find interesting, though, you have to *learn* something about them. This is usually accomplished by creating a system that is able to collect users' preferences and then make some predictions based on those preferences. For example, if a user has shown interest in basketball, it is likely that he might enjoy a video like "Best game winner in NBA history." The resulting predictions can be used for a variety of services, from search engines to resource suggestions and targeted advertising. The system's functionality thus relies on users implicitly or explicitly revealing their activity and personal preferences, which are ultimately used to generate personalized recommendations.

In order to create profiles of your users' activities, you might start to collect different information. The kind of information that you might be interested in includes not only what videos they have actually watched, but also if they have decided to watch certain videos again, what time of the day they are most likely to log in at, and which days of the week they are most likely to share videos.

As you start considering which events to store and to analyze, you might find out more about the users of your platform. For example, you might notice that some of your users are more likely to watch a video from the beginning to the end, while others will tend to skip part of it or even close it before it has finished. Some users are more likely to share on other platforms what they have watched, while others will just ignore the platform recommendations.

As you start analyzing raw event data, you might start to ask yourself some questions:

- What patterns can you isolate about events in your platform or your users' behavior?
- What is the average activity on your platform? What does this look like?
- What raw information can you translate into a predictive model?
- What raw information can be used to create useful metrics about your platform?

As you start asking yourself questions about your data, you will be able to create more meaningful data points that correspond to particular actions happening on your platform, and display aggregated data about these actions.

In our example scenario, users would be presented with a video that had been recommended to them. They could watch the video, share it, or just skip it by moving to the next video.

Each user can therefore perform three possible actions:

- Watch
- Share
- Skip

The three actions do not need to be exclusive. This means every combination of the three actions is possible in our app. Users can watch a video, then share it, then skip it and move on to the next video. They can also share it without watching it, or watch it for a while and then skip it, and so on.

Each action can also be analyzed from different points of view. For example, we can count how many videos were watched or shared in a certain time frame, or how many users skipped a certain video.

Once you start aggregating data, you will discover what metrics make the most sense for your platform. But once again, as you start counting and measuring you will start asking yourself some new questions:

- If you are measuring the number of videos watched, are you counting unique views or total number of views?
- If you are measuring the number of shares, are you counting the number of videos that were shared or the total number of sharing actions performed?
- What time ranges are you choosing for your aggregated metrics? Why?
- Are your metrics localized on your time zone or on the user's time zone?
- What models, algorithms, and analyses should you consider and implement?

How you answer all these questions depends on a number of factors that are mostly dictated by your application problem and real-world context.

Plotting Data

There are different solutions available nowadays for visual time series analysis and plotting of statistical data.

We will concentrate on importing and plotting data with *Graphite* (*http://graphite.wikidot.com/*), a monitoring solution originally developed by Chris Davis at Orbitz back in 2006. Graphite is released under the open source Apache 2.0 license and its source is available on GitHub (*https://github.com/graphite-project*). Documentation is available online (*http://bit.ly/graphite-docs*).

Graphite was designed to run on cheap hardware and do two main things: store numeric time-series data and render graphs of this data on demand. It consists of three software components: Carbon, a set of daemons that make up the storage backend; Whisper, a simple database library for storing time-series data; and the Graphite web app (*graphite-web*), a Django app that renders graphs on demand using Cairo.

The component responsible for receiving data into Graphite is Carbon. All Carbon daemons listen for and accept time-series data over a set of common protocols, but they do different things with that data once they have received it. There are three kinds of Carbon daemons in Graphite: *carbon-cache, carbon-relay,* and *carbon-aggregator.*

In a simple installation, only the *carbon-cache* daemon is typically used. *carbon-cache* accepts and writes metrics to disk. Metric values are first cached into RAM as they are received, and then flushed to disk at intervals using the underlying Whisper library.

As traffic increases, one *carbon-cache* instance may not be able to handle the load. In this case multiple *carbon-cache* instances can be run behind a *carbon-aggregator* or a *carbon-relay*, possibly on multiple machines.

The *carbon-relay* daemon has two roles: replication and sharding. If run with `RELAY_METHOD = rules`, a *carbon-relay* instance can run as a *carbon-cache* server and relay all incoming metrics to multiple backend *carbon-cache* daemons running on different ports or hosts. If run with `RELAY_METHOD = onsistent-hashing` instead, you can use a `DESTINATIONS` setting to define a sharding strategy to spread reads across multiple *carbon-cache* backends.

Finally, a *carbon-aggregator* daemon can be run in front of a *carbon-cache* instance in order to buffer metrics over time before reporting them in Whisper. This reduces the I/O load, and is useful when granular reporting is not required.

 For further details on Carbon daemon configuration, see the Graphite documentation (*http://bit.ly/carbon-daemons*).

Feeding your data

To feed data into Graphite, we have three main methods available: plain text, Pickle, and the Advanced Message Queuing Protocol (AMQP).

The plain text protocol is the most straightforward option. Data must be formatted as *<metric path> <metric value> <metric timestamp>*. Carbon will then translate each line of text into a metric that Whisper and the web app understand.

The Pickle protocol supports sending batches of metrics to Carbon in one go, by formatting data into a list of multilevel tuples:

```
[(path, (timestamp, value)), ...]
```

The last option is AMQP, an open standard used for passing messages between applications or organizations. In order to use AMQP with Graphite, when AMQP_METRIC_NAME_IN_BODY is set to True in your *carbon.conf* file, the data should be in the same format as with the plain text protocol. When AMQP_METRIC_NAME_IN_BODY is set to False instead, you should omit the *<metric path>* component.

> Carbon's config files are all located in */opt/graphite/conf/*. For a fresh Graphite installation, none of the *.conf* files will exist yet; you will instead find a *.conf.example* file for each one. You can simply copy the example files, removing the *.example* extension, and customize your settings.
>
> The main Carbon configuration file is *carbon.conf*. This defines the settings for each Carbon daemon (the settings are documented by comments within the file itself). For more information on this and the other config files available, see the documentation (*http://bit.ly/carbon-config*).
>
> The documentation (*http://bit.ly/graphite-feeding*) also provides further details on the protocols you can use for sending data to Graphite.

All data stored in Graphite has a path with components delimited by dots. Therefore, before sending your data into Graphite you need to decide on a naming scheme and data hierarchy. For example, for our Walks application, *citywalks.walks.london* would represent the number of walks created for the city of London by our Citywalks API.

If you have already planned ahead which time series to feed into Graphite and what these mean, it should be easy to define a clear data hierarchy.

> If you'd like to learn more about using Graphite to store and render time-series data, Matt Aimonetti has written a great blog post on the topic; check out his "Practical Guide to StatsD/Graphite Monitoring" (*http://bit.ly/aimonetti-statsd*).

Another aspect to consider is that Graphite is built on a fixed-size database: *Whisper*. Therefore, you have to create the right configuration beforehand, depending on how much data you intend to store and at what level of precision.

Whisper is similar in design to a round-robin database (RRD), like that used by RRDtool (*http://bit.ly/rrdtool*). An RRD stores time-series data in a circular buffer, which allows you to keep the system storage footprint constant over time.

A circular buffer is a particular data structure. To understand how it works, imagine a buffer where the beginning is connected to the end. A structure like this is particularly suited for data stream buffering.

The precision of your data defines the time interval between two consecutive data points. If you store your data with one-second precision, it means you will have one data point for each second.

The storage cost is determined by the number of data points you want to store; the finer your precision, the more data points you will store in memory.

Graphite's documentation (*http://bit.ly/data-into-graphite*) provides a set of questions to help you determine the best retention configuration for your needs:

1. How often can you produce your data?
2. What is the finest precision you will require?
3. How far back will you need to look at that level of precision?
4. What is the coarsest precision you can use?
5. How far back would you ever need to see data?

Data points are stored on-disk by Whisper as big-endian double-precision floats. Each value is paired with its timestamp, in seconds since the Unix epoch (01-01-1970).

Each Whisper database contains one or more *archives*. Each archive has a specific data resolution and retention policy, which is defined in number of data points or maximum timestamp age. The ordering of archives goes from highest resolution and shortest retention period to lowest resolution and longest retention period.

The archive with the longest retention period determines the total retention time of the database, as the time periods covered by the archives overlap. That is, a pair of archives with retention periods of 2 months and 12 months will provide only 12 months of storage—the length of its longest archive—and not 14 months.

This latest policy is one of the reasons why Whisper is somewhat inefficient in its usage of disk space: when a data point is written, Whisper stores the same data in all archives at once. Each archive will store that data point until its retention period is exceeded. To avoid too much duplication, lower-resolution archives should be configured to have significantly lower resolution and higher retention intervals than their higher-resolution counterparts.

As noted, Whisper also stores each data point with its timestamp, rather than inferring a timestamp from the data point's position in the archive. The reason behind this design choice is that timestamps are used during data retrieval to check the validity of each data point: if a timestamp does not match the expected value for its position relative to the beginning of the requested series, the data point is considered out of date and a null value is returned instead.

When Carbon receives some data, it determines where on the filesystem the Whisper data file is located for each metric. If the data file does not exist, Carbon creates it. At this point Carbon needs some parameters, which it retrieves from the schemas file (which you create by creating/editing *opt/graphite/storage-schemas.conf*). In order of priority, from the highest to the lowest, Carbon looks for the first schema whose pattern matches the metric name. If no match is found, the default schema is used: two hours of minutely data. When the appropriate schema is determined, Carbon uses the retention configuration for the schema to create the Whisper data file appropriately.

Once you have completed the configuration steps, you are ready to start sending data into Carbon and visualizing that data in Graphite. There is much more that you will be able to do with Graphite in terms of monitoring and visualization, but that doesn't fall within the scope of this book. If you are interested in the topic, you should check out the quickstart guide (*http://bit.ly/graphite-quickstart*) on Graphite.

Wrapping Up

In this chapter we learned about data analytics and how to manage different data sources in our applications or API platforms. In the next chapter we will see how we can scale Rails applications gracefully.

Scaling Gracefully

Scaling has always been a controversial issue for Rails applications, yet there are many examples of apps that have been able to scale successfully. The key is always being able to identify bottlenecks and distribute the load across different services to handle different tasks efficiently. In this chapter, we are going to see how we can break down the complex task of scaling an application, and how this doesn't simply mean scaling a specific framework (in this case, Rails). We are going to introduce the concept of middleware and see how we can use it to distribute the load across the different server instances and APIs that we are going to use, in order to scale horizontally. We will take a look at Nginx and the Lua programming language to see how these can be used to create a front-facing HTTP server and load balancer for our APIs.

Scaling Rails

As mentioned, scaling is a controversial issue in Rails. But let's tackle this issue with the appropriate preparation.

First of all, there are a couple of concepts about scaling that we should have clear. Scaling a service isn't just about the framework used to code the service functions. It is about the architecture, the databases, how you use caching, how events are queued, disk I/O, content distribution networks, and a variety of other things.

So to answer the question "Does Rails scale?" as straightforwardly as possible, the response is definitely "Yes!"

Furthermore, to comment on that question, Rails is among the most efficient frameworks available right now to quickly build an application—so you shouldn't worry about the scalability of the framework you are using, but actually design your architecture for scalability independently of Rails.

Deploying an application can technically mean a range of different things, and the processes involved might take place at very different levels. Rails can in fact be deployed with different servers, and the deployment process can be automated using different tools.

If we were to consider a very simple scalable application, we would identify the following two levels in our service architecture:

- Application server (Unicorn, Puma)
- Front-facing HTTP server/load balancer (Nginx)

There are different application servers that can be used for Rails, but I have mentioned Unicorn and Puma specifically. Both Unicorn and Puma are designed for running Rack applications only. Rack is a middleware providing a minimal interface between web servers that support Ruby and Ruby frameworks. Rack considers an application to be any object that responds to the `call` method, which takes the environment hash as a parameter and returns an array with three elements:

- The HTTP response code
- A hash of headers
- The response body, which must respond to `each`

The array is passed from the web server to the app, and the response is sent back to the server.

Unicorn (*http://unicorn.bogomips.org/*) is a very mature web application server for Ruby, "designed to only serve fast clients on low-latency, high-bandwidth connections and take advantage of features in Unix/Unix-like kernels." Specifically, processes are used in Unicorn to handle multiple requests concurrently, while the operating system kernel takes care of performing load balancing. It is a fully featured server, but by design Unicorn is principally and only a web application server. It uses forked processes to allow Rails applications to handle multiple requests concurrently.

Puma (*http://puma.io/*) is a web server built specifically for Ruby and based on Mongrel, designed with speed and parallelism in mind. It is described as "a small library that provides a very fast and concurrent HTTP 1.1 server for Ruby web applications." Puma has several working modes: you can set the minimum and maximum number of threads it can use to do its job, but it can also work in a clustered mode whereby you can use forked processes to handle requests concurrently.

Depending on your service requirements, you could choose to use either Puma or Unicorn.

Past the application server we find the HTTP server. We will now focus on preparing a production environment and configuring an HTTP server, using Nginx (*http://wiki.nginx.org/Main*) as our example. With Nginx, either Unicorn, Puma, or another web app server can be used.

There are many reasons behind the choice of Nginx over another HTTP server, such as Apache. Notably, Nginx is usually faster than Apache, and quicker to set up and configure. The Nginx HTTP server has been designed from the ground up to act as a multipurpose, front-facing web server. In addition to serving static files (e.g., images, text files, etc.), it can balance connections and deal with some exploit attempts. It acts as the first entry point for all requests, distributing them to web application servers for processing.

We will use Nginx as a middleware enabling our different APIs to communicate. This will allow us to eventually distribute the traffic to all our endpoints. More generally, Nginx can act as a proxy and load balancer, helping integrate different APIs into a product or service, or even allowing you to wrap different API requests in code snippets written in a language similar to JavaScript.

So, the scaling of our Rails app can be split into different subtasks:

1. Preparing, maintaining, and deploying the Rails application servers
2. Preparing the Nginx-based front-facing server with the load balancer and the reverse proxy to distribute the load across the Rails application servers
3. Scaling the storage options and databases
4. Scaling the infrastructure hardware (if you actually own this)

As you can see, scaling a Rails application involves much more than just scaling the Rails framework. On the contrary, you are scaling a whole set of different services.

In general terms, there are two main scaling strategies:

- Horizontal scaling
- Vertical scaling

Scaling horizontally means you are adding more servers, while when you are scaling vertically you are altering and tweaking a server's resources, for example by increasing its size or adding more memory to it. A reasonable scaling strategy often involves scaling both vertically (up) and horizontally (out). To scale horizontally you will have to add a middleware to route traffic to your different servers according to a set of defined rules. We are going to see how this is accomplished in the next sections.

Using Processes Efficiently

A problem with scaling is managing the background workers and jobs that an application needs to handle and schedule. Foreman is a tool that can be used to configure the various processes that your application needs to run, using a *Procfile*.

More information about Foreman can be found at David Dollar's blog (*http://bit.ly/intro-foreman*).

Creating a Middleware for Different APIs to Communicate

To understand what an API middleware is, we need to borrow some concepts from the field of distributed systems. After all, web applications using different APIs to communicate are de facto distributed systems.

The simplest definition of a middleware is that of *a component that lies in between two systems*. If you think of a client/server application, the middleware is the *slash* between the client and the server, or in other words the component making the communication between the two possible.

There are different advantages to using such a solution when dealing with and integrating APIs. First of all, a middleware really facilitates the development of distributed systems by accommodating the heterogeneity of the different parts (in our case, the different APIs). It does this by hiding the individual details of the single services and providing a set of common and domain-specific endpoints.

The different services and applications in our architecture will communicate directly with the middleware, and this will be responsible for distributing the traffic to our different APIs according to the methods and the resources requested.

It follows that when an API changes, you do not have to modify all the applications and services that use that API. You just have to apply the change in the middleware, modifying the logic that handles the new calls and methods; all the different applications can keep calling the same methods they were using before.

Another advantage of using a middleware is that you will be able to monitor how your applications are using the different APIs from a single point in your architecture. You will have a clear picture of the traffic load on each component, since all the calls and requests will go through the middleware. This means you will not have to develop and maintain different analytic solutions on a per-service basis.

Within RESTful applications the middleware can also function as a REST connector with non-RESTful components. These could be legacy services or even external services that are being integrated into your architecture, like WebSockets or streaming services.

Configuring a Reverse Proxy with Nginx

In this section we are going to set up Nginx on OpenShift, so we can start using it with our APIs.

To create an OpenShift application, you can use the client tools that you installed in Chapter 10. We'll name the application *nginx* and use the "do-it-yourself" cartridge type, *diy-0.1*:

```
$ rhc app create nginx diy-0.1
```

We can then show the newly created application's information:

```
$ rhc app show -a nginx
```

When you go to your application page in OpenShift, on the righthand side you will find a Remote Access section. You will have to copy the ssh command shown there to open a secure shell session to your application. The command will look something like this:

```
$ ssh <random-strings>@nginx-<your-namespace>.rhcloud.com
```

 OpenShift offers a whole set of environment variables that you can use to configure your application to run properly. You can check them all out at the OpenShift website (*http://bit.ly/env-variables*).

You can now proceed to install Nginx. Navigate to the *tmp* directory and download the Nginx source files:

```
$ cd $OPENSHIFT_TMP_DIR
$ wget http://nginx.org/download/nginx-1.7.8.tar.gz
$ tar zxf nginx-1.7.8.tar.gz
$ cd nginx-1.7.8
```

You may need to install some libraries from source. If you run:

```
$ ./configure --prefix=$OPENSHIFT_DATA_DIR
```

you will get the following errors:

```
checking for PCRE library ... not found
checking for PCRE library in /usr/local/ ... not found
checking for PCRE library in /usr/include/pcre/ ... not found
checking for PCRE library in /usr/pkg/ ... not found
checking for PCRE library in /opt/local/ ... not found
./configure: error: the HTTP rewrite module requires the PCRE
library.
You can either disable the module by using
--without-http_rewrite_module option, or  install the PCRE library
```

```
into the system, or build the PCRE library statically from the
source with Nginx by using --with-pcre=<path> option.
```

Since we cannot install the PCRE library into the system, we have to build it from
source directly:

```
$ cd $OPENSHIFT_TMP_DIR
$ wget ftp://ftp.csx.cam.ac.uk/pub/software/programming/
  pcre/pcre-8.36.tar.bz2
$ tar jxf pcre-8.36.tar.bz2
```

We have now the possibility to modify the makefile to suit our needs. When configuring the makefile, we can enable a list of standard and optional HTTP modules that
are supported by Nginx. The full list can be found in the Nginx documenation (*http://
bit.ly/nginx-modules*). We will keep the defaults for now and just run the configure
command:

```
$ cd nginx-1.7.8
$ ./configure --prefix=$OPENSHIFT_DATA_DIR
  --with-pcre=$OPENSHIFT_TMP_DIR/pcre-8.36
```

If the configuration runs successfully you should see the following output:

```
Configuration summary
  + using PCRE library: /tmp//pcre-8.36
  + OpenSSL library is not used
  + md5: using system crypto library
  + sha1: using system crypto library
  + using system zlib library
nginx path prefix: "/var/lib/stickshift/
    c45cdc9a27944dc5b1cd7cb9e5c9f8c7/nginx/runtime/"
nginx binary file: "/var/lib/stickshift/
    c45cdc9a27944dc5b1cd7cb9e5c9f8c7/nginx/runtime//sbin/nginx"
nginx configuration prefix: "/var/lib/stickshift/
    c45cdc9a27944dc5b1cd7cb9e5c9f8c7/nginx/runtime//conf"
nginx configuration file: "/var/lib/stickshift/
    c45cdc9a27944dc5b1cd7cb9e5c9f8c7/nginx/runtime//
    conf/nginx.conf"
nginx pid file: "/var/lib/stickshift/
    c45cdc9a27944dc5b1cd7cb9e5c9f8c7/nginx/runtime//
    logs/nginx.pid"
nginx error log file: "/var/lib/stickshift/
    c45cdc9a27944dc5b1cd7cb9e5c9f8c7/nginx/runtime//
    logs/error.log"
nginx http access log file: "/var/lib/stickshift/
    c45cdc9a27944dc5b1cd7cb9e5c9f8c7/nginx/runtime//
    logs/access.log"
nginx http client request body temporary files: "client_body_temp"
nginx http proxy temporary files: "proxy_temp"
nginx http fastcgi temporary files: "fastcgi_temp"
nginx http uwsgi temporary files: "uwsgi_temp"
nginx http scgi temporary files: "scgi_temp"
```

This information will be needed to configure Nginx. Now we can compile and install:

```
$ make install
```

Once the installation has finished, you can navigate to *$OPENSHIFT_DATA_DIR*, where your Nginx is installed.

OpenShift currently allows one internal IP address and port for your application; these are available through the *$OPENSHIFT_DIY_IP* and *$OPENSHIFT_DIY_PORT* environment variables. These values may change, so you will want to include these environment variables directly in the *nginx.conf* file by using the env directive. Please note that these env variables can only be referred to in the main block of the config, not the http, server, or location blocks.

Let's then edit the Nginx configuration file:

```
$ nano $OPENSHIFT_DATA_DIR/conf/nginx.conf
```

Change the listen value to:

```
http {
    ...
    server {
        listen          $OPENSHIFT_IP:$OPENSHIFT_PORT;
        server_name     localhost;
        ...
    }
    ...
}
```

Then copy the modified configuration file:

```
$ mv $OPENSHIFT_DATA_DIR/conf/nginx.conf \
  $OPENSHIFT_DATA_DIR/conf/nginx.conf.template
```

We have just bound the internal IP address and port in the Nginx configuration dynamically. We now need to modify the *$OPENSHIFT_<cartridge-name>_IP* and *$OPENSHIFT_<cartridge-name>_PORT* values when the *start* action hook is called.

To start up your application automatically, you'll need to edit the local *.openshift/action_hooks/start* file, adding ${OPENSHIFT_RUNTIME_DIR}/nginx/sbin/nginx. Exit from your *ssh* session. Then run these commands on your machine:

```
$ cd nginx
$ nano .openshift/action_hooks/start

#!/bin/bash
# The logic to start up your application should be put in this
# script. The application will work only if it binds to
# $OPENSHIFT_DIY_IP:8080
# nohup $OPENSHIFT_REPO_DIR/diy/testrubyserver.rb
# $OPENSHIFT_DIY_IP $OPENSHIFT_REPO_DIR/diy |
# & /usr/bin/logshifter -tag diy &
```

```
#
sed -e "s/`echo '$OPENSHIFT_IP:$OPENSHIFT_PORT'`/`
echo $OPENSHIFT_DIY_IP:$OPENSHIFT_DIY_PORT`/"
$OPENSHIFT_DATA_DIR/conf/nginx.conf.template >
$OPENSHIFT_DATA_DIR/conf/nginx.conf
nohup $OPENSHIFT_DATA_DIR/sbin/nginx >
$OPENSHIFT_DIY_LOG_DIR/server.log 2>&1 &
```

And finally, execute the following commands:

```
$ git add .
$ git commit -a -m "start nginx when starting up the app"
$ git push
```

Then use your browser to navigate to *http://nginix-<your-namespace>.rhcloud.com*. The welcome page will be displayed (Figure 15-1).

Welcome to nginx!

If you see this page, the nginx web server is successfully installed and working. Further configuration is required.

For online documentation and support please refer to nginx.org. Commercial support is available at nginx.com.

Thank you for using nginx.

Figure 15-1. Nginx welcome page

Use the `rhc tail -a nginx` command to troubleshoot if you are having problem with the start script.

Also, you might have to run:

```
$ $OPENSHIFT_DATA_DIR/sbin/nginx -s reload
```

to force Nginx to reload the configuration every time you make some changes.

We now need to configure Nginx to act as a reverse proxy. We will configure Nginx to do the following:

- Pass requests to a proxied server
- Distribute content from different services
- Configure responses from different services

In particular, we will configure Nginx to proxy calls to the Wikipin API and distribute its responses.

According to the Nginx documentation:

> When NGINX proxies a request, it sends the request to a specified proxied server, fetches the response, and sends it back to the client. It is possible to proxy requests to an HTTP server (another NGINX server or any other server) or a non-HTTP server (which can run an application developed with a specific framework, such as PHP or Python) using a specified protocol. NGINX supported protocols include FastCGI, uwsgi, SCGI, and memcached.

To pass a request to an HTTP proxied server, the `proxy_pass` (*http://bit.ly/proxy-pass*) directive is specified inside a `location` block:

```
location /some/path/ {
  proxy_pass http://www.example.com/link/;
}
```

We can set up a location for our Wikipin API as follows:

```
location /api/v1/pins/ {
  proxy_pass
    http://wikipin-<openshift-namespace>.rhcloud.com/api/v1/pins/;
  proxy_intercept_errors          on;
  proxy_redirect                  off;
  proxy_set_header X-Real-IP       $remote_addr;
  proxy_set_header X-Forwarded-For $proxy_add_x_forwarded_for;
}
```

Meet Lua

As described on its project page (*http://www.lua.org/about.html*), "Lua is a powerful, fast, lightweight, embeddable scripting language[, combining] simple procedural syntax with powerful data description constructs based on associative arrays and extensible semantics. Lua is dynamically typed, runs by interpreting bytecode for a register-based virtual machine, and has automatic memory management with incremental garbage collection, making it ideal for configuration, scripting, and rapid prototyping."

Lua was designed to be embedded within larger systems written in other languages, and since it has remained minimal and easy to integrate it is a popular choice in certain fields, like video game development (*World of Warcraft* used it as a scripting language), security and monitoring applications (Wireshark used it for prototyping and scripting), and the Web (Wikipedia has been using it as a template scripting language since 2012).

Lua can be used to extend Nginx into a self-contained web server. Being a scripting language, Lua can be used to write powerful applications directly inside Nginx without the need to use CGI, FastCGI, or uWSGI. Small features can also be implemented easily, just by adding a bit of Lua to an Nginx config file.

To extend Nginx, we need to add a bundle that supports Lua. There are bundles that already have Lua built in for your convenience, such as OpenResty (*http://openresty.org/*) and Tengine (*http://bit.ly/tengine*).

OpenResty (aka *ngx_openresty*) is a web application server that bundles together the standard Nginx core with a set of third-party Nginx modules (*http://bit.ly/3rd-party-nginx*) (and their external dependencies), Lua libraries, and more. Tengine is another web server based on Nginx that is known to be very stable and efficient.

You can also install the Lua modules yourself. The modules you will need are:

- ngx_lua module (*http://bit.ly/ngx-lua*)
- The HTTP proxy module (*http://bit.ly/ngx-http*)

The ngx_lua module exposes the Nginx environment to Lua via an API, while also allowing us to run Lua code snippets during the Nginx rewrite, access, content, and log phases.

A simple example of Lua scripting could be adding the following to *$OPEN-SHIFT_DATA_DIR/conf/nginx.conf*:

```
location /hello {
    default_type 'text/plain';
    content_by_lua '
        local name = ngx.var.arg_name or "Anonymous"
        ngx.say("Hello, ", name, "!") ';
}
```

Bundle Things Together

Lua brings the possibility of using a scripting language to write both simple and complex rules in your *nginx.conf* file. This actually means that a part of your routing and proxy logic can be relegated to the Nginx server and doesn't have to go into your application logic.

As mentioned at the beginning of this chapter, Nginx can also be used as a load balancer across multiple application instances, to optimize resource utilization, maximize throughput, reduce latency, and ensure fault-tolerant configurations.

There are different load-balancing methods that you might consider implementing on Nginx; here we'll only discuss some of them superficially, with the objective being to point you in the right direction should you need to do more research on the topic.

Nginx supports three approaches to load balancing:

Round-robin
> Requests to the application servers are distributed in a round-robin fashion.

Least connected
> Each incoming request is assigned to the server with the least number of active connections.

IP hash
> A hash function is used to determine what server should be selected for the next request, based on the client's IP address.

The simplest configuration for load balancing with Nginx involves specifying multiple instances of the same application running on a number of servers: *srv1–srv3*. When a load-balancing method is not specifically configured, Nginx defaults to the round-robin mechanism. All requests are proxied to the server group *myapp1*, and Nginx applies HTTP load balancing to distribute the requests. The following configuration shows how this can be accomplished:

```
http {
    upstream myapp1 {
        server srv1.example.com;
        server srv2.example.com;
        server srv3.example.com;
    }
    server {
        listen 80;
        location / {
            proxy_pass http://myapp1;
        }
    }
}
```

With the least-connected method you have a bit more control over the load on the application instances, and can account for situations when some requests take longer to complete than others. Nginx will try not to overload an already busy application server with excessive requests, and instead will distribute the new requests to servers that are less busy.

To use the least-connected strategy, you just have to specify it in your *nginx.conf* file, as in the following example:

```
upstream myapp1 {
    least_conn;
    server srv1.example.com;
    server srv2.example.com;
    server srv3.example.com;
}
```

If you are interested in trying IP hash load balancing, you need to replace the least_conn directive with ip_hash. This method ensures that requests from the same client are passed to the same server, unless that server is unavailable.

A different load-balancing strategy involves using server weights to further influencing the algorithm. If no server weights are configured, like in the previous example, Nginx will treat all specified servers as equally qualified for a particular load balancing method. With the round-robin method, this results in requests being distributed fairly equally across the servers (provided there are enough requests, and the requests are processed in a uniform manner and completed quickly enough). This can be seen as similar to the least-connected method.

When a weight parameter is specified for a server, this will be considered as part of the load-balancing decision. For example, with this configuration:

```
upstream myapp1 {
    least_conn;
    server srv1.example.com weight=3;
    server srv2.example.com;
    server srv3.example.com;
}
```

Nginx will distribute three out of every five requests to *srv1*; the remaining requests will be distributed equally across *srv2* and *srv3*.

Nginx also includes in-band server health checks in its reverse proxy implementation. This implies that if a response from a certain server fails with an error, Nginx will mark the server as failed and will try to avoid it for the following inbound requests.

You can set the max_fails directive to indicate the maximum number of consecutive unsuccessful communication attempts that can be made to a particular server within the period specified by fail_timeout in order for that server to be marked as failed. max_fails is set to 1 by default; setting it to 0 for a particular server disables health checks for that server.

The fail_timeout parameter also defines how long the server is marked as failed once the health check is triggered. Following that interval, Nginx will start to gracefully probe the server with the live client's requests. If the probes are successful, the server will be marked as live again.

Caching

Generally speaking, a cache is a computing component that transparently stores data so that future requests for that data can be answered faster. That data kept in the cache might be duplicates of values that are stored elsewhere, allowing faster access, or the result of previously executed operations that it is believed might be requested again in the near future.

Rails supports three types of caching natively, without the use of third-party libraries or plug-ins:

- Page Caching
- Action Caching
- Fragment Caching

In order to start playing with caching, you first need to set the following in the corresponding *config/environments/*.rb* file:

```
config.action_controller.perform_caching = true
```

This flag is normally disabled by default for development and testing, and enabled for production.

The first caching mechanism that you will find in Rails is *Page Caching*. It allows the web server (e.g., Nginx) to fulfill requests for generated pages without having to go through the Rails stack at all, resulting in very fast response times. Page Caching has been removed from the core dependencies in Rails 4, and needs to be installed as a gem. To use Page Caching, add the following line to your application's *Gemfile*:

```
gem 'actionpack-page_caching'
```

This mechanism cannot be applied to every situation—for example, it won't work when the app is requesting some information that might change the page, such as for a page that needs authentication—and since the web server is just serving a file from the filesystem, you'll need to deal with the issue of cache expiration.

Since we are dealing with APIs, we might want to use Action Caching instead to cache particular actions. Action Caching has also been removed in Rails 4, but can be used through a gem. Add the following to your *Gemfile*:

```
gem 'actionpack-action_caching'
```

Then, to enable Action Caching, you use the `caches_action` method:

```
class Api::V1::CategoryController < ApplicationController
  caches_action :show
  def show
    category = params[:category] ? params[:category] : \
      "Main_topic_classifications"
    @category = Category.where(:cat_title => category.capitalize).first
    if @category
      render :json => @category, serializer: CategorySerializer, root: "category"
    else
      render :json => {:error => {:text =>  "404 Not found", :status => 404}}
```

```
    end
  end
```

In this example we have added caching to our `CategoryController` and considered our *show* action. The first time anyone requests a certain category Rails will generate the JSON response, and subsequently use `Rails.cache` behind the scenes to cache the generated JSON.

Please refer to the Action Caching repository (*http://bit.ly/rails-action-caching*) for further information and available options.

The action cache is responsible for handling caching for different representations of the same resource. By default, these representations are stored by in the Rails *public* folder, where cache fragments are named according to the host and path of each request.

The default action cache path can be modified via the `:cache_path` option.

We might want additional control over how we use the caching mechanism provided. For example, we might want to add an expiration to our cache:

```ruby
class Api::V1::CategoryController < ApplicationController
  respond_to :json
  caches_action :show, cache_path: { project: 1 }, expires_in: 1.hour
  def show
    category = params[:category] ? params[:category] : \
      "Main_topic_classifications"
    @category = Category.where(:cat_title => category.capitalize).first
    if @category
      render :json => @category, serializer: CategorySerializer, root: "category"
    else
      render :json => {:error => {:text => "404 Not found", :status => 404}}
    end
  end
end
```

What the action cache does behind the scenes is serve cache fragments after an incoming request has reached the Rails stack and Action Pack. This way, a mechanism like `before_filter` (*http://bit.ly/before_filter*) can still be run before the cache fragments are returned and served. This allows the action cache to be used even in situations where certain restrictions apply, like authenticated sessions.

You can clear the cache when needed using `expire_action`.

If you are using memcached or Ehcache, you can also pass `:expires_in`. In fact, all parameters not used by `caches_action` are sent to the underlying cache store.

As with Page Caching, Action Caching cannot always be used. Sometimes, especially with dynamic web applications, it is necessary to cache specific parts of the page independently from others, as well as with different expiration terms.

For such cases, Rails provides a mechanism called Fragment Caching that allows you to serve fragments of view logic wrapped in cache blocks out of the cache store when subsequent requests come in.

Fragment Caching really means that you are actually caching only certain parts of the answer to a request.

A very important technique involving Fragment Caching is called the *Russian doll* approach to caching. If you think of a Russian doll, you will picture a container with many smaller containers nested inside the first one.

The Russian doll caching mechanism works like this: cache fragments are nested and expire when an object's timestamp changes.

There is yet another approach to caching that you might consider: it falls somewhere between Action and Fragment Caching and is referred to as *model caching*.

Model-level caching is often ignored since we tend to either cache the action or the view. This low-level approach is particularly useful for applications integrating different APIs: in such a situation you might have a model that, before an update, looks something up from another service through an API call.

> To find out more about low-level caching, check out the Ruby on Rails Guide (*http://bit.ly/rguide-low-level*).

For model-level caching we can go back to using Redis, since we do not require long-term persistence of caches. We met Redis in Chapter 12 when creating a temporary resource to be queried to get the status of an asynchronous REST request; as you'll recall, it's a very fast in-memory key/value store. WRedis is particularly suited for storing cache fragments due to its speed and support for advanced data structures.

To initialize Redis, add the following to your *Gemfile*:

```
gem 'redis'
gem 'redis-namespace'
gem 'redis-rails'
gem 'redis-rack-cache'
```

The *redis-rails* gem provides caching support (among other things) for Ruby on Rails applications. You can configure *redis-rails* in *config/application.rb*:

```
config.cache_store = :redis_store,
  'redis://localhost:6379/0/cache', {
    expires_in: 90.minutes
  }
```

You also need to add the *redis.rb* initializer in *config/initializers*:

```
$redis = Redis::Namespace.new("wikicat", :redis => Redis.new)
```

Now, all Redis functionality is available across the entire app through the $redis global. If you run the Rails console you can try it yourself:

```
$ rails console
```

If you want to test Redis you can try the following test key and value:

```
$redis.set("test_key", "Hello World!")
```

Then, to retrieve the key, simply run:

```
$redis.get("test_key")
```

The same mechanisms are used behind the scenes when getting and setting values within the view or the controller. If certain conditions are met, you can execute the get or set methods to retrieve or store values in the Redis cache instead of querying your database directly.

To set a certain expiration time on the Redis cache you can simply call:

```
# Expire the cache, every 3 hours
$redis.expire("categories",3.hour.to_i)
```

Please note that whether you decide to use Redis or another key/value store for your cache mechanism is independent from how you decide to cache in your app. Once you have set the cache_store and added the *redis-rails* gem, Rails will automagically switch to Redis for caching fragments instead of using memcached.

Scaling Is Not Necessarily Difficult and Painful

The intention of this chapter was to show how it is possible to scale a Rails application gracefully without being limited by the very same framework.

Scaling a Rails application involves having a clear architectural picture of your service and keeping things relatively simple.

Most of the claims against being able to scale a Rails application trace back to the story of Twitter abandoning Ruby on Rails (*http://bit.ly/twitter-ror*) because it could not support the growing user base.

First of all, we are not in 2008 anymore. Rails is a mature enough technology to make scaling easy if well planned and architectured. Furthermore, the microservices/microapps approach to building complex applications is already a scaling paradigm. You keep your applications minimal and simple enough that you can easily extract complex logic into a different service if you need to, or isolate slow actions into background jobs.

A background job is some task that needs to be executed asynchronously by the server. This can be a slow action or a long series of processes that will otherwise block an HTTP request/response for a longer time than is needed or ideal. We want to send the client an answer as soon as possible, even if this means telling the client that it needs to wait and will have to check back to get the status of a resource.

The most common approach to running these longer "jobs" is to hand them off to a separate process to execute them independently of the web server. There are plenty of great libraries out there that provide the "background job" functionality for you.

Background Jobs on RoR

There are different libraries to run background jobs on Ruby. The most popular of these are Resque (*https://github.com/resque/resque*) and Sidekiq (*https://github.com/mperham/sidekiq*); check out their GitHub pages for details.

The idea behind writing microapplications is to avoid writing complex applications that are difficult to run and maintain. If a service has to perform only a limited number of functions, its logic can be kept simpler and therefore easier to scale, evolve, integrate, and modify. The number of tests of a microservice does not need to grow exponentially, as happens with a monolithic application once it has reached a certain level of complexity.

Therefore, microservices can be tested faster and more frequently, which means they will be more robust and the code will be less prone to errors.

Wrapping Up

This chapter has been about scaling our platform and our Rails applications. I have tried to bust some myths about the concept that Rails doesn't scale. In the next chapter, we will talk about the privacy and security of a Rails app and of data in general.

Privacy and Security

This chapter considers privacy and security issues that should be evaluated while writing a RESTful application or service. Our discussion will go beyond the usual Rails recommendations and security best practices; we will also explore the implications of handling and collecting data about users' behavior and preferences.

How to Protect User Privacy

Privacy is currently one of those hot topics in information technology. This is probably because there are two primary opposing views on the subject:

1. Users do not care about privacy.
2. Users wouldn't want to be "social" if they knew what it really meant for their privacy.

Both views are utterly right and utterly wrong at the same time. The truth in fact is that users do see a benefit in disclosing their preferences and in having websites collect their data. They receive value back in terms of utility, or in other words a better service already filtered and tailored for their needs and tastes. Still, by collecting user data, over time you will end up with a history of your users' behavior on your platform, and some information about their activity on other platforms as well. This can be a potential source of a whole class of issues.

The first important step when it comes to security is understanding what kinds of sensitive data your service is storing. This may include anything from credit card and banking information, to physical addresses or personal preferences that the users would like to keep private.

Once you know what kind of data you are storing about your users, you should try to understand how this data can be shared by the users (if that's possible) and who could have access to it.

This question might seem trivial, but it is actually crucial when you are dealing with user data. To understand why, I will introduce the notion of a *quasi-identifier*. We are all familiar with the concept of a unique identifier; we use it constantly. A unique identifier (*http://bit.ly/wiki-unique-id*) is "any identifier which is guaranteed to be unique among all the identifiers used for [a class of] objects and for a specific purpose." This could be for example a social security number, a serial number, a credit card number—something that is never repeated.

A quasi-identifier (*http://bit.ly/wiki-quasi-id*) instead is not unique in itself, but combined with other quasi-identifiers can be sufficiently well correlated with an entity as to create a unique identifier.

To understand this notion, imagine that you are in a remote location and you are using Twitter with the location sharing services enabled. Nobody knows your username, yet some people might know your location and use that information to find your identity on Twitter, since very few people might be tweeting from that location.

This is certainly an extreme case, considering how many people use Twitter worldwide. But you might be working on an application for which the number of users at a certain time or in a specific location is very low, and a simple action by an individual could become a quasi-identifier for a possible attacker.

For example, think of a smart transportation service that is sharing online the number of people getting on and off of certain buses at a certain time. Imagine that someone always catches the bus at the beginning of the run and gets off only toward the end. More often than not, only a few users get on at the beginning of the route and off at the end.

Therefore, with some other information that could be used as quasi-identifiers in correlation with the relative frequency of people hopping on and off the bus, it would be relatively easy to make assumptions regarding who those few users are.

When you think of private information, think of it like puzzle pieces. Each piece of information, or in other words each quasi-identifier, can be used to assume other information and eventually create a complete picture of a user and her activities.

This can particularly be an issue when data from different services is combined. Each activity, each data point, each preference expressed probably corresponds to a little piece of the puzzle, and before you realize it the user's identity has been leaked to third parties.

Reasoning about user privacy implies understanding the trade-off between providing a tailored and useful service and protecting users' private data from involuntary leaks.

Up to now, in an online context, the right to privacy has commonly been interpreted as a right to "information self-determination." Acts typically claimed to breach online privacy concern the collection of personal information without consent, the selling of personal information, and the further processing of that information.

This definition of privacy breach can be considered valid as long as the users have direct control over the data they have created and who they are sharing it with. The problem with this approach is that users have practically lost direct control over their data, considering the amount of user information that is constantly created, shared, and consumed online by a complicated network of applications and services.

As application developers, we should always give users an intuitive way of controlling who has access to their data and how that data is shared on our platforms and with third parties.

Furthermore, you might consider anonymizing the data before third parties can access it through your APIs, in a way that reduces the possibility that some user activity might be used as a quasi-identifier.

In such a situation, your API will only request data from an anonymized database that will contain only data that is considered safe to be accessed by third parties (i.e., some features of the original dataset will have been removed to avoid leakage of sensitive information).

There are different techniques here that might seem a bit academic, but in my opinion they are worth considering if you are dealing with potentially sensitive user data.

Two very common strategies of anonymization are k-anonymity and differential privacy. We are going to briefly introduce both of them.

k-anonymity

k-anonymity (*http://bit.ly/wiki-k-anon*) is a concept that was first formulated by Latanya Sweeney (*http://bit.ly/wiki-lsweeney*) in a paper published in 2002. *K*-anonymity is concerned with reducing the possibility that a quasi-identifier can be used to infer unique properties about a user. More specifically, the problem that *k*-anonymity tries to solve can be formulated in the following terms: "Given user-specific field-structured data, is it possible to produce a release of the data with scientific guarantees that the individuals who are the subjects of the data cannot be re-identified while the data remain practically useful?" Therefore, a release of some data is said to have the *k*-anonymity property "if the information for each person contained in the release cannot be distinguished from at least *k*-1 individuals whose information also appear in the release."

K-anonymity algorithms are usually intended to be used when complete databases of sensitive information are disclosed to the public. As a concept, it can also be used to assess the possibility that information contained in a certain set of data could be used for a privacy attack.

Differential Privacy

Differential privacy (*http://bit.ly/wiki-diff-privacy*) is a concept rooted in the notion of statistical disclosure control (SDC). In 1977, Tore Dalenius wrote what is now considered a classic paper on SDC,[1] providing a formal definition of the topic and theory of statistical disclosure and finally proposing a methodology for SDC. The objective of SDC is summarized in the question: "How is it possible to publish some useful information regarding a group of individuals?" That is, how can we disclose a statistic about a population, without violating the privacy of individuals?

SDC is connected to the notion of semantic security for cryptographic systems. Given a clear text and a ciphertext, the definition of semantic security formulates that: "Whatever is efficiently computable about the cleartext given the ciphertext, is also efficiently computable without the ciphertext." Alternatively, it could be said that no information can be learned regarding a given plain text by seeing the ciphertext, which could not be learned without seeing the ciphertext.

Per Dalenius, in the database field, the notion of semantic security could be translated into: "Having access to a statistical database should not enable one to learn anything about an individual that could not be learned without access." Cynthia Dwork in her work on differential privacy (*http://bit.ly/dwork-diff-privacy*) states that this kind of privacy cannot be achieved, since possible attackers might possess some auxiliary information that could help them isolate key features regarding a specific individual.

This concept is translated into practical terms by Dwork's definition of differential privacy: "the risk to one's privacy, or in general, any type of risk, such as the risk of being denied automobile insurance, should not substantially increase as a result of participating in a statistical database." Differential privacy is, therefore, a mechanism designed to provide strong privacy guarantees for an individual's input to a (randomized) function, regardless of whether any individual opts into or out of a database.

Privacy-Enhancing Technologies

While the notions of *k*-anonymity and differential privacy might seem like academic, abstract mathematical concepts, they are often the theoretical foundation for safely disclosing user data or sharing information on the Internet or in a network of distributed services and applications.

---

1 Dalenius, T. "Towards a methodology for statistical disclosure control." *Statistik Tidskrift* 15 (1977): 429–444.

Privacy-enhancing technologies (PETs) are therefore a set of measures that can be adopted to protect information privacy by eliminating or minimizing personal user data and preventing unwanted leaks, without a considerable loss of system functionality. One or several PETs can be adopted with different objectives in mind, including:

- Increase user control over their personal data
- Minimize the personal data collected and used by third-party service providers and merchants
- Allow for a degree of anonymity and *unlinkability*, i.e., the possibility that profiles from different service or virtual identities can be linked to a unique identifier or physical persona
- Facilitate the exercise the user legal rights
- Achieve informed consent regarding data usage and dissemination policies
- Allow users to safely log and track their activity on your platform
- Technically enforce terms of service and conditions over the use of data and your privacy policy

Is My Data Safe?

Data security means protecting your data from any possible destructive agents and the unwanted actions of unauthorized parties. Whether you are deploying your own infrastructure or using a cloud-based service, there are different issues in data security that need to be considered:

- Where is your data stored? Are you infringing any law in the country where your data is stored?
- Is your data encrypted?
- Who could potentially access your data?
- Is your data backed up?

These are the questions that will need to be answered to secure your data—and these are all questions related to system security.

Generally speaking, system security is a wide topic, covering several layers and influencing the application and service design at many different levels.

Since you have reached the last chapter of this book on RESTful Rails development, by now you might have noticed that the approach that we have followed is to break down complex problems into smaller ones. Each small problem was solved with a new API, and the APIs were consumed by a set of different services and applications.

This approach certainly has various benefits, while also carrying with it various intrinsic issues. Some of these issues can be dealt with at the microservice level, while some others need to be identified and resolved at the macro application level.

We will try to follow the same approach when it comes to security. Some security concerns can be analyzed at the service level, but others will need to be evaluated at the distributed application level.

There are a number of common sources of insecurity when reasoning about data. Some can be dealt with at the framework level (Rails), and others need to be addressed with design choices.

There are different ways and techniques to address the security of an application or system. If you are familiar with software testing strategies, you have probably heard of *white box* testing and *black box* testing. These are two opposite testing strategies: in white box testing you consider the system design and its functionality, and you test different cases that are considered appropriate; in black box testing instead you basically try to break the system and see what happens.

White box testing in the security development lifecycle (SDL) attempts to highlight possible vulnerabilities within the architectural design of the application and/or the actual code implementation of a single service.

White box analysis often implies the use of formal mathematical methods to prove that some function(s) or a certain routine can or cannot contain runtime errors. These methods are often approximate, as it was proven by Alan Turing in 1936 that a general algorithm to solve the halting problem (*http://bit.ly/wiki-halting-problem*) (i.e., "the problem of determining, from a description of an arbitrary computer program and an input, whether the program will finish running or continue to run forever") for *all* possible program-input pairs cannot exist.

Static analysis often uses data-flow analysis (*http://bit.ly/wiki-data-flow-analysis*), "a technique for gathering information about the possible set of values calculated at various points in a computer program." With this technique, a program's control flow graph (CFG) is used to determine how a particular value is propagated when assigned to a variable. The information gathered is often used to understand if the program or the unit examined is functioning according to the specification.

Another analytical procedure used in static analysis is taint analysis (*http://bit.ly/static-code-analysis*), which "attempts to identify variables that have been 'tainted' with user controllable input and traces them to possible vulnerable functions also known as a 'sink.'" Tainted variables that slip through and are passed to a sink without first being sanitized are flagged as vulnerabilities.

Static analysis can be performed at different levels of an application (or sometimes, organization). The lowest level is the unit level. Here, a specific portion of the application is considered in isolation. At the next level, the technological level, interactions between different units are taken into consideration. Then we consider interactions at the system level, taking into account different units, programs, and services. At the last level we consider interactions at the business level.

Common Sources of Insecurity

A common source of insecurity in web application is just about anywhere the user can input data.

Data inputs can be used by a possible attacker in many different ways. We'll look at a few of them here.

XSS

XSS attacks use a data input field to inject some code in a web application. The injected malicious code can just be executed to retrieve some data or perform an action, or stored to obtain access to the application database and server.

Command-line injection

Command-line injection might also be possible if your application executes commands in the underlying operating system. In this situation you have to be especially careful if the user is allowed to enter the whole command, or even just a part of it. This can be particularly dangerous since in most cases you can theoretically execute another command at the end of the first one, by concatenating them with a semicolon (;) or a vertical bar (|).

To prevent this type of attack, consider using a method that passes command-line parameters safely, like the `system` command:

```
system([env,] command... [,options]) -> true, false or nil
Executes command... in a subshell. command... is one of following forms.
commandline : command line string which is passed to the standard
shell cmdname, arg1, ... : command name and one or more arguments
(no shell) [cmdname, argv0], arg1, ... : command name, argv[0] and
zero or more arguments (no shell)system returns true if the command
gives zero exit status, false for non zero exit status. Returns nil
if command execution fails. An error status is available in $?.
```

HTTP header injection

Another possible attack is HTTP header injection. HTTP header injection attacks work by the attacker injecting certain fields, or text, into the header of a request to the server. Header fields should always be escaped when used in your application, especially if any of these fields are based on user input (even partly).

HTTP response splitting

An attack related to HTTP header injection is HTTP response splitting. The Security Guide gives the following example:

In HTTP, the header block is followed by two CRLFs and the actual data (usually HTML). The idea of Response Splitting is to inject two CRLFs into a header field, followed by another response with malicious HTML. The response will be:

```
HTTP/1.1 302 Found [First standard 302 response]
Date: Tue, 12 Apr 2005 22:09:07 GMT
Location: Content-Type: text/html

HTTP/1.1 200 OK [Second New response created by attacker begins]
Content-Type: text/html

<html><font color=red>hey</font></html>
[Arbitary malicious input is shown as the redirected page]
Keep-Alive: timeout=15, max=100
Connection: Keep-Alive
Transfer-Encoding: chunked
Content-Type: text/html
```

SQL injection

SQL injection attacks are carried out with the goal of influencing database queries and actions by manipulating web application parameters. A popular goal of these attacks is to bypass authorization and hence gain access to data in the database.

Ruby on Rails already contains a number of measures to prevent SQL injection attacks. A good source to learn more about possible attacks, how they are implemented, and how to prevent them is Rails SQL Injection Examples (*http://rails-sqli.org*). The web app contains a list of possible situations where it is actually possible to perform a SQL injection attack in Rails. It also lists all query methods and options in Active Record that should be treated with extra attention since they do not sanitize raw SQL arguments.

Is Rails Secure?

To answer the question "Is Rails secure?" we should start by considering why Rails was developed and how it is actually used.

Generally speaking the purpose of a web application framework is to help developers create web applications. As part of the framework, some security mechanisms to help you in securing your app are also included.

Having said this, no framework is particularly more secure than any other. In general, if they're used correctly it is possible to build secure applications with many different frameworks. Each of them will offer its own features to solve issues that you might encounter when developing an app, security issues included.

The Rails team handles support by categorizing changes made to the framework into four groups: new features, bug fixes, security issues, and severe security issues. They are handled as follows:

1 New Features

New features are only added to the master branch and will not be made available in point releases.

2 Bug Fixes

Only the latest release series will receive bug fixes. When enough bugs are fixed and [it's] deemed worthy to release a new gem, this is the branch it happens from.

In special situations, where someone from the Core Team agrees to support more series, they are included in the list of supported series.

Currently included series: 4.2.Z, 4.1.Z (Supported by Rafael França).

3 Security Issues

The current release series and the next most recent one will receive patches and new versions in case of a security issue.

These releases are created by taking the last released version, applying the security patches, and releasing. Those patches are then applied to the end of the x-y-stable branch. For example, a theoretical 1.2.3 security release would be built from 1.2.2, and then added to the end of 1-2-stable. This means that security releases are easy to upgrade to if you're running the latest version of Rails.

Currently included series: 4.2.Z, 4.1.Z.

4 Severe Security Issues

For severe security issues we will provide new versions as above, and also the last major release series will receive patches and new versions. The classification of the security issue is judged by the core team.

Currently included series: 4.2.Z, 4.1.Z, 3.2.Z.

5 Unsupported Release Series

When a release series is no longer supported, it's your own responsibility to deal with bugs and security issues. We may provide backports of the fixes and publish them to git, however there will be no new versions released. If you are not comfortable maintaining your own versions, you should upgrade to a supported version.

It is important to understand that there is no library or tool or gem that will give you security out of the box. It is often said that the only secure system is the isolated system, meaning that as soon as something is able to communicate with the outside world, it will have to face some risks.

Security in a web app, as we saw in the previous section, depends on different layers of the web application environment, and possibly also on other services as well. Therefore, in order to keep your web application secure you have to think about security issues at all layers, keep up-to-date with current issues, read security blogs, update your libraries, and try to identify possible malicious activity on your platform.

Sessions

HTTP is a stateless protocol, yet both server and client in certain situations need to keep track of the state of the user or the application itself. This is accomplished using sessions.

A session in Rails consists of a hash object, with some key/value pairs and a session ID. The session ID is usually a 32-character string; it identifies the hash.

The session ID is included both in information saved on the browser side, like cookies or local-storage data, and in the requests from the client to the server. This way the client doesn't have to authenticate at each request.

Rails creates a new session automatically whenever a new user accesses the application, and if the user has already used the application it will load the existing session. You can save and retrieve values using the `session` method:

```
session[:user_id] = @current_user.id
User.find(session[:user_id])
```

In Rails the session ID is built as a 32-byte MD5 hash value of a random string. The random string is generated from the current timestamp, a random number between 0 and 1, the process ID number of the server's Ruby interpreter, and a constant string. The Rails session ID is very difficult to compromise and can be considered secure in its default implementation. MD5 remains uncompromised, but collisions in MD5 hashes are in fact possible. So, theoretically, an attacker could create an input text with the same hash value.

If an attacker steals the user's session ID, he could impersonate the victim and use the web application on his own behalf.

There are different ways a session ID could be stolen. To understand how this could be accomplished, let's take a step back and look at how authentication systems work in general.

When a user authenticates to a web app, she provides a username and password. The web application checks them and stores the corresponding user ID in the session hash (Figure 16-1). From now on, the session is valid. On every request the application will query the database and use the profile of the user identified by the ID in the session, without the need to authenticate again. The session ID in the cookie identifies the session.

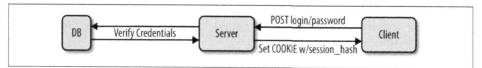

Figure 16-1. Simple authentication system where login credentials are posted to the server and, once verified, a cookie is set with the session ID

The cookie serves as a temporary authentication for the web app, which means anyone in possession of the cookie could act on behalf of the user. Possible ways to hijack the session include:

- Cookie sniffing in an insecure network, such as an unencrypted wireless LAN, where it is trivial to listen to the traffic of connected clients. A countermeasure in this case would be to force SSL connections in your application via `config.force_ssl = true`. Yet, since most people do not clear out their cookies even when they are using a public terminal, session IDs could remain stored there and be easily stolen. To avoid this, always provide an easy-to-access logout button in the user interface.
- XSS exploits aimed at obtaining the user's cookie.
- Session fixation, where the attacker obtains a session ID and forces the victim's browser to use this ID.

Session storage

Different storage mechanisms are provided in Rails for safekeeping session hashes, including `ActionDispatch::Session::CookieStore`.

CookieStore has been used in Rails since version 2 to save session hashes directly in a cookie on the client side. With CookieStore the server retrieves the session hash from the cookie. This mechanism eliminates the need to use a session ID.

CookieStore represents a great improvement for application speed. However, storing the session hash in the cookie is not ideal for security purposes. Drawbacks of this approach include:

- The maximum size of a cookie is 4 KB. (This is fine for most applications and for the functionality supported by CookieStore.)
- Everything you store in a cookie can be accessed and read by the client. The information stored is Base64-encoded, but not encrypted. Please be aware that storing secrets in a cookie is inherently insecure.

The security of the CookieStore option depends on the application secret that is used to calculate the digest.

Replay attacks for CookieStore. Imagine an online game of some sort. The user has been playing the game and the application has stored the score in the session (this is bad practice anyway since it should be stored in the server, but let's pretend this doesn't matter at this point).

The user plays the game a bit more and his score decreases for some reason. The application will update the new score in the session.

Now, for some other reason, imagine that the user has saved the cookie with the previous score value. He can use the old cookie to replace the new cookie and get back his higher score. This is illustrated in Figure 16-2.

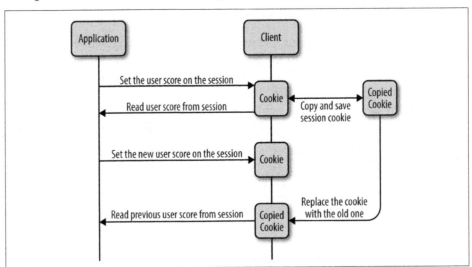

Figure 16-2. In a replay attack, the cookie is replaced and the server reads an older amount stored in the session

To avoid this type of replay attack, you could store some random value that is valid only once (a *nonce*) in the session so that a possible attacker cannot tamper with the cookie. This strategy can get complicated if the server needs to keep track of large series of nonces that will have to be stored in the database, though, and since the purpose of using CookieStore is not having to access the database, using this technique would nullify its benefits.

The best solution to avoid this type of attack is not to store sensitive information in the session. Store only the logged-in user's ID in the session, and all other information in the database.

Session fixation attacks

The idea of a session fixation attack is that both the attacker and the victim (user) share the same session ID. To accomplish this, the attacker creates a valid session ID by loading the login page of the web application where she wants to fix the session, and notes the session ID stored in the cookie sent with the response.

The attacker will try to maintain the session for as long as possible, accessing the web application at regular intervals in order to keep the session alive. Therefore, expiring sessions greatly reduces the chances of such attacks succeeding.

Once the attacker has obtained a valid session ID, she will need to force the same ID into the user's browser. This may be done by injecting JavaScript code like the following (an XSS attack) into the application that the user will execute when visiting the page: `<script>document.cookie="_session_id=1234";</script>`.

Then, when the user visits the login page himself, his browser will replace the session ID that's assigned by the app with the trapped session ID. The user will be asked to authenticate (as the attacker trapped the session ID but didn't actually provide credentials to log in to the web app), and from now on the victim and the attacker will both be able to use the application with the same session. Figure 16-3 illustrates how this attack works.

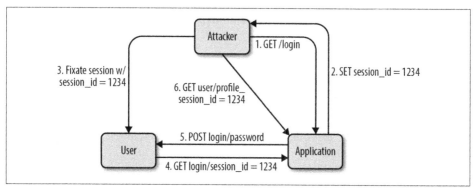

Figure 16-3. A session fixation attack where the attacker forces the victim's browser to use a specific session ID

Different countermeasures are possible for session fixation attacks. The most effective is to issue a new session ID after a successful login while also declaring the old one invalid. This way, an attacker cannot tie the session to the victim. This is a good countermeasure for session hijacking as well.

The Rails method to tell your application to reset the session is `reset_session`. Note that this method removes all values from the session, so any values you want to maintain must be transferred to the new session.

It is also important to stress that session expiration information cannot be stored in the cookie. The cookie is always stored on the client side and therefore can be edited. It is better to set the expiration on the server side to avoid tampering.

Another possible countermeasure is to save user-specific properties into the session that can be verified by the application. This is sometimes referred to as "user fingerprinting"; it takes into consideration a variety of characteristics from the user's machine, such as browser settings that can uniquely identify a user online.

Cross-Site Request Forgery

A *cross-site request forgery* (CSRF) is a security attack that either uses malicious code stored in the database or loads it through external links. If a user is logged in, an attacker might try to use this technique to steal user data or execute unauthorized commands.

Imagine that a user is logged into a certain application and accesses a page where the `src` attribute of an image has been modified in such a way as to make it possible to destroy some of the user's data. The user will not notice that a command was executed when an attempt was made to load the image; she will just see a broken image link.

It is important to notice that the actual engineered image or link doesn't necessarily have to be situated in the web application's domain—it can be anywhere, such as in a forum or blog post or an email.

CSRF attacks can be easily avoided by using HTTP verbs correctly. For example, fetching a particular URL should not be able to trigger a dangerous action (a POST or PUT request should be used instead when deleting a database record).

Rails includes a required security token to protect applications against forged requests. This one-liner in your application controller (included by default in all newly created Rails apps):

```
protect_from_forgery
```

will cause a security token to be included in all forms and Ajax requests generated by Rails. If the security token in a request doesn't match what is expected, the session will be reset.

Redirection

Redirection is a simple attack to construct. The most obvious situation would be a redirect to a fake web application that looks and feels like the original one.

The link that the attacker uses starts with the URL to the web application, and the URL to the malicious site is hidden in the redirection parameter: e.g., *http://www.example.com/site/redirect?to=www.attacker.com*.

Generally speaking, whenever the user is allowed to pass (parts of) the URL for redirection, it is possibly vulnerable.

Possible countermeasures to this common attack include using a whitelist or regular expression to check that the URL or domain being redirected to is an approved one and, for self-contained XSS attacks, not allowing the user to supply the URL to be redirected to (or any parts of it).

File Upload

There are many possible security issues that can come with allowing users to upload their own files. For example, files can include viruses or malicious programs that could compromise your server. Often it is beneficial to use a whitelist approach to filter filenames that the user can upload. Also, it is better not to process uploaded files synchronously. An attacker might take advantage of this to start several file uploads at the same time and take your service offline (a denial of service attack). Also, always check for executable code in file uploads.

File Download

Although it might seem counterintuitive, there are also a set of security issues around file downloads. Here are a few tips:

- When sending files to the user, again use a whitelist approach to filter filenames that the user may choose. Although this might seem counterintuitive, it is important to take all possible security precautions.
- Store the allowed filename patterns in the database and name the files on disk after the IDs or patterns stored. This is also a good approach to avoid possible code in an uploaded file from being executed.

Logs

A commonly overlooked mistake in application development is that of copying passwords to log files. *Remember to tell Rails not to put passwords in the logs!*

Rails logs all requests being made to a web application by default, but you don't need log files to contain login credentials, credit card numbers, and other private user data.

The Ruby on Rails Security Guide offers this tip: "You can *filter certain request parameters from your log files* by appending them to `config.filter_parameters` in the application configuration. These parameters will be marked [FILTERED] in the log."

Conclusions

This was the last chapter of this book. I hope that you have had fun building different applications, and that you have also learned a lot.

This chapter was about security and privacy, and it is no coincidence that it was the final chapter of the book. Sometimes developers and startups in general do not consider user privacy or API security early enough in their ventures. I can only recommend that you do not commit this mistake and overlook the importance of designing a secure product from the beginning. Building an insecure application can destroy your users' and partners' trust in your product. Not protecting your users' privacy or respecting their personal information shows that you do not really care about them. This is something that cannot easily be patched later on.

HTTP Quick Reference

Everything Started with Hypertext

The term *hypertext* was first defined in 1965 by Ted Nelson, as text containing links to other text. The World Wide Web Consortium defines hypertext as "text that is not constrained to be linear."

Generally speaking, we can think of hypertext as text displayed on electronic devices that references or links to other text.

The term *hypermedia* is an extension of this term. Generally speaking, hypermedia means hypertext that includes images, videos, and sounds. Ted Nelson was again the first to use the term.

REST is an architectural style introduced by Roy Thomas Fielding in 2000, which has been at the core of web design and development ever since.

REST actually defines the architecture of the Web: the way clients and servers communicate on the Web nowadays is dictated by REST principles.

REST principles emphasize *scalability*, both of components and of interactions between them. REST advocates for generality of interfaces and protocols and independent deployment of components. Furthermore, REST architectures make use of intermediary blocks, to reduce latency, enforce security, or simply encapsulate legacy systems.

Ted Nelson's idea of hypertext was a little bit different from what we know today. He envisioned the possibility not only of tracking links, but also of versioning of documents. His vision was translated into Xanadu (*http://bit.ly/wiki-xanadu*), a software system that was meant to be a universal library (like Wikipedia), a worldwide hypertext publishing tool, and a means for resolving copyright issues, as well as a forum for discussion and debate.

Xanadu was meant to provide most of the services that we can find nowadays on the Web in a single application; its ultimate purpose was to eliminate ignorance and misunderstanding, and to fix politics and communications. Xanadu was supposed to change the world for the better. Instead, the project went many times to the brink of bankruptcy and became one of the biggest vaporware stories in the history of the Internet.

The project has been developed and redeveloped but never released, although a working prototype (*http://www.xanadu.com*) is available.

While Xanadu was being rewritten and redesigned, the Web developed into a distributed hypermedia system, thanks to the collective effort of numerous cooperative projects and technological companies.

The Web consumes and generates enormous quantities of data, as a consequence of the constant interchange of information between users, client software, and services. These streams of data have often been referred to as *hyperdata*, or in other words interconnected data snippets that could therefore be explored.

Hyperdata represents the evolution of the Web as we now know it. When Tim Berners-Lee envisioned the Semantic Web in 2001, the Web of Data was described as a framework where autonomous agents could access structured information and conduct automated reasoning. These agents can be imagined as interconnected services accessing resources through a set of protocols or interfaces.

APIs can provide such interfaces by specifying how software components can interact with one another through one or more protocols. When a request is sent to a certain service through an API, one or more data objects are streamed through the network as a reply. This reply is expressed in a format that can be parsed and interpreted.

A hypermedia API would additionally specify links between the data objects returned, and a hypermedia browser would be able to explore the resulting flow of information just as a web browser can navigate through the hyperlinks in a web page.

From this point of view the "Web of Data," as the future evolution of the Web has already been defined, does not present too many innovative concepts. We have been surfing websites and using web apps for many years now, and the idea of what hypertext is and how hypertext documents can be explored through the links that interconnect them has almost become intuitive.

This appendix provides some basic information about the HTTP protocol—the protocol that makes the Web, hypertext, and hypermedia possible—that can serve as a quick reference when you're using this book. While our aim in the opening chapters of the book was to get up and running with Rails quickly, the more theoretical information you'll find here will give you a deeper understanding of how things work behind the scenes.

Creating an HTTP Server in Ruby, Quickly

Before diving into the HTTP protocol, let's try to grasp the basics. When the browser sends an HTTP request, a TCP socket connection is opened to *website.com* on port 80. The server accepts the connection and opens a socket for bidirectional communication. When the connection is established, the HTTP client sends an HTTP request:

```
GET /index.html HTTP/1.1
User-Agent: MyBrowser/1.0
Host: website.com
Accept: */*
```

The server parses the request. The first line defines the HTTP method (GET, in this case), the Request-URI (*/index.html*), and the HTTP protocol version (1.1).

The following line defines the request headers, consisting of key/value pairs separated by a colon (:).

Using the same connection, the server answers the request with the content of the requested file:

```
HTTP/1.1 200 OK
Content-Type: text/html
Content-Length: 145
Connection: close
<!DOCTYPE html>
<html>
<head>
  <title>Hello HTTP</title>
</head>
<body>
  <h1>HELLO WORLD</h1>
  <p>My first HTTP request.</p>
</body>
</html>
```

You can quickly try this out with this one-liner Ruby script:

```
$ ruby -rwebrick -e'WEBrick::HTTPServer.new(:Port => 3000,
  :DocumentRoot => Dir.pwd).start'
```

The web server will run on 127.0.0.1 on port 3000.

We can now create a simple HTML document so that we can request it from the server:

```
<!DOCTYPE html>
<html>
<head>
```

```
  <title>Hello HTTP</title>
</head>
<body>
  <h1>HELLO WORLD</h1>
  <p>My first HTTP request.</p>
</body>
</html>
```

To try this out, we can use *telnet*:

```
$ telnet 127.0.0.1 3000
```

We will get the command prompt:

```
Trying 127.0.0.1...
Connected to localhost.
Escape character is '^]'.
```

At which point we can request the index page:

```
GET /
```

We will then receive the HTML document in response, and the server will close the connection.

WEBrick

WEBrick (*http://bit.ly/ruby-webrick*) is an HTTP server toolkit available in Ruby that can be configured as an HTTPS server, a proxy server, or a virtual-host server. It offers complete logging of server operations as well as HTTP access and supports basic and digest authentication.

The HTTP Protocol

HTTP is an application protocol designed with lightness, speed, and hypermedia in mind. Between 1991 and 1992 the Internet Engineering Task Force (IETF) introduced the first documented versions of HTTP (HTTP v0.9 and HTTPv1.0) as a "stateless object-oriented protocol," with the capability to negotiate data representation, thereby allowing software systems to be built independently of the data format used for the actual communication.

The 1991 definition of the protocol implemented three actions:

- Request
- Response
- Disconnection

The request action consisted of sending a document request. This request was formed with the word "GET," a space, the document address (omitting the "http:"), the host name, and the port number.

The response consisted of the actual HTML document that had been requested, sent as a byte stream of ASCII characters.

When the whole document had finished transferring, the connection with the server was broken (the disconnection action).

HTTP has been extended and developed up to version 1.1 (RFC 7230 (*http://bit.ly/ rfc-7230*)), where it has been defined as a "generic interface protocol for information systems." One interesting aspect of the protocol's definition is that HTTP requests can be considered in isolation—i.e., the server can transparently ignore specific aspects of the client itself or a defined sequence of application steps. The protocol can hence be used in a wide range of contexts, where the actual implementations can evolve independently.

HTTP can also be implemented as an intermediate protocol used to translate communication messages between non-HTTP systems. In this particular implementation, HTTP proxies are responsible for translating their own sets of protocols into a hypertext format that can be interpreted and manipulated by HTTP clients and services.

The HTTP protocol's flexibility resides in the idea that it only defines the syntax of the communication between the parties involved, the intent of the received communication, and the expected behavior of the recipients. What happens behind the interfaces of the communicating parties is out of the scope of the protocol definition.

To understand the basics of HTTP and be able to reason about the protocol, let's start by getting some HTTP manually. We are going to "pretend" we are a web browser and request a resource through *telnet*.

From a terminal window, type:

```
$ telnet google.com 80
```

This will open a *telnet* request to *google.com* on port 80:

```
Trying 173.194.45.174...
Connected to google.com.
Escape character is '^]'.
```

Now let's request the index page:

```
GET /
```

To which we will get the reply:

```
HTTP/1.1 302 Found
Cache-Control: private
Content-Type: text/html; charset=UTF-8
```

```
Location: http://www.google.es/?gfe_rd=cr&ei=6xwvVOTHIcnBUOrygsAD
Content-Length: 256
Date: Fri, 03 Oct 2014 22:02:19 GMT
Server: GFE/2.0
Alternate-Protocol: 80:quic,p=0.01
<HTML><HEAD><meta http-equiv="content-type" content="text/html;
charset=utf-8">
<TITLE>302 Moved</TITLE></HEAD><BODY>
<H1>302 Moved</H1>
The document has moved
<A HREF="http://www.google.es/?gfe_rd=cr&ei=6xwvVOTHIcnBUOrygsAD">
here</A>.
</BODY></HTML></p>
```

Google is telling us that it has moved the page.

Architecture

HTTP was created to support the World Wide Web, and its development over time has reflected the Web's needs and its scalability challenges.

HTTP's architecture is based on a client and server model. The definitions of client and server only define the particular roles that the programs or services fulfill for a particular connection, though. This means the same party can be a server in one connection and a client in others.

HTTP is stateless. This means that the communication protocol treats each request independently from previous ones and that the server does not retain session or status information regarding the parties involved in a certain communication.

The message exchange pattern used by HTTP is request/response. Messages are exchanged over a reliable transport or session layer connection.

The client in a HTTP communication is the party that establishes a connection to a server for sending one or more HTTP requests. Other terms that complete the HTTP protocol glossary are *user agent, origin server, sender,* and *recipient.*

A user agent is a software client originating an HTTP request. This can be a browser, a spider (robot program) crawling the Web, or any generic application. An origin server is a program that can originate authoritative responses for a certain resource. This is the server where the specified resource resides.

Sender and recipient are the terms used to indicate any party that sends and receives messages, respectively.

It is important to note that HTTP has been designed to be implemented in a wide range of situations. Not all user agents are general-purpose browsers accessing large public websites served by origin servers.

A user agent can be any sort of application, from mobile apps, to household appliances, to environmental sensors, to personal devices like fitness activity trackers.

The same applies when considering origin servers: these can be anything from city traffic cameras to networking components.

Most HTTP communication consists of a request for some resource indicated by a Uniform Resource Identifier (URI). The URI is a standard for identifying local and remote resources and describing the relationships between resources.

HTTP considers URIs as formatted strings identifying specific resources, composed from a limited set of characters and some graphic symbols and consisting of a hierarchical sequence of components: the scheme identifying the protocol, host name and port number, absolute path, query, and fragment. The format is (with optional components indicated by square brackets):

```
"http:""//"host[":"port][abs_path["?"query]["#"fragment]]
```

HTTP also allows the use of intermediaries between the client and server (as illustrated in Figure A-1), to handle requests through a chain of connections. Generally speaking, it is possible to identify three common HTTP intermediaries:

Proxy

> A proxy's function is to forward messages. The client selects the proxy via some local configuration rule to receive requests for all or some absolute URIs and redirects these requests through the HTTP interface toward some origin servers, in the attempt to satisfy them.

Gateway

> A gateway, or *reverse proxy*, acts as an origin server translating received requests and forwarding these inbound to other servers. A gateway may communicate with inbound servers using different protocols, but if it wants to interoperate with third-party HTTP servers it will have to respect the user agent requirements for the inbound connections.

Tunnel

> A tunnel is a relay between two connections that doesn't change the messages exchanged in any way. Once it has been activated, a tunnel is not considered a party in the HTTP communication itself, and it is terminated when both ends of the connections are closed. An example of where tunnels are used is when Transport Layer Security (TLS) is used to establish a confidential communication.

This categorization is actually very versatile, as a single intermediary might act as an origin server, proxy, gateway, or tunnel in different communications, while at the same time handling many requests simultaneously.

HTTP moreover distinguishes between *upstream* and *downstream* communications, to describe directional requirements in relation to the message flow (messages always originate upstream and flow downstream). The terms *inbound* and *outbound* are instead used to describe directions regarding the request route, where inbound means toward the origin server and outbound means toward the user agent.

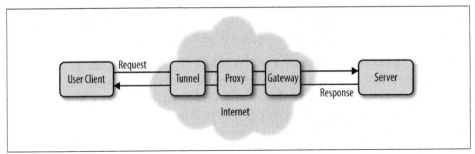

Figure A-1. A simple HTTP communication, initiated from a user client toward an origin server, can pass through a series of intermediaries

Parameters

Within HTTP request and response messages, colon-separated name/value pairs are transmitted in clear-text string format and terminated by a carriage return (CR) and line feed (LF) character sequence. These constitute the header fields of the HTTP message and define the operating parameters of an HTTP transaction. The end of the header fields is marked by two consecutive CRLF pairs.

If you were to visit *http://www.oreilly.com*, your browser would send a number of HTTP requests; if you captured one of these, the "headers" part of the request would look more or less like this:

```
GET / HTTP/1.1 Host: www.oreilly.com
Accept-Encoding: gzip,deflate,sdch
Accept-Language: en-US,en;q=0.8,es;q=0.6,it;q=0.4,en-GB;q=0.2,ca;
q=0.2
Cookie: <Some garbled cookie data>
User-Agent: Mozilla/5.0 (Macintosh; Intel Mac OS X 10_9_2)
AppleWebKit/537.36 (KHTML, like Gecko) Chrome/35.0.1916.153
Safari/537.36
X-Client-Data: <Some garbled client data>
HTTP/1.1 200 OK Accept-Ranges: bytes
Cache-Control: max-age=14400
Connection: keep-alive
Content-Encoding: gzip
Content-Length: 16813
Content-Type: text/html; charset=utf-8
Date: Sat, 12 Jul 2014 16:59:01 GMT
Expires: Sat, 12 Jul 2014 20:59:01 GMT
Last-Modified: Sat, 12 Jul 2014 08:28:40 GMT
```

```
Server: Apache
Vary: Accept-Encoding
```

The Internet Engineering Task Force (IETF) has standardized a core set of field names (*http://bit.ly/rfc-3864*) that must be implemented by all HTTP-compliant protocol implementations. In addition to the core set, each application can also define their own field names and permissible values.

The Internet Assigned Numbers Authority (IANA) maintains the permanent registry of headers (*http://bit.ly/iana-msg-headers*) and a repository of provisional registrations. Up to June 2012, nonstandard header fields were conventionally marked by prefixing the field name with "X-"; however it was decided to deprecate this convention to avoid issues when nonstandard fields became part of the standard set.

Among the message headers, an HTTP-Version field is also specified to indicate the version of HTTP in use. This allows the sender to specify the format of a message and its capacity to understand further HTTP communications.

 Although a detailed analysis of HTTP parameters is outside of the scope of this book, a particularly interested reader might find the following RFC documents useful:

- RFC 2616 (*http://bit.ly/rfc-2616-3*) (Hypertext Transfer Protocol—HTTP 1.1, Section 3, Protocol Parameters)
- RFC 4229 (*http://bit.ly/rfc-4229*) (HTTP Header Field Registrations)
- RFC 3986 (*http://bit.ly/rfc-3986*) (Uniform Resource Identifier (URI): Generic Syntax)

Messages

HTTP messages are either *requests* from client to server or *responses* from server to client.

Both requests and responses consist of a start line, zero or more header fields, an empty line (i.e., a line containing just a CRLF) that indicates the end of the header fields, and possibly a message body with the payload of the message. The format is therefore:

```
start-line
*(message headers CRLF)
CRLF
[ message-body ]
```

The header fields include general headers, request headers, response headers, and entity header fields.

The message body of an HTTP message (if there is one) carries the entity body associated with the request or response. The entity body might be encoded as defined by the Transfer-Encoding field. In this case it will differ from the message body:

```
message-body = entity-body
             | <entity-body as encoded per Transfer-Encoding>
```

 HTTP messages are described in greater detail in RFC 2616, Section 4 (*http://bit.ly/rfc-2616-4*).

Although request and response messages use a generic format for transferring the message payload, some syntax differences apply between the two.

Request messages

An HTTP request is always sent from the client to the server. The first line of the message includes the method of the request, the resource identifier (URI), and the protocol version.

HTTP defines a list of common methods; in addition, resources might specify allowed methods in an Allow header field. When a request message specifies a certain method, the return code of the response message notifies the client whether that method is allowed or implemented.

Whenever the method is implemented by the server but not allowed for the requested resource, the origin server should return the status code 405 (Method Not Allowed); it should return 501 (Not Implemented) if the method is not recognized or not implemented. We'll look at status codes in more detail shortly.

The client can use the request headers to pass additional information to the origin server. The request header fields act as modifiers, following semantics equivalent to those of parameters in a programming language method invocation.

The complete list of core HTTP methods includes the following:

```
Method = "OPTIONS" ;
       | "GET" ;
       | "HEAD" ;
       | "POST" ;
       | "PUT" ;
       | "DELETE" ;
       | "TRACE" ;
       | "CONNECT" ;
       | extension-method
       | extension-method = token
```

For a detailed discussion of several of these methods and how they are mapped to controller actions in Rails, please see "HTTP Semantics" on page 61 in Chapter 4. The HTTP methods are defined in RFC 2616, Section 9 (*http://bit.ly/rfc-2616-9*).

Response messages

Once the origin server receives and interprets a request message, it will respond with an HTTP response message.

The response message starts with a status line, comprised of the protocol version, a numeric status code, and its associated textual phrase:

```
Status-Line = HTTP-Version SP Status-Code SP Reason-Phrase CRLF
```

Status codes are three-digit identifiers that the server sends in its response after parsing and interpreting a request. They are intended to be used by the client software to understand the server's reply. The reason phrase is just a human-readable explanation of the status code, which the client is not required to examine or display.

Following the status line, the response message contains the response headers. These allow the server to pass additional information about itself and the requested resource.

Entity

Both request and response messages may contain an *entity* consisting of entity headers and an entity body.

The headers define metainformation regarding the entity body or the requested resource. Some of this information is optional, and some might be required by the protocol specification.

An entity body can only be included in a message when a message body is present. When an entity body is included, the Content-Type and Content-Encoding fields determine the data type of the entity body.

The entity body follows a two-layer, ordered model:

```
entity-body := Content-Encoding( Content-Type( data ) )
```

The Content-Type field specifies the media type of the enclosed data, while the Content-Encoding field may indicate additional content codings applied to the data (e.g., for the purpose of data compression). No default encoding is specified in the protocol definition.

Connections

HTTP supports the possibility of using a single TCP connection to send and receive multiple HTTP request/response messages. This method is called *persistent connection*, *keep-alive*, or *connection reuse*. Under HTTPv1.0, if the client supports the Keep-Alive header field, it will add it to the request:

```
Connection: Keep-Alive
```

Then, when attempting to handle this request, the server will add the same header field to the response. For following messages, the connection is kept open. When the client sends another request it will therefore use the same TCP connection. The connection will be interrupted only when either the client or the server drops it, signaling that the communication is over.

In HTTPv1.1 all connections are considered persistent unless otherwise specified. A short connection timeout is also implemented to allow origin servers to deliver multiple components of a web page rapidly enough, while not consuming excessive resources.

Clients supporting persistent connections may also wish to "pipeline" their requests, i.e., sending multiple requests without waiting for each response. The origin server will serve the responses in the same order that the requests were received.

Status Code Definitions

Status codes are three-digit codes that define the response of the server to a certain request. The first digit corresponds to the class of response. HTTP defines five classes:

```
1xx: Informational - Request received, continuing process
2xx: Success - The action was successfully received,
    understood, and accepted
3xx: Redirection - Further action must be taken in order to
    complete the request
4xx: Client Error - The request contains bad syntax or cannot
    be fulfilled
5xx: Server Error - The server failed to fulfill an apparently
    valid request
```

HTTPv1.1 also defines individual values of the status codes, with corresponding reason phrases that are intended to be used as recommendations for individual implementations (these can be replaced without affecting the protocol). Codes that you will probably use most frequently are:

```
Status-Code = 100 : Continue
| 200: OK
| 201: Created
| 202: Accepted
| 204: No Content
```

```
| 301: Moved Permanently
| 302: Found
| 303: See Other
| 304: Not Modified
| 400: Bad Request
| 401: Unauthorized
| 403: Forbidden
| 404: Not Found
| 500: Internal Server Error
| 501: Not Implemented
| 502: Bad Gateway
| 503: Service Unavailable
```

HTTP status codes are defined in RFC 2616, Section 10 (*http://bit.ly/rfc-2616-10*).

Access Authentication

HTTP provides different optional challenge-response authentication mechanisms, which can be used either by the server to challenge a client request, or by a client to provide authentication information.

These are defined separately from the protocol specification in RFC 2617 (*http://bit.ly/rfc2617*). Note, however, that the authentication scheme provided by HTTP is not considered to be a secure method of user authentication unless used together with other external secure methods, such as SSL.

Content Negotiation

Content negotiation is the process of selecting a representation for a given response when multiple representations are available, in terms of type, language, encoding, and so on. HTTP defines two kinds of content negotiation: server-driven and agent-driven. The two methods are orthogonal and therefore can be used either independently or in combination. Transparent negotiation is one type of combination, where the negotiation work is taken over by the cache.

For details on the supported forms of content negotiation, see RFC 2616, Section 12 (*http://bit.ly/rfc-2616-12*).

Caching

HTTP was designed for distributed information systems, where caching is known to improve performance. Therefore, the protocol definition includes a number of methods and elements to make the use of response caches as efficient as possible.

The ultimate goal of caching in HTTP is to reduce the need to send requests or response message in as many cases as possible, therefore limiting the number of network round-trips and network bandwidth required for a given communication.

Caching is an important aspect of HTTP and REST. Within RESTful architectures, the most efficient network request is one that doesn't use the network, but efficiently relies on caching.

When defining its caching capabilities, HTTP introduces the concept of *semantic transparency*. It is said that a caching method is semantically transparent regarding a certain response when its use affects neither the client nor the origin server, except to improve performance. In other words, if the caching method is semantically transparent, the client receives the response from the cache exactly as it would have received it if the origin server had handled the request.

HTTPv1.1 allows clients, servers, and caching methods to explicitly reduce semantic transparency when necessary to improve performance.

HTTP also defines *cache correctness* as the idea that the cache, or caching method, responds to a certain request with the most up-to-date response possible that is appropriate to the request.

If the response returned by the cache is neither firsthand nor considered "fresh enough," a Warning header is attached to the response so that the client can handle it properly.

Client and server caching and cache control mechanisms were discussed in detail in Chapter 12, where we saw how to best integrate external resources into our own application.

Security Considerations

HTTP clients and servers often exchange large amounts of user-generated data, and this should be handled carefully to prevent leakage to external sources through the HTTP protocol.

Chapter 16 discussed a number of security challenges that developers face, but it's worth repeating a few key points.

Particularly, a server is in the position to log personal data contained in users' requests that might reveal more than intended about them, and can be used by a potential attacker in a variety of ways. Users often reveal information regarding their thoughts, actions, tastes, and preferences by sharing them either indirectly, through their request messages, or directly, by voluntarily publishing this information online.

It is also important to note that as users' online interactions become more complex and as shared documents are enriched with different media content, it is often difficult for the users to understand and ponder what kind of information is actually being shared with a single post, or what they might consider just innocuous activity.

It is therefore the responsibility of the application developer to implement methods and practices to safeguard privacy and protect user data from unintended leakages and unauthorized accesses.

Index

testing, 53
WikiCat hypermedia API (example), 73-78
Wikipedia
  category system, 42
  geolocated articles, 106
Wikipin API (example), 106
  configuring Nginx as reverse proxy/load
    balancer for, 223
  creating the app, 107
  defining controllers for pin and block
    resources, 114
  defining module to handle REST requests/
    responses, 124
  defining the models, 112
  deploying on OpenShift
    preliminary steps, 156
  documenting blocks API methods with api-
    Doc, 165
  generating the models, 109
  installing PostgreSQL for, 107
  working with requests' IP addresses, 115
Windows systems
  installing MySQL, 43

Ruby installer, 16
workers, 81
  creating and scheduling, 86
WoT (Web of Things), 186
WWW (World Wide Web), 1
  architectural needs, analysis from different
    viewpoints, 2
  design concepts, 5
  identification, representation, and format as
    separate concepts, 3
  W3C definition of, 4

X
XSS (cross-site scripting) attacks, 239, 245

Y
YAML format, database configuration in, 108
YouTube Data API, using, 173
YouTube videos, searching for, 170

Z
zones, 202

About the Author

Silvia Puglisi is a software engineer based in Barcelona, Spain. She is also part of the Information Security Group in the Department of Telematics Engineering at Universitat Politècnica de Catalunya (UPC) as a PhD candidate and research engineer. Previously Silvia worked for Google, Inc., as an Operations Engineer and Enterprise Engineer.

She has a passion for technology and the Web and likes building open applications and services for fun and profit. When she needs to rest her eyes away from the computer screen, she loves hanging out at the beach and surfing.

Colophon

The animal on the cover of *RESTful Rails Development* is Desmarest's hutia *(Capromys pilorides*, also known as the Cuban hutia), a large rodent found only in Cuba. It is named for Anselme Gaëtan Desmarest, a 19th-century French zoologist. Hutias live in a wide range of habitats throughout Cuba, including mangrove forests, plains, and swampland.

Desmarest's hutias are stocky animals with short legs and a waddling gait. They have coarse black or brown fur, as well as large claws to help them climb. Hutias normally live in pairs, and are most active during the day. At night, this animal sleeps in hollows among trees or rocks (it does not create burrows). Its omnivorous diet is made up of bark, leaves, nuts, and fruit, with an occasional lizard or insect. The hutia's stomach is among the most complex of all rodents, because it has three separate compartments.

These are the largest species of hutia, averaging 12–24 inches long and up to 19 pounds in weight. They were traditionally hunted for food in Cuba due to their size and agreeable taste, but became protected in 1968 when legislation made it illegal to kill the animals without a permit. Today, their population is so abundant that they damage crops and are considered pests.

It is likely that the first meat Christopher Columbus ate in the New World was hutia, which are common on Caribbean islands and were a staple in the diet of the indigenous people.

Many of the animals on O'Reilly covers are endangered; all of them are important to the world. To learn more about how you can help, go to *animals.oreilly.com*.

The cover image is from Lydekker's *Royal Natural History*. The cover fonts are URW Typewriter and Guardian Sans. The text font is Adobe Minion Pro; the heading font is Adobe Myriad Condensed; and the code font is Dalton Maag's Ubuntu Mono.

Get even more for your money.

Join the O'Reilly Community, and register the O'Reilly books you own. It's free, and you'll get:

- $4.99 ebook upgrade offer
- 40% upgrade offer on O'Reilly print books
- Membership discounts on books and events
- Free lifetime updates to ebooks and videos
- Multiple ebook formats, DRM FREE
- Participation in the O'Reilly community
- Newsletters
- Account management
- 100% Satisfaction Guarantee

Signing up is easy:

1. Go to: oreilly.com/go/register
2. Create an O'Reilly login.
3. Provide your address.
4. Register your books.

Note: English-language books only

To order books online:
oreilly.com/store

For questions about products or an order:
orders@oreilly.com

To sign up to get topic-specific email announcements and/or news about upcoming books, conferences, special offers, and new technologies:
elists@oreilly.com

For technical questions about book content:
booktech@oreilly.com

To submit new book proposals to our editors:
proposals@oreilly.com

O'Reilly books are available in multiple DRM-free ebook formats. For more information:
oreilly.com/ebooks